T0408713

Creating Pathways for Prosperity

EMERALD STUDIES IN SUSTAINABLE APPROACHES TO POVERTY ALLEVIATION

Series Editors:
Dr Richa Goel
Symbiosis Centre of Management Studies, Noida;
Symbiosis International Deemed University, Pune, India

Dr Tilottama Singh
Uttaranchal University, India

Md. Mashiur Rahman
Bank Asia Ltd., Bangladesh

Quazi Tafsirul Islam
North South University Bangladesh

Dr Sukanta Kumar Baral
Indira Gandhi National Tribal University (A Central University of India), India

Emerald Studies in Sustainable Approaches to Poverty Alleviation serves as a hub for researchers, professionals and practitioners to share innovative research and effective solutions aimed at reducing global poverty.

Poverty is a major global issue that affects millions of people around the world. It poses a serious threat to human development, well-being and social fairness. Global poverty is a complicated and complex issue driven by different economic, social, political and environmental elements that vary by location. As per UNDP, today, one in every five people on the planet (1.2 billion) lives on less than a dollar a day. Fifty-six percent of the developing world lacks basic sanitation, and over 50 nations now have poorer real per capita incomes than they did a decade ago.

Drawing on a global authorship, *Emerald Studies in Sustainable Approaches to Poverty Alleviation* tells the stories of effective interventions and programmes that have made a difference, providing hope and inspiration for those working in the area and inspiring others to become involved. Also using various indicators like HDI, MDPI, Income Consumption index, Poverty headcount ratio, Ginni coefficient data & Welfare index, this book series will try to cover even those masses who do not fall in the above criteria and will touch poverty from its grassroots level. It is critical to employ a combination of these methodologies and indicators when assessing poverty in order to present a full picture of the worldwide poverty situation.

This series will include economics, sociology, development studies, public policy and other disciplines to present a comprehensive and multidimensional assessment of worldwide attempts to eradicate poverty. Each work provides policymakers, practitioners, scholars and concerned citizens with insights, research findings, case studies and practical help in the battle against poverty. *Emerald Studies in Sustainable Approaches to Poverty Alleviation* will allow for in-depth investigation of numerous elements of poverty and its core causes, including income disparity, access to education, healthcare and economic opportunities, social justice, child marriages, micro rural finance, food security, resource mobilisation, women entrepreneurship, war impacted countries and more.

Published Titles in This Series

Understanding the Multi-Dimensional Nature of Poverty
Richa Goel, Tilottama Singh, Md. Mashiur Rahman, Quazi Tafsirul Islam, and Sukanta Kumar Baral

Creating Pathways for Prosperity

EDITED BY

RICHA GOEL
Symbiosis Centre of Management Studies, Noida;
Symbiosis International Deemed University, Pune, India

TILOTTAMA SINGH
Uttaranchal University, India

Md. MASHIUR RAHMAN
Bank Asia Ltd., Bangladesh

QUAZI TAFSIRUL ISLAM
North South University, Bangladesh

AND

SUKANTA KUMAR BARAL
Indira Gandhi National Tribal University (A Central University of India), India

United Kingdom – North America – Japan – India – Malaysia – China

Emerald Publishing Limited
Emerald Publishing, Floor 5, Northspring, 21-23 Wellington Street, Leeds LS1 4DL

First edition 2025

Reprints and permissions service
Contact: www.copyright.com

British Library Cataloguing in Publication Data
A catalogue record for this book is available from the British Library

ISBN: 978-1-83549-122-5 (Print)
ISBN: 978-1-83549-121-8 (Online)
ISBN: 978-1-83549-123-2 (Epub)

Printed and bound by CPI Group (UK) Ltd, Croydon, CR0 4YY

INVESTOR IN PEOPLE

Dedicated to all who played an important role in the development of this edition of the book our families, friends, readers, authors, reviewers and of course the Emerald Team with whom this seems to be a true success, and we are deeply grateful to all of them.
– Prof. (Dr) Sukanta Kumar Baral & Dr Richa Goel

To my wife, Ronayat Ramiz Diya, who fanned the flames of my ambition during our fledgling days and remained my unwavering compass through tides both high and ebbing, and to my brother, Quazi Tahsinul Islam, a source of pride and unwavering reliability – this book is for both of you.
– Quazi Tafsirul Islam

To the Almighty who gives me a life on earth, my parents, wife, kids and siblings; those are inspiring and supporting me as and when required – I am grateful to you all.
– Md. Mashiur Rahman

Dedicated to all the real heroes who are on grounds to bring the smiles to those little hands by which we take hold of heaven.
– Dr Tilottama Singh

Contents

List of Contributors

Dr Chakir Aziza	Hassan II University, Morocco
Dr Sukanta Kumar Baral	Indira Gandhi National Tribal University, India
Dr Bhubaneswari Bisoyi	KIIT University, India
Nishita Chatradhi	Government of Alberta, Canada
Dr Biswajit Das	KIIT University, India
Dr Rajshree Dutta	Fakir Mohan University, India
Dr Vijay Prakash Gupta	Institute of Business Management, G.L.A University, India
Dr Syed Far Abid Hossain	BRAC Business School, BRAC University, Bangladesh
Vijay D. Joshi	Dr. Ambedkar Institute of Management Studies and Research (DAIMSR), India
Aurodeep Kamal	KIIT University, India
Dr Saslina Binti Kamaruddin	Universiti Pendidikan Sultan Idris (UPSI), Malaysia
Juairya Ashger Khan	BRAC Business School, BRAC University, Bangladesh
Rakesh Kumar	Uttaranchal University, India
Dr K. Latha	Department of Commerce, Ramanujan College, University of Delhi, India
Shahid Lone	National Institute of Technology, Srinagar, India
Abhiraj Malia	KIIT University, India
Dewan Nailat Islam Neera	BRAC Business School, BRAC University, Bangladesh
Zarin Tasnim Nira	BRAC Business School, BRAC University, Bangladesh

Dr Megha Ojha	JustAuto Solutions Pvt. Ltd., India
Dr Manisha Paliwal	Sri Balaji University, India
Ameya Patil	Dr. Vishwanath Karad MIT World Peace University, India
Manish M. Pitke	Prin. L. N. Welingkar Institute of Management Development & Research (WeSchool), India
Yash Ranga	PYXERA Global, India
Dr Rakhi Raturi	NMIMS (Deemed-to-be) University, India
Dr Ipseeta Satpathy	KIIT University, India
Dr Archana Saxena	Uttaranchal University, India
Rajeev Sengupta	Dr. Vishwanath Karad MIT World Peace University, India
Arfan Shahriar	BRAC Business School, BRAC University, Bangladesh
Dr Vinay Pal Singh	Quantum University, India
Dr Sasikanta Tripathy	University of Bahrain, Bahrain
Kamal Kant Tyagi	COER University, India
Nazmul Hasan Wanjan	BRAC Business School, BRAC University, Bangladesh
Dr Arti Yadav	Department of Commerce, Ramanujan College, University of Delhi, India
Dr Parul Yadav	Department of Commerce, Ramanujan College, University of Delhi, India
Dr N. Yogeesh	Government First Grade College, India

Foreword

The comprehensive reference source of this book *Creating Pathways for Prosperity* offers individualised, approachable and well-designed experiences through its rich contents. 'No Poverty' is the most crucial of the 17 Sustainable Development Goals (SDGs). Studies on poverty reduction have substantially increased in terms of their research views, methodologies and issue integration with the development of praxis in the 21st century.

The second volume in *Emerald Studies in Sustainable Approaches to Poverty Alleviation* will bring the topic of poverty eradication and its comprehension to the forefront, as well as show how rising economies are grappling with poverty challenges at its heart. It focuses on the key concerns that nations throughout the world are experiencing, such as pandemic-related poverty, environmental-related poverty, energy crisis, implementation issues and how new creative models and methods that use current technology may help make economies and enterprises more sustainable. Poverty is the greatest barrier to long-term development, which is why eradicating it has become one of the most pressing global concerns of the 21st century. It also provides an overview of current research and suggest that, in the future, cross-disciplinary collaboration and attention to the contribution of marginal fields to poverty reduction research should be prioritised. There has been a lot of debate on how developing economies' economic development and structural transformation influence poverty. This book revisits these themes, using a newly constructed dataset of global poverty measures.

I assume that this book is anticipated to be highly valuable for a wide range of readers with a variety of interests, and it is not limited to academics, postgraduate students and research associates, but also to corporate executives, entrepreneurs and other professionals and masses in all fields who can improve and expand their knowledge with the learning of the basic trends and activities in this book. This book will have an edge over the other few existing books as it presents customised economic models, essential policy tools, suggestions and strategies designed to eradicate poverty with respect to innovative technology, sustainable development, industry 5.0 especially within the context of the 2030 Agenda.

It gives me great pleasure to write this preface because the book's editors have worked tirelessly to find an excellent answer and creativity. The chapters in this book were all chosen based on peer reviews by reviewers who were quite knowledgeable about the field.

Prof (Dr) Arceloni Neusa Volpato
Professor, Head of Foreign Affairs & Coordinator of
Transcultural Practices Master
UNIFACVEST University Centre (Centro Universitário Facvest), Brazil

Preface

The second volume in *Emerald Studies in Sustainable Approaches to Poverty Alleviation* highlights the issue of eradicating poverty and understanding it, as well as demonstrate how difficulties related to poverty are being addressed by emerging economies. It focuses on the main issues that countries around the world are facing, including poverty linked to pandemics, poverty linked to the environment, the energy crisis, implementation problems and how new innovative models and methods that make use of current technology may help make economies and businesses more sustainable. Based on current discussions on the subject, the study emphasises varying viewpoints on the concept of poverty as well as variations in interpretations in developing countries.

In the modern world, a book on sustainable approaches to alleviating poverty is essential since it tackles the pressing need to do so while preserving the future of our planet. Millions of people worldwide continue to experience poverty, which calls for complex answers. It is crucial that attempts to reduce poverty are sustainable, ensuring that economic advancement does not come at the expense of our environment as environmental challenges loom. A book like this serves as an essential information base, providing insights into the connections between social equality, environmental sustainability, and poverty. It provides policymakers, practitioners, educators, and communities the evidence-based concepts, real-world examples, and tools necessary to break the cycle of poverty without endangering the welfare of the present or future generations. In a society that aspires to inclusive and environmentally responsible development, this book offers a road map for dramatic transformation and a glimmer of hope for a more equitable and sustainable future.

It increases understanding of the various elements of poverty in major developing economies and how the definition of poverty has expanded beyond economic indicators. This book provides tailored economic models, important policy tools, recommendations and methods to end poverty in light of cutting-edge technology, sustainable development and industry 5.0, particularly in the context of the 2030 Agenda. It implies that strong institutions are needed to carry out locally specific poverty reduction policies that are essential to enhancing the well-being of the poor, rather than widely accepted solutions, in order to ensure sustainable poverty reduction and development in developing nations.

The following chapters are listed under this book:
Chapter 1 talks about the Role of Hybrid Leadership Style to Face Uncertain Market Turbulence. In this research, we magnify the role of hybrid leadership

style in facing uncertain turbulence in the market. Due to the rapid change in innovation and other macroeconomic developments, the already existing market turbulence has become uncertain. This uncertainty has further been accentuated by recent events like COVID-19 and Russia–Ukraine invasion. One solution that is crucial in facing this uncertainty is effective leadership. However, taking the wide groups of individuals present in the market into account, this leadership has to be tailored for each and this is where the topic for this research, hybrid leadership style to face uncertain market turbulence, comes to play. Here, we gather the existing roles of different leadership styles in different businesses that help in facing the uncertainties and explore the possibilities of new ones. This work can therefore act as a guide to practice hybrid leadership style during market turbulences where following a single specific style may prove unhelpful or lead to dissatisfaction and aggravation.

Chapter 2 talks about Entrepreneurship and Innovation – A Way towards Sustainable Development and Poverty Alleviation. The importance of entrepreneurship as a force for economic progress and poverty alleviation has grown in recent years. Innovation is at the core of entrepreneurship, whereas entrepreneurship is a tool for Innovation. Forbye, social innovation has become a new way of thinking and strategy for solving social problems. Against this backdrop, this chapter presents to accentuate the role of social innovation and entrepreneurial strategies in mitigating poverty. Additionally, to study the ever-growing and dynamic space of entrepreneurship followed by an analysis of the actors in the ecosystem, including an emphasis on its outcome and social impact on poverty. Drawing on the insights from the framework of the Theory of Change, the authors present the case of PYXERA Global. Using a qualitative research method to generate rich findings from the organisation's work and experience of working in over 100 countries, we exhibit the entrepreneurial ecosystem approach followed and implemented by them. Through meticulous interviews, the chapter produces in-depth insights from the strategists and entrepreneurs of the organisation that create a balanced and focused social impact. The study reveals the importance of entrepreneurial training, education, technical skills, and gender balance in poverty alleviation. Through collaborations with the private, public, and social sectors, the organisation ensures to the creation of an ecosystem that provides technical support and access to skills to develop an entrepreneurial mindset. The Theory of Change undertaken by PYXERA informs how tri-sector partnerships and deep organisational involvement can aid towards sustainable development and poverty alleviation. The findings contribute to the development of an attitude that poverty reduction and community development can be achieved through co-creation, which is possible through Entrepreneurship and innovation. The chapter concludes with a summary of insightful information and suggestions, which could trigger more empirical research on the subject.

Chapter 3 talks about Role of Government in Eradication of Poverty in India. The problem of poverty is particularly acute in India. Eradication of poverty is an important objective of economic policy. One of the biggest challenges to planned economic progress is the eradication of poverty. Since each state's experiences with economic growth and poverty reduction have been so unique, it is challenging to recommend a universal course of action. States that focused on a high agricultural expansion and effectively reduced poverty include Punjab and Haryana. Success was also achieved by other states that followed the path of human resource development (Kerala). Although social security programmes in India have greatly reduced poverty, they are not without difficulties. The gains were undone by COVID-19, which also disrupted the informal sector and particularly hurt migrant workers. Millions of people are now living in even greater poverty. Government officials and communities in need are looking for programmes like MGNREGA to combat unemployment. This article is an attempt to study the role of government and its policies, plans and programs for poverty eradication.

Chapter 4 talks about Climate Change Adaptation Challenges Require Technical Expertise and Data Management. The multifaceted issue of climate change, sometimes known as global warming, has a variety of effects on both society and the economy. The number of media and public attention given to this topic has skyrocketed in recent years. The goal of this chapter, 'Technical Area and Data Management on Climatic Changes Adaptation Challenges of the 21st Century', is to give a comprehensive review of the key components of global warming and how society as a whole understands and addresses it both locally and globally. This chapter looks at efforts from outside of climate modelling to measure and predict the complex effects of future climate change on populations and ecosystems. It looks at how we can assess how vulnerable these ecosystems are and how we may modify our way of life to lessen the effects of climate change. This information also has broader implications for the ongoing global debate about sustainable development. The chapter discusses how social, economic and ecological systems are all impacted by climate change in a variety of ways, leading to significant economic losses that will probably get worse the longer we wait to take action. Because of this, the main goal of this chapter is to encourage planning and capacity building at the local, regional, national, and international levels to deal with the effects of climate change at the local, regional, national, and international levels. This is done by using a unified approach to improve coordination and develop climate resilience in nations that are more likely to be affected by climate change. Overall, this chapter shows how hard climate change is by looking at both the problems and the chances of adapting to and reducing the effects of climate change.

Chapter 5 talks about Revisiting Microfinance as an Instrument of Sustainable Development. In the past, financial viability and the creation of social value were seen as competing goals, but today they are linked and form the main axis for the operation of inclusive firms. However, depending on who offers the ideas for inclusive enterprises, there can be questionable presumptions regarding what is promised in relation to poverty. The most important but dubious premise is that all problems, especially poverty, can be solved by the market on its own. It seems more appropriate to consider markets as a prerequisite but not sufficient condition for resolving the social problems that face contemporary societies. Financial inclusion through microfinance, which is particularly effective in reducing income inequality and poverty by giving underprivileged populations previously unachievable prospects for upward mobility, is a crucial facet of social inclusion. At the World Summit for Social Development (WSSD) in March 1995, governments pledged to eradicate poverty on a global scale, citing it as a moral, social, political, and economic imperative. One of the three main objectives of the WSSD was the eradication of poverty. According to the United Nations System Conference Action Plan, conducting international conferences will be primarily focused on eliminating poverty (UNSCAP). Microfinance provides financial services for persons living below the poverty line and for small businesses that do not have access to conventional banking and related services. Microfinance refers to a broad range of services, including microcredit. Microcredit is the lending of small amounts of money to underserved consumers. Though its reach is modest, microfinance succeeded where institutional financing failed. Microfinance organisations' viability is in question. To assist the development of the emerging microfinance industry and handle the trade-off between outreach and sustainability, a comprehensive effort is needed. It is well known that only efficient institutions can greatly lower the long-term expense of serving irregular and low revenues. The poor and severely poor can then get these lower costs in the form of affordable finance charges, which will entice them to participate in their effective income-generating activities.

Chapter 6 talks about E-Governance as a Strategy for Poverty Alleviation: An Analysis. E-governance is the term used to describe the use of communication and information technologies for government. It guarantees information flow transparency, aiding in the improvement and redefinition of social, environmental, and economic values. The implementation of numerous Central and State initiatives is the responsibility of the Rural Development Department. The execution of almost all systems makes use of Management Information Systems (MIS) software. The state government's policy aims to provide top-notch internet services with a focus on the needs of the citizenry. A number of programmes, including CRISP, NEGP, NIC, E-choupal, Gyandoot, etc. have already been put into use, and more e-Government initiatives are in the operation. In a country like India, where demand is high owing to a huge population, alleviating poverty is more crucial and infrastructure is a significant determinant for faster economic growth. By providing improved access to essential commodities like roads, water, drainage, energy, transportation, infrastructure would raise inhabitants' quality of life. One thing is certain: the development of the Indian economy will be fuelled by technologically driven e-governance solutions as it strives to become a global superpower. The initiatives made in the field of e-governance that can hasten economic development are therefore the main emphasis of this chapter, which is based on secondary sources. E-governance initiatives can aid in advancing good governance. E-promotion of governance can be of more inclusive governance and can aid in resolving the enormous global issues associated with poverty alleviation. The chapter will go on to outline how e-governance software enables stakeholders to not only monitor quality, cost, and schedule but also regulate deviations through ongoing automated monitoring, escalations, and transparency. The anticipated problems and limitations of e-governance initiatives are also described.

Chapter 7 talks about E-Inclusiveness in Business & Financial System. According to G20, 'Inclusiveness basically signifies the accessibility of the various resources (goods, services, and livelihoods) on a commercially viable basis to the economically vulnerable section of the society through making them part of the organizations' value chain as customers, retailers, distributors, and suppliers'. With the increased application of digital technology in every sphere of life the concept of inclusiveness has moved to e-inclusiveness. So, the present chapter tried to investigate the conceptual journey from inclusiveness to e-inclusiveness from business and financial system aspects. Further, it presents an insight into how the e-inclusiveness aspect impacts the poverty level mainly from the developing country's perspective. The study also suggests that from the perspective of developed as well as developing economies, the public and private sector players strive to develop an effective financial system incorporating an inclusiveness aspect.

Chapter 8 talks about Economic and Social Dimensions of Indian Trade towards Transformation in the 21st Century. The COVID-19 epidemic has rendered the current state of the world economy unworkable. Because services are interdependent and demand close closeness between the provider and the client, the lockdown mechanism and social distancing have created a dire scenario for international trade in general and services (in particular). Given the outstanding contribution of services in India's foreign trade, this study examines the changing international trade pattern for India. It ultimately seeks to highlight key opportunities, challenges, and suggestions to protect and promote India's international trade with the existence of certain global disruptions. We reviewed trade data (for imports and exports) for the last 15 years. This was obtained from suitable secondary sources and published information. Also, data from government sources such as the Ministry of Commerce and the Reserve Bank of India are reviewed. The analysis highlights a growing trade surplus in services, and an increasing trade deficit (i.e., imports higher than exports) in goods. The growing trade surplus in services for India is not enough to cover the trade deficit in goods. This has taken a toll on the rupee. However, when looked at from another perspective, it calls for the strengthening of the domestic manufacturing sector. By doing this, India will achieve a comparative edge in the trade of goods with an aim of 'becoming a manufacturing hub of the world'. The growing economy and supportive government policies offer greater opportunities for the country in the longer period if urgent policy initiatives and support are extended to existing and potential manufacturing and services sectors. Besides achieving economic growth, it is important to have social inclusion that will ensure the creation of jobs and economic progress of the low-income people in the country.

Chapter 9 talks about Economic Perspectives on Poverty: Analysing Its Measurement Across Different Economics and Contexts. Poverty prevents individuals from meeting their fundamental requirements for food, clothing, medical care, education, and sanitation. Poverty has several definitions and varies by location and time. Each nation has its own poverty level and poverty rate. Our economy is affected by increased health care, education, and other bad services. Poverty, isolation, undereducation, and sickness undermine society. Despite progress in measuring and analysing poverty, the World Bank Group is working to establish indicators for other aspects. This chapter aims to study the numerous settings of poverty in India and around the world, as well as its relevance, causes, methods of measurement, and various programs to end it in different sectors of different economies. The findings of this chapter will give readers a strong understanding of various concepts related to poverty, such as its causes and effects in the real world, especially in India. Individuals, decision-makers, the government, researchers, and industries who use the poverty index for planning and development will find it beneficial.

Chapter 10 talks about An Analytical Study on the Role of Private Sector in Bringing Economic Development and Equality in India. India's privatisation era is always praised for its capacity to create opportunities and more effective business models to support growth. By excluding the weaker, less skilled, and more vulnerable groups in society, private enterprises may also be more likely to exacerbate economic imbalances and inequality, according to the current study. Recent data show that inequality in India has significantly increased in a variety of ways. Additionally, it has been asserted that the private sector makes the wealth gaps worse. In a similar vein, most people would only have limited access to a premium knowledge base or service. This is a worry since the government began disinvesting by selling public sector firms to the private sector, which resulted in a progressive decline in State ownership and control over resources. Privatisation results in the State's loss of control over decision-making and price setting. This may increase the likelihood that expensive, high-quality items and services will be. The study makes an effort to offer solid proof of how the private sector contributes to the country's unequal wealth distribution and low levels of knowledge exchange. The study will also explore if the Indian government can reduce income inequality and poverty rates by enacting sound policies that apply to both the public and private sectors. The results would encourage changes in policy aimed at reducing economic inequality in India and advancing welfare.

Chapter 11 talks about Sustainable Environment with respect to Go- Green. The purpose of this chapter is to explore the function of a sustainable environment in terms of environmental-friendly behaviour. Author identified the best practices of sustainability initiatives across different parts of the world, because humanity's inability to fit its activities into that pattern is profoundly altering the planetary systems (Elbasiouny & Elbehiry, 2020). Many development changes are endangering the life. There is no way out of this new reality, so it needs to be acknowledged and managed. First and foremost, it is a fact that sustainable development places a premium on the environment, human well-being and economic growth. According to Che Rusuli et al. (2016), many members of society lost their lives as a result of the severe haze with a high API that an open burning generated, and steps should be taken to address this condition. Therefore, in order to mitigate global warming, people and society must change their behaviour (e.g. public trash disposal, recycling, and reduced use of plastic bags) stated by Che Rusuli et al. (2016). Slowly and gradually people are getting awareness regarding go-green practice. People are now conscious that their consuming habits may cause environmental issues (Tsen et al., 2006). Green consumers are those people or customers who are aware of and concerned about environmental issues (Soonthonsmai, 2007). At last, this chapter's goal is to highlight how becoming green has become more prevalent among people as they get older.

Chapter 12 talks about Restructuring Sustainable Strategies for Alleviation of Poverty through a Dynamic Approach. This book chapter explores into the understanding of poverty and mitigating the challenges by revisiting for a sustainable alleviation of the scales of economy. Eventually insufficient income and spending is the bastion of natural deprivation for household problems. Effective measures are critically examined to redefine the obstacles that are key to upliftment and eradication of poverty. It essentially aims to bridging the gap, analysing the SDGs through a trend analysis for a time period. These strategies will introspect into overcoming the emerging areas of concern with a futuristic development. These social, economic, political, legal and technological interventions through their novel strategies can empower and create inclusion for the sharing of equitable wealth distribution, ensuring justice and supporting human rights, providing social security to the poorest of the poor. The research study shall innovatively scan through the new entrepreneurship models to understand the skillsets across the globe in order to foster good governance in a win-win environment. Basically, in review of the aforesaid dimensions, the study shall vividly examine on the SDGs pertaining to poverty alleviation worldwide to adjust for the seamless and uninterrupted continuation trend analysis of the periodic plans of action. It shall adjudge into the befitting global trend admissible under the uncertain future.

Acknowledgements

Writing a book is more difficult than we anticipated, but also more gratifying. None of this would have been possible without the efforts, hardship and, of course, encouragement of our complete team members, and this book would not exist without their experiences and support.

It's as challenging as it sounds to take an idea and convert it into a book. The experience is mentally taxing and satisfying. We want to express our sincere gratitude to everyone who made this possible. The success of this book was made possible by the collaboration of many outstanding researchers, who genuinely provided a new path for this book.

Our entire team, which was dispersed across multiple locations, used to interact several times each day for months on end before developing something creative and in depth, and we still cherish those times. We were only able to put this book together because of God's grace, which gave us the strength to pursue our dreams and put our faith in our interests.

Our sincerest gratitude to our family members who have been a pillar of support for us throughout the difficult process of finishing this book. Also, many thanks to all of the authors and reviewers who contributed to the review process. Without their assistance, this book would not have been possible. We are grateful that many of the writers also served as referees. Those who provided thorough and critical comments on a few chapters pushed us to clarify concepts, study specific elements of insight work and explain the reasoning behind certain recommendations. We also wish to thank everyone who has helped us study and practice networking throughout the years, both directly and indirectly.

Editors
Dr Richa Goel, Dr Tilottama Singh, Md. Mashiur Rahman
Quazi Tafsirul Islam, and Dr Sukanta Kumar Baral

Introduction

Researching the sustainable aspects of eradicating poverty on a global scale necessitates a complex strategy that goes beyond simply raising income levels. First and foremost, the economic aspect is very important. Access to financial services, fair income distribution and chances for good work are all goals of sustainable economic development. We can assist in removing people from poverty and ensuring that the benefits are shared fairly by promoting inclusive and ecologically conscious economic growth. To provide the resources for sustainable livelihoods, this strategy frequently includes investments in infrastructure development, vocational training and education. The social aspect of reducing poverty, which focuses on enhancing the capabilities of marginalised communities, is as significant. Access to high-quality healthcare, social safety nets, education and gender equality are all included in this dimension. Sustainable initiatives to reduce poverty should empower people by boosting their human capital, enabling them to effectively engage in the economy and society. In order to guarantee that vulnerable groups are not left behind and that poverty reduction is both equitable and durable, addressing socio-economic inequalities and advancing inclusive policies are crucial.

An important factor in the analysis of global poverty alleviation is environmental sustainability. The poor's way of life is frequently impacted by poverty's interactions with resource depletion and environmental deterioration. Sustainable strategies place a strong emphasis on protecting the environment, conserving natural resources and managing environmental risks. In addition to reducing poverty, promoting sustainable agriculture, the use of renewable energy and climate resilience measures ensures the long-term well-being of vulnerable communities in the face of environmental difficulties.

Finally, the governance component is crucial to the long-term analysis of eradicating global poverty. Policies and programmes are implemented effectively and transparently by effective governance structures. This factor entails evaluating the effectiveness of institutions, the integrity of the legal system and the level of corruption in programmes to fight poverty. Achieving sustainable outcomes that benefit everyone requires accountable and consultative governance frameworks that involve local communities and give them a voice in their own development. In order to provide long-term, fair and environmentally sound solutions to this complicated global challenge, the study of sustainable components in poverty alleviation involves economic, social, environmental and governance factors.

Chapter 1

The Role of Hybrid Leadership Style in Uncertain Market Turbulence

Syed Far Abid Hossain, Arfan Shahriar, Nazmul Hasan Wanjan, Dewan Nailat Islam Neera, Juairya Ashger Khan and Zarin Tasnim Nira

BRAC Business School, BRAC University, Bangladesh

Abstract

In this research, we magnify the role of hybrid leadership style in facing uncertain turbulence in the market. Due to the rapid change in innovation and other macroeconomic developments, the already existing market turbulence has become uncertain. This uncertainty has further been accentuated by recent events like COVID-19 and Russia–Ukraine invasion. One solution that is crucial in facing this uncertainty is effective leadership. However, taking the wide groups of individuals present in the market into account, this leadership has to be tailored for each, and this is where the topic for this research, hybrid leadership style to face uncertain market turbulence, comes to play. Here, we gather the existing roles of different leadership styles in different businesses that help in facing the uncertainties and explore the possibilities of new ones. This work can therefore act as a guide to practice hybrid leadership style during market turbulences where following a single specific style may prove unhelpful or lead to dissatisfaction and even aggravation.

Keywords: Leadership; uncertainty; market; turbulence; volatility; leader

Introduction

Businesses always have to face some level of turbulence, which is normal and is a part of any normal economy. However, due to the rapid change of macro and microeconomic factors from rapid technological advancements to customer

Creating Pathways for Prosperity, 1–13
doi:10.1108/978-1-83549-121-820241002

empowerment, the market has been facing increasing turbulence. Uncertainty, therefore, is the defining character of business today (Sull, 2009). This in turn raises the stakes for businesses (Kotler & Caslione, 2009, p. 16). In fact, the survival of an organisation depends on adaptation to the environment and the acquisition of necessary resources. As most organisations, small and large, depend on the group performance of the employees, the need for effective leadership to face this uncertainty is inevitable. However, due to the presence of different groups of people, following one leadership style for a certain business is neither efficient nor an option. Therefore, organisations tend to follow different styles at different levels. This approach falls under the hybrid leadership pattern and ensures fulfilling the needs of more employees.

Hybrid leadership means mixed leadership patterns (Gronn, 2009). Although the reviewing of the current literature reveals that the effectiveness of different leadership styles in dealing with market turbulence has already been studied, there remain gaps that need attention, especially considering the fact that the styles in this situation have so far been explored in isolation. This calls for the need to move away from popular methodologies and find out new possibilities, without overlooking the existing ones, for different leadership styles in confronting this uncertainty (Hossain et al., 2020).

In this research, we take the major recent economic events into consideration to collect the recent and possible uncertain scenarios that affect the businesses and create opportunities for leadership. We then look into the existing literature in order to explore how hybrid leadership style is beneficial during market turbulence. Therefore, in the following sections, we start by reviewing the existing literature to find out the role of different leadership styles in solving organisational issues during times of uncertain market turbulence, then we focus on recent economic events that contribute to market volatility and try to find the needs of leadership in that context (Hossain et al., 2019a, 2019b). Later, we provide insights by combining the already existing findings with our interpretation from the current state to show how hybrid leadership style helps in facing uncertain market turbulence. This work may prove helpful to future researchers looking to further explore the possibilities of hybrid leadership and practitioners to enhance their organisational performance in a holistic manner (Hossain et al., 2022).

Background

While there has so far been extensive research on leadership solving organisational problems, most ongoing researchers focus on a particular style of leadership in performing them. Therefore, we first go through these existing isolated works to understand the needs and effectiveness of different leadership styles both in an organisational context in general and during market turbulence. Hybrid leadership in today's world is not a new type to be learnt or acquired. It simply emerges from the way organisations operate. This is echoed in Gronn (2009)'s work on exploring the role of hybrid leadership under distributed style in educational institutions. He pointed out that going away from popular phenomena of being either normative or adjectivalist, hybrid leadership does not designate a new type of leadership. Rather, it is simply a way to characterise the emerging state of affairs.

Particular to his research, hybridity represents an attempt by schools to accommodate contingency (Gronn, 2009, p. 35). He mentions that, to speak of a constantly shifting leadership mix or configuration would make sense in any particular organisational setting when speaking of hybridity in organisation. The overall composition of this style should then be understood as an adaptive or emergent response, rather than a different style, to wider environmental and immediate situational challenges specific to that context. This therefore allows different kinds of both individualised focused and distributed patterns of leadership to coexist in each organisational context where leadership may be manifest (Gronn, 2009, pp. 19–20). By examining an educational institute and interviewing its leaders, it also occurred to him that the trigger for hybrid leadership practices is the need for intelligence.

Shadraconis (2013)'s research provides a broad overview of how transformational leadership in organisations during uncertain times may help them adapt, involve with and cope up with the situation. The author recognises the need for transformational leadership in the current fluctuating market and from the characteristics of transformational leadership derives the precise benefits that such leaders present to an organisation.

Linking the authentic leadership style to subordinate behaviours, Liu et al. (2017) provide empirical evidence to prove that the relation between authentic leadership and subordinate behaviour is positive. He further shows the negative relationship of the mentioned leadership style with the subordinates' workplace deviance factors. From this, the authors conclude that the authentic style results in a positive work climate within which employees feel safe to contribute their effort to their jobs.

From the belief that recent events largely contribute to uncertainty in market turbulence, we went through the existing literature that focuses strictly on connecting those developments to different markets and tried to create a critical overview of the current scenario. Adekoya and Oliyide (2021)'s work provides an insight on the effect of the pandemic on the connectedness among different markets by using both casualty and non-causality tests. The authors analyse the market condition before and after events like announcements of death rate, etc. to reveal the connectedness among financial and commodity markets. The authors also explore how such announcements create panic among the investors of one market and cause them to reach for the other, either to act as a safety net or to completely replace the previous investment decision. The focus of their work is on the volatility connectedness among gold, oil and financial markets, and they use infectious diseases-based equity market VIX (Volatility Index) to derive their relation. They conclude with the definite relationship among different commodity and financial markets, which may be interpreted as a shift from one to others during crises, causing turbulence.

In an attempt to investigate the effect of new cases of COVID-19 infection and fatality ratio on the volatility of financial markets in the United States, Albulescu

(2021), through empirical method, found that reports of new infection cases globally and within the United States increases financial volatility among other findings. This in turn creates the possibility of market turbulence.

Among other factors that create uncertainty in the already existing market turbulence, in recent times, just like COVID-19, the Russia–Ukraine invasion has been shown to be one of the most prominent ones. Alam et al. (2022), in their research to investigate the impacts of the invasion on global markets and commodities, found extreme connectedness among five commodities and the G7 and BRIC markets. Their findings suggest that gold and silver in the commodity market, and United States, Canada, China and Brazil stock markets are the shock receivers from the transmitters such as platinum, natural gas, silver and crude oil markets during this crisis. The authors also mention that the financial markets across the world have experienced a strong dynamic due to the ongoing conflict. To get a solid grasp of the crisis, the invasion has augmented gas prices to USD 3.54 per gallon and caused gold prices to cross the figure of USD1900 per ounce (Liadze et al., 2022).

These new and significant uncertainties aggravate the already existing decision-making challenges for the leaders. This requires a rapidly adaptive response that is not usually found in usual turbulent times (Anderson, 2018). One of the key challenges of a pandemic as mentioned by Ahern and Loh (2020) is that a large-scale change in human behaviour is required to carry out an effective management of the situation. Another key point that has been identified by the same authors is that, in order to trust their leaders, followers need access to objective information while being able to speak up and ask questions. They argued that when creating and sustaining trusting relationships, it is not only leaders who play the dominant role. Rather, it is done mutually by both leaders and followers. Leaders must therefore trust their followers, especially if they plan to delegate responsibility or share the process of decision making (Ahern & Loh, 2020).

Leadership in Different Facets of Business

We now look into some notable characteristics of successful businesses today. This is useful due to the fact that each leadership style has to align differently in order to be effective in catering to the different attributes presented by these characteristics. However, it has to be noted that these are only a few of the many defining characteristics of current successful businesses that have been identified so far.

First, we present two most relevant capabilities that every successful business today must have from the three component factors of the dynamic capabilities presented in (Wang & Ahmed, 2007).

(1) *Adaptive capability* is defined by a firm's ability to sort out and explore new market opportunities (Wang & Ahmed, 2007). It refers to an optimal state of the firm's survival stage where this helps to find balance and explore

strategies. It also measures the elasticity of the available resources of the firm. Organisations use different evaluation methods that help them to metre the firm's adaptability. Firms can undergo changes throughout each financial year in order to adapt to the turbulent market and unpredictable consumer behaviour in the near future. This can in turn contribute to the embitterment of the organisation's environment which is clearly observed when a company goes through uninterrupted change in the products, capabilities, resources, and other operational functionalities. This dynamic nature of the organisation is also reflected in their adaptive capabilities when there is a change in the firm's position, internal environment, resources, new threats, challenges etc. In many cases, firms that have high dynamic qualities tend to perform better in the long run for both inside as well as outside in the consumer market.

(2) *Innovative capability* refers to a firm's ability of innovation in developing new products or ideas. It has become of crucial importance for the companies looking to succeed in this technological era. Every firm faces the challenge or threat from their rivals coming with new products where consumers will feel eager to buy new and updated alternatives (Wang & Ahmed, 2007). In such cases, it is essential for the firms with the non-upgraded products to face the challenge of innovation. In this updating process each project leader needs to come up with a new leadership style to encourage each of the employees for the betterment of their, and resultantly the overall firms, innovative capabilities. Additionally, leaders need to utilise the employees' thinking style and prioritise their opinions for the sake of the firm/company to gather more ideas about how they can innovate products with a better outcome while keeping the investment to a minimum (Wang & Ahmed, 2007). Here, seeking unusual and novel solutions using smart methods like brainstorming might bring greater innovation.

Next, we present two of the many concerns that drive the firms to strive for the above capabilities and also the role expected from the leaders.

(1) *Financial impact:* While the motivation for different leaders may differ, the end goal for both innovation and adaptation capabilities of the firm still circles around the financial impact of the organisation. Therefore, earning a good profit and having a larger market share is an important driving factor for every organisation, even with the changing customer minds, behaviour and needs. Also, market share is very essential for a noticeable marketing effort (Anderson, 2018) which most of the leaders believe to measure the firms' effectiveness. An increase in revenue and management of the expenditure is required for that desired financial impact. Often, investments are contemplated as marketing expenditure while Return on Investment is estimated as financial return. At length, firms must analyse the changing needs of the consumers and offer required products to them, all while maintaining the expenses in the raw materials and maximising the profit. For this reason,

leaders need to manage their employees in such a way that they are aware of what actions they are taking to meet the desired profit margin (Rust et al., 2004). Also, financial risks are considered by financial returns and that can lead to a firm in a big loss, big profit or anything in between. Nonetheless, these types of financial risks are always being calculated by the firm's finance section. So, to make a good outcome, the leader must come up with an effective leadership style for a specific period of time to lead the key employees in that role as well as throughout the organisation in order to prevent financial loss.

(2) *Impact on the value of the firm*: Marketers tend to measure the financial implications of their previous actions for valuing the firm. Keeping that in mind, customers are the main revenue source and also work as assets (Gupta & Lehmann, 2003) that may determine the value of that firm. Enterprises basically focus on reaching the state where its consumers act as a metric for its stocks' price. However, we believe that this view can be misleading as assets must be owned by the firm and customers are not the firm's property to own. Although effective customer relationship management can lead to better customer satisfaction, the firm cannot guarantee the customers' loyalty. Therefore, when a firm claims the previous point, it should not make any conclusion. A firm should rather earn loyalty of its consumers using different marketing strategies. Maintaining good metrics of value per subscriber, course of period, positive reviews may lead to the ultimate benefit to the firm (Rust et al., 2004). Here, the leader has to integrate the marketing department with the financial and make sure all the previous strategies are exercised throughout the regular financial periods of that organisation.

Leadership During the Turbulence

Market turbulence is one of the bitterest factors that a business leader needs to face. In order to keep up with that on top of leading the diverse teams with their various needs, it is important for the leaders to be alert and respond to the situations so that the business does not take big hits of the wave. This is exactly the reason why the role of hybrid leadership is inevitable. An organisation can be seen as a place for working as a large team where the different individuals (maybe working in smaller teams) play different roles. Sticking to a particular leadership style hence may prove costly. For leaders to deal with uncertain challenges, they need to be capable of stepping out of their comfort zones and thinking from the perspectives of the different individuals while tailoring different styles to approach them.

From our secondary research, we have identified two basic patterns in the hybrid leadership that are practiced in the organisations.

(1) Different leaders with their personal styles to suit different groups within the organisation.
(2) Individual leader practicing multiple leadership styles.

In order to succeed for any organisation at any business, being able to mix multiple approaches is very important. The styles and patterns of leadership are no exception. It is as important to be capable of possessing mixed leadership styles as it is necessary to understand which type of leadership is more appropriate and suitable in which situations. It is especially relevant today because although encouraging the inclusion of multiple cultures, races, genders, ethnicity and nationality within the same organisation has been around for a while (Cox Jr, 1991), with the addition of generation Z in the workplace (Schroth, 2019), increasing number of market leaders are finding novel benefits of having them (Duchek et al., 2020; Fine et al., 2020; Gomez & Bernet, 2019).

For an organisation to flourish, at first, they need to have knowledge about the employees and what type of leaders there are. For instance, if the employees always get straightforward directions from the leaders, they may feel dominated, and that will cause a decline of enthusiasm in the workplace. In general, the employees may feel the need for emotional support while carrying out simple tasks, which is exercised in the supportive leadership styles (Northouse, 2020, p. 479). Similarly, there could be employees who like directive leadership, which provides a framework for the employees' decision-making (Stogdill, 1974, p. 309), and get the necessary tasks done by due time with efficiency. As a matter of fact, it is important for today's leaders to come out of their selective pattern and pursue a hybrid style to keep the balance in the team. Moreover, mixtures of different leadership approaches are also significant in order to keep the workflow according to plan.

Looking at the need for leadership style outside the workplace, in order to be the market leader, the organisation needs to stand out in the crowd of its competitors. One activity that helps in this process is taking measured risks. From Pratono (2021)'s analysis, we get to know about the opportunities that risk-taking behaviour offers. According to the author, if a company has the tendency or the confidence to take some risky decisions while other competitors may tend to avoid them due to the uncertainties, it could open the door of a big competitive edge for them over the rivals, which in turn helps in leading the market. Despite that, generally, the top management considers the risk-taking personnel to be costly, avoidable and a negative resource. However, from the modern perspective, the results show otherwise. They show that if the leaders are reluctant to take risks when necessary or when opportunities arise, not taking them may bring poorer results. Therefore, vision, which is considered one of the four major factors accounting for extraordinary performance of leadership (Bass & Avolio, 1994), is a required quality that leaders need to have.

Again, using hybrid leadership approaches and taking risky decisions in isolation does not guarantee success. There is no certainty that the risky moves will bring about positive outcomes. Hence, comes the challenge of uncertainty, and as discussed earlier in this chapter, it is understandable that hybrid leadership is not only necessary but also effective to deal with the situations. If a leader knows about the skills, needs and competencies of his subordinates and the availability of the resources, then this knowledge can give him the confidence to take the risks without being afraid of the negative outcomes. This is only possible through the integration of the leadership style practices both inside the workplace as well as outside. During the innovation process, the risk and uncertainty are made clear. This capability can exhibit how many businesses can target and identify the major risks at different innovation processes with the view to reduce the negative effects of such implementation to the least (Games & Rendi, 2019). Therefore, we first look into the wider practice, that is, the mix of leaders with their individual styles throughout the organisation to suit different groups.

(1) *Different leaders with their personal styles to suit different groups within the organisation.*

As pointed out by Drucker (1993, p. 02), any attempt to manage in turbulent times must start with the most predictable of all developments: demographics. Confronting today's population characteristics, a leader has to realise the shift from manual work to knowledge work as the central resource and utilise it accordingly. They then have to work on empowering, motivating and raising conscientiousness in others to embrace this change. From the literature review, it is evident that a leader needs to create connections with the followers and respond to any fluctuating environment rapidly. Therefore, the leaders in this scenario must have the ability to motivate others. This in turn creates an improved output performance and job meaningfulness (Yukl, 2010). This aligns with the characteristics of transformational leadership, which describes how leaders can initiate, develop and carry out significant changes in organisations.

However, the motivation required for keeping up with this change might not be the same for everyone in the organisation. Some may prefer exchange, which mostly translates to rewards, over emotional motivation. Here, a leader needs to have the ability and power to reward or punish the subordinates. This in short defines the purpose of transactional leadership, which is also characterised by reliance on rewards and punishments to get optimal job performance.

Another crucial role of leaders during uncertain market turbulence is the management of organisational knowledge. All the tacit and explicit knowledge that are possessed by individuals and the explicit knowledge that are codified in manuals, databases and information systems are included in organisational knowledge. It also includes the collectively shared tacit knowledge within the firm in the form of routines, culture and know-how embedded in social processes (Grant, 1996; Nahapiet & Ghoshal, 2000; Nonaka & Takeuchi, n.d.), and knowledge management, according to Grey (1996), is the collaborative and integrated approach for creating, capturing, organising, accessing and using of an enterprise's intellectual assets.

Bryant (2003) in his paper states that leaders provide vision, motivation, systems and structures at all levels of the organisation that facilitate the conversion of knowledge into competitive advantages, and it is essential to effectively lead organisational knowledge processes to achieve and sustain competitive advantage. Although during times of uncertainty, it may often be the case that most of the competitors or rival organisations are taking the blow and each of them is faced with the same scenario; it is an effective leader's task to use the knowledge available, may it be few as is mostly the case during uncertainties, and use them efficiently to overcome the state.

In the same paper, the author reveals the role of transformational and transactional leadership in managing knowledge and argues that the role of leadership in converting knowledge into competitive advantages is important. He suggests an effective usage of the blend of transformational and transactional leadership in managing organisational knowledge by implying that at creating and sharing of knowledge at the level of individual groups, transformational leadership may be more effective, while at the organisational level of exploiting knowledge, transactional leadership is more effective. This further strengthens the need for both leadership styles to be present in an organisation during the times of uncertain market turbulence.

Also, due to the presence of constant turbulence, in today's market, it is essential for businesses to thrive through them instead of trying to change the scenario. One of the characteristics found from the demographics is the movement of population from manual to knowledge work. To manage in turbulent times, therefore, means to face up to the new realities (Drucker, 1993, p. 2). This is exactly where adaptive leadership fits in, which is characterised by the practice of mobilising people to tackle tough challenges and thrive. Adaptive leaders engage in activities that mobilise, motivate, organise, orient and focus the attention of others (Heifetz et al., 1994, 2009).

One possible style of leadership that may be incorporated in the hybrid leadership mix in an organisation is servant leadership, of which the chief motive is to serve first (Greenleaf, 2002). Servant leadership emphasises on developing and empowering people, authenticity, expressing humility, interpersonal acceptance and stewardship and providing direction (Van Dierendonck, 2011). This in turn helps the organisation create leadership among the followers, who require lesser direction from the leader. This is crucial during market turbulence as the more people there are in the decision-making process of an organisation, the better the chance of more unique and effective solutions to emerge that in turn help the organisation to get ahead in the competing environment. One of the defining characteristics of servant leadership which makes it especially relevant in leading during today's uncertain environment is the building of community (Spears, 2010), which during the times of uncertainty helps the employees of an organisation stay motivated, develops courage and keeps them focused on the goals, may it be modified or not.

(2) *Individual leader practicing multiple leadership styles.*

Now, we shift the attention to the more individualistic approach which, from the surface, might be confused for a new style of leadership. In this approach, the same leader possesses and applies multiple leadership characteristics to suit members of the same group of people, often at the same time. During the times of such uncertainty, leaders in organisations take different drastic steps to help them survive the turbulence. One such step that has been followed and practiced during

COVID-19 globally, as pointed out by Dulebohn and Hoch (2017) in their research, is shifting from physical teams to virtual ones, or a mix of both by using electronic communication media, primarily due to the lockdown and government restrictions, but later to reduce the costs of travelling, relocation, overhead, etc. He also mentioned the importance of the leaders to possess relevant team skills combined with appropriate leader behaviours that are crucial in dealing with the lack of face-to-face contact with team members.

According to the authors, one of the drawbacks faced by the leaders while leading virtual teams was difficulties in creating trust and shared responsibility among team members when compared to the co-located teams. This can be solved by following the charismatic approach, which is defined by the perception of the followers that a leader possesses a divinely inspired gift and is somehow unique and larger than life (Weber, 1968).

The indicators of charismatic leadership, as indicated by House (1977), include followers' trust in the correctness of the leader's beliefs, willing obedience, unquestioning acceptance of and affection for the leader, which might prove beneficial in leading virtual or mixed teams. Also, as pointed out by Dulebohn et al. (2016), communication skills, depth of understanding in collaborative technology, ability to influence and facilitate team member engagement, appreciation for cultural diversity and an ability to influence and build trust and relationships with the geographically dispersed team members are some of the few skills that a hybrid leader may require. This resonates with the characteristics of transformational, transactional and authentic leadership altogether.

The above-mentioned is a broad classification of the types of hybrid leadership specifically in organisations. Using this for other situations may require modification, which is expected from future researchers, as well as practitioners.

Conclusion

In this study, we have emphasised the need of a hybrid leadership style in navigating uncertain market turbulence. The already present turbulence has grown unpredictable as a result of the innovation's quick transformation and other macroeconomic events. Recent events only served to magnify this uncertainty. Effective leadership is one approach that is essential in dealing with this unpredictability. The theme of this research, hybrid leadership style to meet unpredictable market turbulence, came into play because this leadership had to be adjusted for each of the diverse groups of people present both inside the organisation and outside in the marketplace. Here, we've included the roles that several leadership philosophies currently followed in various firms that aid in navigating uncertainty and exploring the potential for new philosophies. This study could therefore serve as a manual for using a hybrid leadership style during market upheavals because sticking with a single particular style may prove ineffective or result in annoyance and frustration.

References

Adekoya, O. B., & Oliyide, J. A. (2021). How COVID-19 drives connectedness among commodity and financial markets: Evidence from TVP-VAR and causality-in-quantiles techniques. *Resources Policy, 70*, 101898. https://doi.org/10.1016/j.resourpol.2020.101898

Ahern, S., & Loh, E. (2020). Leadership during the COVID-19 pandemic: Building and sustaining trust in times of uncertainty. *BMJ Leader*, 1–4.

Alam, M. K., Tabash, M. I., Billah, M., Kumar, S., & Anagreh, S. (2022). The impacts of the Russia–Ukraine invasion on global markets and commodities: A dynamic connectedness among G7 and BRIC markets. *Journal of Risk and Financial Management, 15*(8), 352. https://doi.org/10.3390/jrfm15080352

Albulescu, C. T. (2021). COVID-19 and the United States financial markets' volatility. *Finance Research Letters, 38*, 101699. https://doi.org/10.1016/j.frl.2020.101699

Anderson, L. (2018). Leadership during crisis. *Leader to Leader, 2018*(90), 49–54. https://doi.org/10.1002/ltl.20389

Bass, B. M., & Avolio, B. J. (1994). Transformational leadership and organizational culture. *International Journal of Public Administration, 17*(3–4), 541–554.

Bryant, S. E. (2003). The role of transformational and transactional leadership in creating, sharing and exploiting organizational knowledge. *Journal of Leadership & Organizational Studies, 9*(4), 32–44. https://doi.org/10.1177/107179190300900403

Cox Jr, T. (1991). The multicultural organization. *Academy of Management Perspectives, 5*(2), 34–47.

Drucker, P. F. (1993). *Managing in turbulent times*. Routledge.

Duchek, S., Raetze, S., & Scheuch, I. (2020). The role of diversity in organizational resilience: A theoretical framework. *Business Research, 13*(2), 387–423.

Dulebohn, J. H., Davison, R. B.Lee, S. A.Conlon, D. E. McNamara, G. & Sarinopoulos, C. (2016). Gender differences in justice evaluations: Evidence from fMRI. *Evidence from fMRI. Journal of Applied Psychology, 101*(2), 151.

Dulebohn, J. H., & Hoch, J. E. (2017). Virtual teams in organizations. *Human Resource Management Review, 27*(4), 569–574. https://doi.org/10.1016/j.hrmr.2016.12.004

Fine, C., Sojo, V., & Lawford-Smith, H. (2020). Why does workplace gender diversity matter? Justice, organizational benefits, and policy. *Social Issues and Policy Review, 14*(1), 36–72.

Games, D., & Rendi, R. P. (2019). The effects of knowledge management and risk taking on SME financial performance in creative industries in an emerging market: The mediating effect of innovation outcomes. *Journal of Global Entrepreneurship Research, 9*(1). https://doi.org/10.1186/s40497-019-0167-1

Gomez, L. E., & Bernet, P. (2019). Diversity improves performance and outcomes. *Journal of the National Medical Association, 111*(4), 383–392.

Grant, R. M. (1996). Toward a knowledge-based theory of the firm. *Strategic Management Journal, 17*(S2), 109–122. https://doi.org/10.1002/smj.4250171110

Greenleaf, R. K. (2002). *Servant leadership: A journey into the nature of legitimate power and greatness*. Paulist Press.

Grey, D. (1996, March). *What is knowledge management*. The Knowledge Management Forum (KM Forum). https://www.km-forum.org/what_is.htm

Gronn, P. (2009). From distributed to hybrid leadership practice. In *Distributed leadership: Different perspectives* (pp. 197–217). Springer Netherlands.

Gupta, S., & Lehmann, D. R. (2003). Customers as assets. *Journal of Interactive Marketing, 17*(1), 9–24.

Heifetz, R. A., Grashow, A., & Linsky, M. (2009). *The practice of adaptive leadership: Tools and tactics for changing your organization and the world.* Harvard Business Press.

Hossain, S. F. A. (2019). Social networking and its role in media entrepreneurship: Evaluating the use of mobile phones in the context of online shopping–A review. *Journal of Media Management and Entrepreneurship (JMME), 1*(1), 73–86.

Hossain, S. F. A., Nurunnabi, M., Hussain, K., & Saha, S. K. (2019a). Effects of variety-seeking intention by mobile phone usage on university students' academic performance. *Cogent Education, 6*(1), 1574692.

Hossain, S. F. A., Shan, X., & Nurunnabi, M. (2019b). Is M-learning a challenge? Students attitudes toward the sustainable learning and performance. *International Journal of e-Collaboration, 15*(1), 21–37.

Hossain, S. F. A., Xi, Z., Nurunnabi, M., & Anwar, B. (2022). Sustainable academic performance in higher education: A mixed method approach. *Interactive Learning Environments, 30*(4), 707–720.

Hossain, S. F. A., Xi, Z., Nurunnabi, M., & Hussain, K. (2020). Ubiquitous role of social networking in driving M-Commerce: Evaluating the use of mobile phones for online shopping and payment in the context of trust. *Sage Open, 10*(3), 2158244020939536.

House, R. J. (1977). A 1976 theory of charismatic leadership. In J. G. Hunt & L. L. Larson (Eds.), *Leadership: Zhe cutting edge.* Southern Illinois University Press.

Kotler, P., & Caslione, J. A. (2009). *Chaotics: The business of managing and marketing in the age of turbulence.* Amacom Books.

Liadze, I., Macchiarelli, C., Mortimer-Lee, P., & Sanchez Juanino, P. (2022). Economic costs of the Russia-Ukraine war. *The World Economy.* https://doi.org/10.1111/twec.13336

Liu, Y., Fuller, B., Hester, K., Bennett, R. J., & Dickerson, M. S. (2017). Linking authentic leadership to subordinate behaviors. *The Leadership & Organization Development Journal, 39*(2), 218–233. https://doi.org/10.1108/lodj-12-2016-0327

Nahapiet, J. & Ghoshal, S. (2000). Social capital, intellectual capital, and the organizational advantage. *Knowledge and Social Capital,* 119–157. https://doi.org/10.1016/b978-0-7506-7222-1.50009-x

Nonaka, I., & Takeuchi, H. (n.d.). Knowledge-based strategy. *The Palgrave Encyclopedia of Strategic Management.* https://doi.org/10.1057/9781137294678.0350

Northouse, P. G. (2020). *Introduction to leadership: Concepts and practice.* Sage Publications.

Pratono, A. H. (2021). Innovation strategy beyond the COVID-19 pandemic: The role of trust under disruptive technology. *Foresight, 24*(3/4), 358–376. https://doi.org/10.1108/fs-05-2021-0105

Schroth, H. (2019). Are you ready for Gen Z in the workplace? *California Management Review, 61*(3), 5–18.

Shadraconis, S. (2013). Organizational leadership in times of uncertainty: Is transformational leadership the answer? *LUX: A Journal of Transdisciplinary Writing and Research from Claremont Graduate University*, 2(1), 1–15. https://doi.org/10. 5642/lux.201301.28

Spears, L. C. (2010). *Servant leadership and Robert K. Greenleaf's legacy* (pp. 11–24). Servant Leadership. https://doi.org/10.1057/9780230299184_2

Stogdill, R. M. (1974). *Handbook of leadership: A survey of theory and research.* Free Press.

Sull, D. (2009, February 1). How to thrive in turbulent markets. *Harvard Business Review*. https://hbr.org/2009/02/how-to-thrive-in-turbulent-markets

Rust, R. T., Ambler, T., Carpenter, G. S., Kumar, V., & Srivastava, R. K. (2004). Measuring marketing productivity: Current knowledge and future directions. *Journal of Marketing*, 68(4), 76–89. https://doi.org/10.1509/jmkg.68.4.76.42721

Van Dierendonck, D. (2011). Servant leadership: A review and synthesis. *Journal of Management*, 37(4), 1228–1261.

Wang, C. L., & Ahmed, P. K. (2007). Dynamic capabilities: A review and research agenda.*International Journal of Management Reviews*, 9(1), 31–51. https://doi.org/ 10.1111/j.1468-2370.2007.00201.x

Weber, M. (1968). *On charisma and institution building.* University of Chicago Press.

Yukl, G. A. (2010). *Leadership in organizations.* Pearson.

Chapter 2

Entrepreneurship and Innovation: A Way Towards Sustainable Development and Poverty Alleviation

Manisha Paliwal[a], Sasikanta Tripathy[b], Nishita Chatradhi[c] and Yash Ranga[d]

[a]Sri Balaji University, India
[b]University of Bahrain, Bahrain
[c]Government of Alberta, Canada
[d]PYXERA Global, India

Abstract

The importance of entrepreneurship as a force for economic progress and poverty alleviation has grown in recent years. Innovation is at the core of entrepreneurship, whereas entrepreneurship is a tool for innovation. Forbye, social innovation has become a new way of thinking and strategy for solving social problems. Additionally, to study the ever-growing and dynamic space of entrepreneurship followed by an analysis of the actors in the ecosystem, including an emphasis on its outcome and social impact on poverty. Drawing on the insights from the framework of the Theory of Change, the authors present the case of PYXERA Global. Using a qualitative research strategy to create insights from the organisation's activities in over 100 countries, we exhibit the entrepreneurial ecosystem approach followed and implemented by them. Through meticulous interviews, the chapter produces in-depth insights from the strategists and entrepreneurs of the organisation that create a balanced and focused social impact. The study reveals the importance of entrepreneurial training, education, technical skills and gender balance in poverty alleviation. Through collaborations with the private, public and social sectors, the organisation ensures to the creation of an ecosystem that provides technical support and access to skills to develop an entrepreneurial mindset. The Theory of Change undertaken by PYXERA informs how tri-sector partnerships and deep organisational involvement can

Creating Pathways for Prosperity, 15–32
doi:10.1108/978-1-83549-121-820241003

aid towards sustainable development and poverty alleviation. The findings contribute to the development of an attitude that poverty reduction and community development can be achieved through co-creation, which is possible through entrepreneurship and innovation.

Keywords: Entrepreneurship; innovation; poverty reduction; sustainable development; theory of change

Introduction of the Study

In the last decade, there has been a growing importance in the field of entrepreneurship as a mechanism for poverty reduction. Entrepreneurship, according to many definitions, relates to situations in which markets, resources and organisational structures can be established by developing new methods, ends or means–ends interactions (Eckhardt & Shane, 2003; Shane & Venkataraman, 2000; Si et al., 2020). While many approaches have evolved to cope with complicated social issues, the entrepreneurship model is recognised as an effective model for serving multiple challenges connected to the poor and vulnerable parts of society (Tambunan, 2009; Tripathy et al., 2021). Small producer's associations, labour associations, social networks, women-centric units, federations and hybrid models are all examples of organisational forms for entrepreneurship. Their goal is to improve society. It has the potential to bring about long-term, transformational changes in how it handles acute social problems (Alvord et al., 2004; Austin et al., 2006; Carini & Carpita, 2014). According to Hochgerner (2013), social innovation is the development and implementation of innovative solutions that involve conceptual, process or organisational change, with the goal of improving the welfare and well-being of individuals and communities (Degli Antoni & Sabatini, 2017).

Innovating solutions and developing unique business models can serve poor and marginal communities. Through appropriate business models, most social entrepreneurship models serve clients within this segment (Casado-Caneque & Hart, 2015; Putnam, 2000). In addition to finding innovative solutions to community issues, they can design products and services customised to clients and enhance entrepreneurial development. Through social entrepreneurship, entrepreneurs can develop their human capital through mentoring, sharing information and developing trust and ties (Ferdousi & Parveen, 2019; Mair & Schoen, 2007).

Capacity building is an important component of entrepreneurship development, and it largely comprises of training in four areas: technical skills, on-the-job training, bookkeeping, management and marketing. Financing methods, business and social networking are three notable axes of capacity building (Tripathy et al., 2022; Yadav et al., 2022).

While academic interest in entrepreneurship models has attracted many researchers into the field, there are not enough studies about the importance of entrepreneurial training, technical skills, and gender balance in reducing poverty.

Against this backdrop, this chapter presents to accentuate the role of social innovation and entrepreneurial strategies in mitigating poverty. To explore and analyse the factors that foster community development and poverty reduction through entrepreneurship and innovation, the case study of PYXERA Global's flagship project JIVA and Global Pro Bono project Global Mamas have been studied. Additionally, this research is also aimed to study the ever-growing and dynamic space of entrepreneurship followed by an analysis of the actors in the ecosystem, including an emphasis on its outcome and social impact on poverty.

This study makes a significant theoretical contribution to poverty reduction and community development with entrepreneurship and innovation along with *Entrepreneurial Training and Education, Technical Skills and Gender Balance in Poverty Alleviation.*

Likewise, practical implications to have sustainable poverty reduction mechanism through co-creation are also provided. The remainder of the research is structured as follows: Section 'Review of Literature' covers a literature study and investigates the relationship between *Entrepreneurship and Innovation and poverty reduction, community development with theory of change concepts* and outlines a research proposition. Section 'Methodology' discusses methodology, data gathering, and analysis, while section 'Case Study: PYXERA Global' discusses the PYXERA Global case study. Section 'Managerial Implications' covers the study's theoretical and managerial implications, while section 'Conclusion and Way Forward' finishes with a closing remark, limits and future research plan.

Review of Literature

Entrepreneurship and Innovation

Social innovation has an important role in entrepreneurship development. Solis-Navarrete et al. (2021) proposed some elements for considering social innovation as a phenomenon. Their study results in a conceptual framework for social innovation's use. In a similar light, Veiga et al. (2020) examined the effect of public institutions on revolution, competitiveness, and entrepreneurship. The data was collected from all reputed organisations for a period of 13 years, i.e. 2006–2018. The study employed multiple regression analysis with unbalanced panel data. The results found that public organisations' quality positively influences the proposed variables' levels. Entrepreneurship activities influence not only quality of life but also entrepreneurship behaviour (Woodside et al., 2016). The conclusion from their study implies a necessary change in cultural thinking and behaviour for a successful entrepreneur.

The role of innovation by applying technology cannot be ignored for the social change towards poverty alleviation. Poverty alleviation can be done not only through technological innovation, but it can also achieve through financial development and globalisation (Zameer et al., 2020).

However, this poverty alleviation efficiency is ununiformly distributed as per their study, and the impact of globalisation is statistically insignificant. Likewise, Schot and Steinmueller (2018) enumerated the importance of science, technology, and innovation (STI) strategy in three phases. In the first phase, the government supports developing science and technology as alternative sources of knowledge. The second phase enumerated how globalisation shaped the national system in improving competitiveness, knowledge formation and marketability. The third phase relates to modern environmental and social issues like United Nations (UN) sustainable developmental goals (SDGs). In addition, the study links these three phases for dynamic STI for policymaking and recommends having strong technological advancement.

Social innovation has an important role in entrepreneurship development. Solis-Navarrete et al. (2021) proposed some elements for considering social innovation as a phenomenon. Their study results in a conceptual framework for social innovation's use. Innovation has a broader approach described in their work where it could be applicable both in academia and in private and public sectors. In their paper, they highlighted social enterprise partnerships and individual entrepreneurs to focus on fostering innovation practice and value creation for society.

The role of policies adopted by the government cannot be ignored for an effective social enterprise which leads to the economy's growth in the rural sector. They found a positive effect of the innovation system on the growth of the rural economy, but it varies across different geographical locations for their study (Wu et al., 2017). National support for the foster innovation and economic growth depends on certain mechanisms like new institution creation, support for linkage and policies for the enhancement of demand (Surie, 2017). A positive change in social and environmental came to the limelight because of poverty and poor living style. This brings social welfare to the natural environment and potentiality towards entrepreneurship (Ozdemir & Gupta, 2021).

Poverty Reduction

The importance of entrepreneurship as a force for economic progress and poverty alleviation has grown in recent years. One important factor influencing becoming a successful entrepreneur is energy poverty (Cheng et al., 2021). They discovered a link between a higher share of household income spending and the likelihood of becoming an energy industry entrepreneur. Entrepreneurship can address the poverty solution indicated by the growing gap between rich and poor (Morris et al., 2020). Several factors like expanded opportunity, supportive infrastructure, source of differentiation, a platform for entrepreneurs, a well-designed model, etc., can help to break the poverty cycle.

Poverty relationships and entrepreneurship can help to achieve a combination of conversion factors and future prosperity expectations. It demonstrates that supporting conversion characteristics lead to favourable entrepreneurship-enabled future prosperity expectations (Kimmitt et al., 2020). Poverty alleviation can be majorly achieved through entrepreneurship. This can be achieved through resource concern, institutional change and capitalist-based assumption of business. Adopting technology for social mobilisation and empowering the community helps reduce poverty (Sutter et al., 2019). Technological innovation and sustainable development complement each other for the ultimate growth of community development through entrepreneurship (Gupta et al., 2023; Paliwal et al., 2023).

Community Development

The innovation movement for sustainability starts with social and community development (Joshi & Yenneti, 2020). Their results show a complementary relation between innovation and development in the light of technology. An integrated approach through initiative, ownership and broader social movements brings development to the community (Becker et al., 2017). Community development brings fertile ground for advancing social development and social movements. Change became so popular in those days to achieve some target in the light of this Stevanović (2016) study on existing policy change which brings development not only in entrepreneurship area but also rural advancement. Their work focuses on the importance of the private sector for the ultimate development of the community.

Sustainable Development

The role of innovation by applying technology cannot be ignored for the social change towards poverty alleviation. Poverty alleviation can be done not only through technological innovation, but it can also achieve through financial development and globalisation (Zameer et al., 2020).

However, this poverty alleviation efficiency is ununiformly distributed as per their study, and the impact of globalisation is statistically insignificant. Sustainability is one of the most important ways for innovation to meet global challenges. Commitment to sustainability may sometimes be unpractised because of behaviour gaps. Sustainability-oriented innovation as a practice for achieving organisational goals (Luqmani et al., 2017). Their support towards the route to market, making collaborations, and past failures as learning have been identified as significant tools for sustainable development.

Entrepreneurship alone cannot move ahead without sustainable development. Dhahri and Omri (2018) study the competence of activity involved with entrepreneurs to intensify economic growth and boost social conditions. They found a positive relationship between economic and sustainable development. Their causality test indicates interactions among entrepreneurship on one hand and environmental objectives, economic growth and social conditions on the other.

Theory of Change

The concept of technological transformation is critical in the growth of entrepreneurship. Schot and Steinmueller (2018) identified three stages of the importance of science, technology and innovation strategy. In the first phase, the government supports developing science and technology as an alternative source of knowledge. The second phase enumerated how globalisation shaped the national system in improving competitiveness, knowledge formation and marketability. The third phase relates to the modern environment and social issues like United Nations (UN) sustainable developmental goals (SDGs). In addition, the study links these three phases for dynamic STI for policymaking and recommends to have strong technological advancement.

The Theory of Change undertaken by PYXERA Global informs how tri-sector partnerships and deep organisational involvement can aid towards sustainable development and poverty alleviation. Rosca et al. (2020) examined the engagement of women tycoons in social business activities in a dynamic environment. The sample consists of four firms from two emerging economies, India and Colombia. The study employed an effectuation lens and decision-making logic to investigate further. The results found positive nexus between women's social tycoons and social causes. Further, the results analysed that women entrepreneurs are found to be in elusive transition during venture construction progression.

Entrepreneurial Training and Education, Technical Skills and Gender Balance in Poverty Alleviation

The importance of entrepreneurial training and education, technical skills and gender balance in poverty alleviation is always in the limelight for any society. Zameer et al. (2020) enumerated the role of technological advancement, financial stability and globalisation in poverty eradication in China. The study employed system GMM and super efficiency DEA model for a period of 11 years, i.e., 2007–2018. The results found poverty eradication efficiency was improved in several regions of China. Technology advancement and financial improvement were significant in poverty mitigation efficiency. In contrast, globalisation was insignificant in poverty mitigation efficiency. Similarly, Morris et al. (2020) enumerated how empowerment was improved under entrepreneurship in economically deprived countries. The study proposed a conceptual framework called SPIDER to break the problem of poverty. Rosca et al. (2020) examined the engagement of women tycoons in social business activities in a dynamic environment. The sample consists of four firms from two emerging economies like India and Colombia. The study employed an effectuation lens and decision-making logic to investigate further. The results found positive nexus between women's social tycoons and social causes. Further, the results analysed that women entrepreneurs are found to be in elusive transition during venture construction progression.

Through collaborations with the private, public, and social sectors, the organisation ensures to create of an ecosystem that provides technical support and access to skills to develop an entrepreneurial mindset. Zhao and Lounsbury (2016) investigate the nexus between microfinance organisations (MFOs) and institutional logic like religion and markets. The sample is collected from a proprietary database for capital providers and MFOs of different nations over a period of 8 years, i.e. 2004–2012. The results found solid market logic improves public capital and profitability under the scheme of MFOs. Similarly, religious diversity positively impacts market logic and helps increase capital flows into MFOs.

In a similar light, Stevanović (2016) investigated the need to alter the existing policy related to rural development and entrepreneurship in Serbia. The study provides few insights about funding and allocation of resources in the private and public sectors. Firstly, the private sector should increase the funding or source of allocation of funds in the next 10 years. The employment generation was stronger and more stable in the private sector than in the government sector (Surie, 2017). The government of Serbia must use pre-agreement funds for effective rural development.

The effect of public institutions on revolution, competitiveness and entrepreneurship was examined by Veiga et al. (2020). The data was collected from all reputed organisations for a period of 13 years, i.e., 2006–2018. The study employed multiple regression analysis with unbalanced panel data. The results found that public organisations' quality positively influences the proposed variables' levels.

Gregori and Holzmann (2020) enumerated the role of sustainable firms in communicating information through the business model by embedding innovative technology. Their study identified sustainable business model includes mixed value plans, novel value generation and multidimensional values. In addition, the study enumerated supplementary strains of digital sustainability and links with business context. Finally, it briefs about the limitations of technology for framing a dynamic, sustainable business model. Macke et al. (2018) analysed the approaches, drives, analytical aspects and academic production of social business. Sustainable social transformation comes only with the individual social mission and merging the practice with knowledge. In addition, the solution to the established problems and developments in living situations of different conditions falls under the individual social mission of sustainable entrepreneurship. The study was developed based on a literature survey that investigates academic production under sustainable entrepreneurship. Further, the study analysed various dimensions and elements under the social concept. Wu et al. (2017) enumerated the importance of government policies under the national innovation system (NIS) in endorsing social business action. Further, the study investigated the role of NIS in developing rural sectors through the advance of innovative technology. The results found a positive impact of NIS on the interior region, coastal areas, and China's economic growth. Similarly, NIS has positive nexus with high labour mobility and R&D expenditure in China.

In this context, it has become imperative to explore the extent of *Entrepreneurial Training and Education, Technical Skills in Poverty Alleviation, and community development.*

Methodology

A qualitative study methodology was used to better understand the role of social innovation and entrepreneurial tactics in poverty alleviation. Our paper is supported by a focused literature review and an exclusive case study on PYXERA Global's flagship project JIVA and Global Pro Bono Project Global Mamas. Drawing on the insights from the framework of the Theory of Change, the authors present the case of PYXERA Global to generate rich findings from the organisation's work and experience of working in over 100 countries and to exhibit the entrepreneurial ecosystem approach followed and implemented by them. For this study, the data was collected through in-depth virtual interviews with the officials of JIVA, India and Global Mamas, Ghana and additionally reviewed documents provided by Pyxera Global. Through meticulous interviews, the chapter produces in-depth insights from the strategists and entrepreneurs of the organisation that create a balanced and focused social impact. The unit of analysis, or the study's region of emphasis, is an important component of case studies (Merriam, 1988; Yin, 2009). This unit analysis was the organisation and its members who participated in the study for this investigation.

Case Study: PYXERA Global

In developed economies, entrepreneurship has made a significant contribution to poverty reduction, economic growth, economic development and other related issues. However, PYXERA Global recognises that there is a gap in emerging economies since people in underdeveloped areas are ignorant of national opportunities such as microfinance institution loans. While entrepreneurship is vital in industrialised economies, more work needs to be done in emerging ones. The organisation supports entrepreneurs in gaining the skills, digital infrastructure, financial literacy and access to capital and markets they need to improve value chains and create stronger lives and livelihoods. Over the last few decades, they have addressed systemic challenges with zero respect for borders or sectors. They help leaders to connect with one another and innovate for lasting systemic change.

PYXERA Global stands at the intersection of business, social and public sectors, facilitating groundbreaking partnerships worldwide. For over 30 years, PYXERA Global has provided advisory services and programme execution in over 100 countries. Solving World's most pressing problems One Community at a Time is the mission of PYXERA which symbolise the most pressing challenges in the world. They work towards a world where communities thrive by creating and sustaining inclusive, equitable, and regenerative systems. Pyxera Global does this by reconceptualising how public, private, and social interests solve global challenges and transform private sector leadership. Through this approach, the organisation brings resources to under-resourced communities worldwide to build resiliency, access, and capability. In what follows, we discuss two key case studies and collaborative projects of PYXERA Global from India and Ghana.

JIVA – India

From 2012 to 2020, PYXERA Global India implemented JIVA, the Joint Initiative for Village Advancement, a community development project jointly developed with the John Deere Foundation and local communities in rural Rajasthan, India. The programme's mission is to improve the livelihoods and resilience of smallholder farmers, both current and future, by investing in their present and future. The programme uses income diversification to boost farmer resilience and improve agricultural productivity. This comprehensive approach is essential, working with agricultural productivity to increase resilience to shocks. The programme prioritises community needs like agricultural productivity and education. The two main interventions are agricultural training to boost farm productivity, profitability, and sustainability, and youth education to promote opportunities and equity. Higher-educated farmers are more productive, profitable, adaptable, and resilient. In 2013, several farmers eagerly became Agricultural Volunteers, connecting JIVA and the community. They participated in JIVA's farmer training programme to better serve the community. This training helped them master and implement excellent farming techniques, which increased their crop cultivation income. Also, they actively participated in the financial literacy and agripreneurship training and put what they learnt to use. Farmers increased their revenue by reinvesting it in livestock and opening a retail store, which resulted in a more than eightfold increase in their overall household income from 2013 to 2015. Their leadership has evolved over the years, and they now serve as Resource Farmers. They continue to be a reliable source of knowledge and information for farmers throughout the community, providing guidance on effective and sustainable farming practices.

Over the programme's lifetime, JIVA grew from 3 to 24 villages and nine hamlets – reaching approximately 35,000 community members – and is currently being strategically adapted and piloted in communities in Nigeria while scoping is underway for replication in Latin America. Through December 2021, approximately $3,585,857 in additional income has been generated from JIVA's resilient agriculture interventions and an estimated $1,536,483 increase in lifetime earnings from reintegrating dropout students into schools. In total, JIVA anticipates that between 2014 and 2023, based on actual and projected household income generated, an estimated $5,977,488 in additional income will be produced within Sakrawas, Pipli Ahiran, Pipli Acharyan, Junda and Lapsiya panchayats, plus neighbouring non-JIVA villages where JIVA approaches were adopted. While there has been a surge in research on entrepreneurship and innovation in recent years (Godfrey, 2013), the primary goal of such entrepreneurship has often been framed as assisting individuals in meeting their most basic needs. However, the authors of this study argue that limiting the scope of entrepreneurship to addressing basic needs undervalues its potential impact in these environments. Instead, entrepreneurship has the capacity to achieve far-reaching goals. Researchers have identified innovation, knowledge, and training as critical tools for breaking the cycle of poverty (Bruton et al., 2011). These elements are seen as pathways towards a brighter future, offering individuals the means to improve their economic circumstances and overall well-being. In developing economies, agriculture is the main driver of decreasing poverty. Therefore, the development programme strategically invests in the potential of the young farmers by making sure sustainable, high-quality education is available and affordable. This is in addition to working with farmers to improve agricultural practises and ultimately profitability, savings and reinvestment back into the farm.

Researchers and economists are increasingly recognising that entrepreneurship and new ventures have the potential to alleviate poverty worldwide. Importantly, this approach to poverty alleviation does not argue that many economists' and institutions' traditional perspectives are incorrect (Ahlstrom, 2010). In accordance with this recognition and Fig. 2.1 JIVA takes a holistic approach from the start, incorporating the concept of 'sustainable graduation' into its core strategy rather than as an afterthought at the end of the project. This strategy starts with a community-driven pilot programme, which creates a tight feedback loop that allows for iterative adaptations based on changing needs and opportunities. The refined technological and operational strategies are replicated across different regions as the project progresses, ensuring scalability and effectiveness.

JIVA is also testing and refining the concept of 'sustainable graduation' within the pilot project area according to Fig. 2.1. The insights gained from this gradual

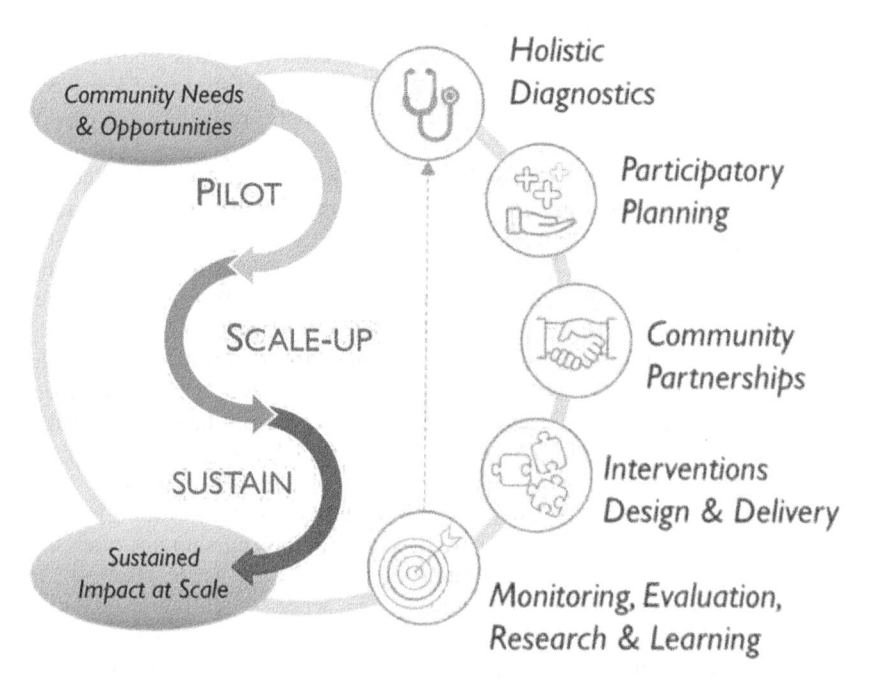

Fig. 2.1.   Strategic Approach of JIVA. *Source:* PYXERA Global website.

reduction in programming help to shape strategies for extending the project's positive impact across the entire region beyond the programme's lifespan. While microlending is frequently promoted as a means of alleviating poverty, it can inadvertently foster subsistence entrepreneurship environments that perpetuate poverty (Viswanathan et al., 2014). Pyxera Global's approach, on the other hand, encourages the development of an entrepreneurial mindset, emphasising that poverty reduction and community development can be accomplished through co-creation, entrepreneurship, and innovation.

Global Mama's – Ghana

Voicing the very mission of Global Mamas, Co-Founder Elizabeth Ampiah shares,

> Having a family, being able to send them to school, and providing a home for them to reside are the definitions of prosperity in my opinion. A family is the foundation of prosperity. When I am entirely dependent on myself and not on anyone else, I will know I have attained prosperity.

The Global Mamas are community leaders, mothers, wives, grandmothers, sisters and entrepreneurs. Six Ghanaian women who were passionate about leveraging their talents as batikers and seamstresses to create a consistent income to support their families formed the organisation in 2003. They were helped by two North American ladies who were passionate about seeing Ghanaian women succeed in business. The Global Mamas group comprises thousands of people from all over the world who are united to bring wealth to African mothers and their families. The Mamas describe prosperity as happiness, good health and financial well-being. They succeed by developing and selling one-of-a-kind, handcrafted items of the finest quality. Being able to make the career they enjoy while still having financial freedom leads to increased pleasure.

Global Mamas' purpose is to help African women and their families live prosperous lives. Prosperity is defined as financial well-being, excellent health and happiness. They make a living by manufacturing and selling high-quality handmade items. They have tried to provide a better living for women and their families in Ghana by producing high-quality handcrafted clothes, accessories, jewellery, and skincare products. Global Mamas is a World Fair Trade Organization (WFT) guaranteed Member, assuring consumers that its production is done responsibly – socially, environmentally and economically. Global Mamas has evolved organically by leveraging talented, skilled craftswomen, local knowledge and extensive sourcing links.

Women constitute an essential component of the labour force in all countries' economies, with a female labour force participation rate of 48.9% (Word Bank, 2019). Evidence also suggests that women entrepreneurs have a positive impact on their communities by participating in entrepreneurial positions, which helps them to attain financially viable, socially and environmentally desirable goals (Allen et al., 2008). Because women entrepreneurs are essential developers of micro-enterprises, it is critical to comprehend the causes and repercussions of entrepreneurship participation (Cesaroni & Paoloni, 2016; Gupta et al., 2023). Today, Global Mamas' programmes are financially sustainable because it re-invests proceeds from product sales into day-to-day operations and capacity-building programmes that complement and enhance the socio-economic lives of women. However, a significant and persistent challenge to the organisation's expansion has been financing on terms that will not jeopardise the sustainability of the business through the pressures of expensive debt. Financing options are notoriously difficult in Ghana and are often identified as one of the main constraints to private sector growth. High-interest rates are not compatible with critical long-term investments. Therefore, Global Mamas relies on grant funding with the sole purpose to scale-up in a manner that is both economically and environmentally sustainable and ultimately results in compelling economic empowerment of women in Ghana.

Entrepreneurship is an example of organisational behaviour. Entrepreneurship requires taking risks, being proactive, and being innovative (Miller, 1983). Slevin and Covin (1990) believed that the three criteria are insufficient to achieve organisational success. "A successful firm does not participate both in entrepreneurial managerial behaviour and the necessary culture and organisational structure to support this behaviour", asserted (Alvarez & Barney, 2014; Alvarez et al., 2015; Greif, 2006). Global Mamas achieves business success by embracing a participatory problem-solving strategy in order to produce local answers and innovations for business activities. First, over 90% of the organisation's management, employees and women-owned enterprises are female, and all are involved in significant business decisions. Second, Global Mamas has a long history of commitment to its employees as well as the women-founded and – owned businesses in its network, which is crucial to fostering trust and encouraging increased engagement. Third, Global Mamas manages most of its supply chain vertically, which has been important to its success in both manufacturing and sales. Finally, Global Mamas does not compete on pricing but rather creates branded, high-quality, and one-of-a-kind products with a compelling story. The vast majority of the organisation's direct recipients are women from rural and suburban regions. Global Mamas believes in the positive ripple effects of economically empowered women: when women work, more children attend school, families receive better health care, local businesses prosper, and everyone's quality of life improves. They have led teams and organisations to implement innovations (Legge & Hindle, 1997).

The organisation worked with entrepreneurs throughout Ghana to make batik fabric and finished clothing. They hired men and women directly to create jewellery and recyclable accessories. They developed patterns, quality control procedures and manage a retail store in Accra, Ghana. GMs' products are available at approximately 150 fair trade merchants in Africa, Europe and North America, as well as on its website. Their business approach supports producers and addresses inclusion and sustainability concerns. Their inclusive business models generate long-term earnings for low-income individuals by incorporating them as employees, producers, and entrepreneurs at various levels in the value chain. The organisation focuses on providing opportunities for local producers to flourish as entrepreneurs and attain financial independence, resulting in healthy, prosperous Ghanaian communities. The foundation is also committed to sustainability, and it collaborates with local producers to create things that use textile scraps rather than burning them, as well as to acquire local cotton textiles whenever possible. Since the founders and administrative staff know and work directly with the producers, the foundation accomplishes a supply chain transparency. The collaborative establishment and growth of the organisation from the ground up, involving both founders and producers in business decisions and prosperity creation, has received a lot of attention because of the partnership between US and Ghanaian entrepreneurs. The collaborative establishment and growth of the organisation from the ground up, involving both founders and producers in business decisions and prosperity creation, has received a lot of attention as a result of the partnership between US and Ghanaian entrepreneurs. The GM case study demonstrates the poor's imaginative and entrepreneurial attempts to find and capitalise on new market opportunities. This case study also looked at how local entrepreneurs might establish disruptive business models that can help people get out of poverty.

Managerial Implications

In many ways, scholars consider entrepreneurship a solution to extreme poverty scholars (Jones Christensen et al., 2015; Peredo & Chrisman, 2006), and this study supports this idea of the previous studies. Using case studies from India and Ghana, this article observed the broader impact of entrepreneurship on poverty. The case studies indicate how by using disruptive innovation as a framework, producers can develop and manufacture innovative new products while also helping the users. They make products more affordable, simpler, and smaller, and thereby affordable to consumers which ultimately produce sustainable solutions to poverty reduction. This also serves to convince aspiring entrepreneurs to launch competitive enterprises, especially at the low end of the market. This study also gave evidence of the local communities entrepreneurial and innovative efforts to discover and capitalise on unique market opportunities. Within this paper, we summarise a number of streams of thought on poverty reduction throughout the last few decades.

Conclusion and Way Forward

This article presents insights derived from the Theory of Change framework from PYXERA Global. Our study illustrates the entrepreneurial ecosystem approach followed and implemented by the organisation and presents rich findings from their work and experience in over 100 countries. Through meticulous interviews, the chapter produces in-depth insights from the organisation's strategists and entrepreneurs that create a balanced and focused social impact. Although extensive empirical work has been done to explore the relationship between poverty and entrepreneurship, theoretical work on the subject is limited, according to the research. Studies that support the positive influence of entrepreneurship on poverty alleviation do not often offer it as a one-size-fits-all answer to economic growth in developing countries. Thus, high-level aspects such as infrastructures and educational, economic and social facilities must be investigated in order to provide more evidence for policymakers to achieve economic growth through entrepreneurship. Policymakers see entrepreneurship as a vital component in the fight against poverty. Despite a substantial body of literature on entrepreneurship, research has focused on the influence on the entrepreneur themselves (Frankish et al., 2017), with most studies concentrating on the impact on the entrepreneur themselves (Bruton et al., 2013).

This article examined the broader influence of entrepreneurship on poverty by presenting case studies from India and Ghana. Disruptive innovation demonstrates how innovative business models can enable producers to develop and manufacture new and useful products while also assisting users in consuming the product by locating a way to deliver simpler, or cheaper products to marginal consumers at an affordable price.

This case study also looked at how local entrepreneurs might establish disruptive business models that can help people get out of poverty. Yet, these theories did little to embrace the entrepreneurial potential in poverty theory. Previous research on poverty reduction through entrepreneurship were heavily affected by external support notions such as microfinance and other traditional props. In this study, we argue that rather than attempting to rely on investment or seeking government and institutional support to combat poverty, rural and local communities in developing countries must rely primarily on their own ability to discover and capitalise on business opportunities through a variety of profit-generating entrepreneurial activities. Such self-sufficiency is required mostly because countries or governments are typically too impoverished to provide such foreign assistance. Second, shifting impoverished people's attitudes and behaviours from passive to active status is critical to encouraging them to pursue economic success and reducing poverty in poor locations. Thus, more effective and causal business relationships in impoverished places may help alleviate poverty through existing community ties.

In addition to the foregoing, the facts and experience gained from this case study will demonstrate how entrepreneurship and innovative business models can enable the producer to create and manufacture new and useful items. It also holds the key to unlocking the purchasing power of the very poor through innovation in the delivery of simpler, smaller or cheaper products at a price they can afford. The importance of rising entrepreneurs as role models for entrepreneurship and poverty reduction for the poor should not be overlooked, as should how to inspire future innovation and new venture formation.

Acknowledgements

We would like to thank Mr Virendra Khatana of JIVA, Ms Reene Adams of Global Mamas and Ms Barbara Gbologah-Quaye of PYXERA Global for their invaluable assistance in the completion of this case study and personal interviews. We are grateful to every one of the staff and members of PYXERA Global for their assistance.

References

Ahlstrom, D. (2010). Innovation and growth: How business contributes to society. *Academy of Management Perspectives, 24*(3), 11–24.

Allen, S. D., Link, A. N., & Rosenbaum, D. T. (2008). Entrepreneurship and human capital: Evidence of patenting activity from the academic sector. *Entrepreneurship Theory and Practice, 31*(6), 937–951.

Alvarez, S. A., & Barney, J. B. (2014). Entrepreneurial opportunities and poverty alleviation. *Entrepreneurship Theory and Practice, 38*(1), 159–184.

Alvarez, S. A., Barney, J. B., & Newman, A. (2015). The poverty problem and the industrialization solution. *Asia Pacific Journal of Management, 32*(1), 23–37.

Alvord, S., Brown, L., & Letts, C. (2004). Social entrepreneurship and societal transformation: An exploratory study. *The Journal of Applied Behavioral Science, 40*, 260–282. https://doi.org/10.1177/0021886304266847

Austin, J., Stevenson, H., & Wei-Skillern, J. (2006). Social and commercial entrepreneurship: Same, different, or both? *Entrepreneurship Theory and Practice, 30*(1), 1–22.

Becker, S., Kunze, C., & Vancea, M. (2017). Community energy and social entrepreneurship: Addressing purpose, organization and embeddedness of renewable energy projects. *Journal of Cleaner Production, 147*, 25–36.

Bruton, G. D., Ketchen Jr, D. J., & Ireland, R. D. (2013). Entrepreneurship as a solution to poverty. *Journal of Business Venturing, 28*(6), 683–689.

Bruton, G. D., Khavul, S., & Chavez, H. (2011). Microlending in emerging economies: Building a new line of inquiry from the ground up. *Journal of International Business Studies, 42*, 718–739.

Carini, C., & Carpita, M. (2014). The impact of the economic crisis on Italian cooperatives in the industrial sector. *Journal of Co-operative Organization and Management, 2*(1), 14–23.

Casado-Caneque, F., & Hart, S. (2015). *Base of the pyramid 3.0: Sustainable development through innovation and entrepreneurship.* Greenleaf.

Cesaroni, F. M., & Paoloni, P. (2016). Are family ties an opportunity or an obstacle for women entrepreneurs? Empirical evidence from Italy. *Palgrave Communications, 2*(1), 1–7.

Cheng, Z., Tani, M., & Wang, H. (2021). Energy poverty and entrepreneurship. *Energy Economics, 102*, 105469.

Degli Antoni, G., & Sabatini, F. (2017). Social cooperatives, social welfare associations and social networks. *Review of Social Economy, 75*(2), 212–230.

Dhahri, S., & Omri, A. (2018). Entrepreneurship contribution to the three pillars of sustainable development: What does the evidence really say? *World Development, 106*, 64–77.

Eckhardt, J. T., & Shane, S. A. (2003). Opportunities and entrepreneurship. *Journal of Management, 29*(3), 333–349.

Ferdousi, F., & Parveen, M. (2019). Role of social business in women entrepreneurship development in Bangladesh: Perspectives from Nobin Udyokta projects of Grameen Telecom Trust. *Journal of Global Entrepreneurship Research, 9*(1). Article 11. https://doi.org/10.1186/s40497-019-0184-0

Frankish, J. S., Roberts, R. G., Coad, A., & Storey, D. J. (2017). Is entrepreneurship a route out of deprivation?. In *Entrepreneurship in a regional context* (pp. 152–169). Routledge.

Godfrey, P. (2013). *More than money: Five forms of capital to create wealth and eliminate poverty.* Stanford University Press.

Gregori, P., & Holzmann, P. (2020). Digital sustainable entrepreneurship: A business model perspective on embedding digital technologies for social and environmental value creation. *Journal of Cleaner Production, 272*, 122817.

Greif, A. (2006). *Institutions and the path to the modern economy: Lessons from medieval trade.* Cambridge University Press.

Gupta, S., Jha, S., Paliwal, M., & Dogra, P. (2023). The impact of entrepreneurial cognitive styles and entrepreneurial orientation on innovation performance of organizations in northern India. *Kybernetes.* https://doi.org/10.1108/K-01-2023-0144

Hochgerner, J. (2013). Social innovations and the advancement of the general concept of innovation. In *Social innovation* (pp. 22–38). Routledge.

Jones Christensen, L., Siemsen, E., & Balasubramanian, S. (2015). Consumer behavior change at the base of the pyramid: Bridging the gap between for-profit and social responsibility strategies. *Strategic Management Journal, 36*(2), 307–317.

Joshi, G., & Yenneti, K. (2020). Community solar energy initiatives in India: A pathway for addressing energy poverty and sustainability?. *Energy and Buildings, 210*, 109736.

Kimmitt, J., Munoz, P., & Newbery, R. (2020). Poverty and the varieties of entrepreneurship in the pursuit of prosperity. *Journal of Business Venturing, 35*(1), 105–113.

Legge, J., & Hindle, K. (1997). *Entrepreneurship: How innovators create the future.* Macmillan Publishers.

Luqmani, A., Leach, A., & Jesson, D. (2017). Factors behind sustainable business innovation: The case of a global carpet manufacturing company. *Environmental Innovation and Societal Transitions, 24*(1), 94–105.

Macke, J., Sarate, J. A. R., Domeneghini, J., & da Silva, K. A. (2018). Where do we go from now? Research framework for social entrepreneurship. *Journal of Cleaner Production, 183*, 677–685.

Mair, J., & Schoen, O. (2007). Successful social entrepreneurial business models in the context of developing economies: An explorative study. *International Journal of Emerging Markets, 2*, 54–68. https://doi.org/10.1108/17468800710718895

Merriam, S. B. (1988). *Case study research in education: A qualitative approach.* Jossey-Bass Publishers.

Miller, D. (1983). The correlates of entrepreneurship in three types of firms. *Management Science, 29*(7), 770–791.

Morris, M. H., Santos, S. C., & Neumeyer, X. (2020). Entrepreneurship as a solution to poverty in developed economies. *Business Horizons, 63*, 377–390.

Ozdemir, S., & Gupta, S. (2021). Inter-organizational collaborations for social inno-vation and social value creation: Towards the development of new research agenda and theoretical perspectives. *Industrial Marketing Management, 97*, 134–144.

Paliwal, M., Chatradhi, N., Tripathy, S., & Jha, S. (2023). Growth of digital entre-preneurship in academic literature: A bibliometric analysis. *International Journal of Sustainable Development and Planning, 18*(6).

Peredo, A. M., & Chrisman, J. J. (2006). Toward a theory of community-based enterprise. *Academy of Management Review, 31*(2), 309–328.

Putnam, R. (2000). *Bowling alone: The collapse and revival of American community.* Simon & Schuster.

Rosca, E., Agarwal, N., & Brem, A. (2020). Women entrepreneurs as agents of change: A comparative analysis of social entrepreneurship processes in emerging markets. *Technological Forecasting and Social Change, 157*, 120067.

Schot, J., & Steinmueller, W. E. (2018). Three frames for innovation policy: R&D, systems of innovation and transformative change. *Research Policy, 47*(9), 1554–1567.

Shane, S., & Venkataraman, S. (2000). The promise of entrepreneurship as a field of research. *Academy of Management Review, 25*(1), 217–226.

Si, S., Ahlstrom, D., Wei, J., & Cullen, J. (2020). Business, entrepreneurship and innovation toward poverty reduction. *Entrepreneurship & Regional Development, 32*(1–2), 1–20.

Slevin, D. P., & Covin, J. G. (1990). Juggling entrepreneurial style and organizational structure. *MIT Sloan Management Review, 31*(2), 43.

Solis-Navarrete, J. A., Bucio-Mendoza, S., & Paneque-Gálvez, J. (2021). What is not social innovation. *Technological Forecasting and Social Change, 173*, 121190.

Stevanović, M. (2016). The role of financial perspective of entrepreneurship and rural development for the purpose of strengthening Serbian economy. *Procedia – Social and Behavioral Sciences, 221*, 254–261.

Surie, G. (2017). Creating the innovation ecosystem for renewable energy via social entrepreneurship: Insights from India. *Technological Forecasting and Social Change, 121*, 184–195.

Sutter, C., Bruton, G. D., & Chen, J. (2019). Entrepreneurship as a solution to extreme poverty: A review and future research directions. *Journal of Business Venturing, 34*(1), 197–214.

Tambunan, T. (2009). Women entrepreneurship in Asian developing countries: Their development and main constraints. *Journal of Development and Agricultural Eco-nomics, 1*(2), 27–40.

Tripathy, K. K., Paliwal, M., & Nistala, N. (2021). Good governance practices and competitiveness in cooperatives: An analytical study of Kerala Primary Agricul-tural Credit Societies. *International Journal of Global Business and Competitiveness, 16*, 153–161. https://doi.org/10.1007/s42943-021-00020-0

Tripathy, K. K., Paliwal, M., & Singh, A. (2022). Women's social entrepreneurship and livelihood innovation: An exploratory study from India. *Service Business, 16*, 863–881. https://doi.org/10.1007/s11628-022-00493-w

Veiga, P. M., Teixeira, S. J., Figueiredo, R., & Fernandes, C. I. (2020). Entrepreneurship, innovation and competitiveness: A public institution love tri-angle. *Socio-Economic Planning Sciences, 72*, 100863.

Viswanathan, M., Echambadi, R., Venugopal, S., & Sridharan, S. (2014). Subsistence entrepreneurship, value creation, and community exchange systems: A social capital explanation. *Journal of Macromarketing, 34*(2), 213–226.

Woodside, A. G., Bernal, P. M., & Coduras, A. (2016). The general theory of culture, entrepreneurship, innovation, and quality-of-life: Comparing nurturing versus thwarting enterprise start-ups in BRIC, Denmark, Germany, and the United States. *Industrial Marketing Management, 53*, 136–159.

World Bank. (2019). *The World Bank annual report 2019*. The World Bank.

Wu, J., Zhuo, S., & Wu, Z. (2017). National innovation system, social entrepreneurship, and rural economic growth in China. *Technological Forecasting and Social Change, 121*, 238–250.

Yadav, H., Paliwal, M., & Chatradhi, N. (2022). Entrepreneurship development of rural women through digital inclusion: Examining the contributions of public programs. In Rajagopal & R. Behl (Eds.), *Inclusive businesses in developing economies. Palgrave studies in democracy, innovation, and entrepreneurship for growth*. Palgrave Macmillan. https://doi.org/10.1007/978-3-031-12217-0_14.

Yin, R. K. (2009). How to do better case studies. In *The SAGE handbook of applied social research methods* (Vol. 2, pp. 254–282).

Zameer, H., Shahbaz, M., & Vo, X. V. (2020). Reinforcing poverty alleviation efficiency through technological innovation, globalization, and financial development. *Technological Forecasting and Social Change, 161*, 120326.

Zhao, E. Y., & Lounsbury, M. (2016). An institutional logics approach to social entrepreneurship: Market logic, religious diversity, and resource acquisition by microfinance organizations. *Journal of Business Venturing, 31*, 643–662.

Chapter 3

Role of Government Programmes and Schemes in Eradication of Poverty in India

Kamal Kant Tyagi[a], Chakir Aziza[b] and Vinay Pal Singh[c]

[a]COER University, India
[b]Hassan II University, Morocco
[c]Quantum University, India

Abstract

India has a serious poverty issue that needs to be addressed immediately. The elimination of poverty should be one of the primary goals of economic policy. The elimination of poverty is one of the greatest obstacles to economic development as it is now envisioned. It is difficult to provide a blanket recommendation for achieving economic growth and reducing poverty because each state's experience has been distinct. The states of Punjab and Haryana are two examples of how a strong emphasis on agricultural expansion can help alleviate poverty. Human resource development has been successful in Kerala; thus, it has been replicated in other states. While India's social safety programmes have helped to alleviate poverty, they aren't perfect. COVID-19 reversed the progress made and harmed migrant workers and others in the informal economy. There are now millions more people living in extreme poverty than before. To tackle unemployment, governments and underprivileged communities are appealing to programmes like MGNREGA.

The purpose of this article is to investigate the measures taken by the state to combat poverty.

Keywords: Eradication of poverty; social protection; economic growth; economic policy; economic development

Creating Pathways for Prosperity, 33–44
Copyright © 2025 Kamal Kant Tyagi, Chakir Aziza and Vinay Pal Singh
Published under exclusive licence by Emerald Publishing Limited
doi:10.1108/978-1-83549-121-820241004

Introduction

In 1901, Dadabhai Naoroji was the first person in the history of India to assess the level of poverty in the country based on the cost of a food item considered necessary for subsistence. In 1938, the National Planning Committee made a proposal for an estimate of the poverty line based on living conditions.

The 1944 Bombay Plan incorporated the recommendation of the National Planning Committee. Since independence, the government has made poverty alleviation a top priority. Numerous academic committees, working groups and individual scholars, such as the Y.K. Alagh taskforce in 1979, Dandekar and Rath in 1971, and the working group in 1962, have attempted to quantify poverty in order to better inform public policy. Lakdawala (1993), Tendulkar (2009) and the Rangarajan Committee (2014) all assembled expert panels to do similar study into the magnitude of poverty. One of the Millennium Development Goals is to decrease the number of people in the world living on less than $1.25 per day by the year 2015. This goal reflects the worldwide effort to alleviate poverty. From 1990 through 2015, we shall evaluate our progress towards this goal.

On 25 September 2015, the General Assembly of the United Nations adopted a resolution that called for the establishment of 17 Sustainable Development Goals (SDGs). The first Sustainable Development target (SDG 1) aims to 'end poverty in all its manifestations everywhere'. This target is multimodal in both its reach and its idea. Half of those living in multidimensional poverty, as defined by national standards, are to be alleviated as part of Target 1.2. People who live on less than $1.25 (later increased to $1.90) per day are considered to be in extreme poverty. The goal of Target 1.1 is to eradicate this level of poverty. Since 2010, the United Nations Development Programme has incorporated the Multidimensional Poverty Gauge (MPI) in its annual Human Development Report (Godinot & Walker, 2020). The MPI is the non-monetary poverty indicator that is used the most commonly all across the world. It displays intersecting levels of deprivation in health, educational opportunities, and living standards (UNDP, 2010).

Since the turn of the millennium, India has witnessed a significant decline in the country's rate of absolute poverty. According to the World Bank, nearly 90 million individuals were rescued from conditions of extreme poverty between 2011 and 2015. In order to bring about this change, the government instituted a number of poverty-alleviation programs with the goals of meeting the needs of the impoverished, generating employment opportunities, and providing food and shelter to those in need. In this study (UNDP), we analyse India's achievement in eradicating poverty by using a modified version of the Multidimensional Poverty Index (MPI), which is a worldwide measure of poverty developed by Alkire and Santos (2010) in collaboration with the United Nations Development Programme.

This article makes an effort to examine the various government programmes and how well they work to end poverty.

What Is Poverty?

Poverty is defined as the lack of the resources and essentials needed to maintain a basic quality of existence. The International Poverty Line, which is set at $1.90 per day (World Bank). The poverty limit set by the Asian Development Bank is now $1.51 per person per day. The Tendulkar Committee in India sets the national poverty line.

The Tendulkar Committee determined poverty levels for 2004–05 at a level equal to Rs. 33 per day in terms of purchasing power parity.

What Is Poverty Eradication?

Poverty alleviation refers to a range of economic and humanitarian efforts to eradicate poverty in a country. According to the World Bank, extreme poverty, which now impacts 767 million people globally, is defined as having a daily income of $1.90 or less. 268 million Indians, according to the most recent official statistics, survived on less than $1.90 per day in 2011. In order to end poverty and give disadvantaged households access to basic essentials, the Indian government has created a variety of programmes and plans.

SDG and Poverty

The first of the 17 Sustainable development objectives, as established in 2015, is SDG 1: Zero poverty. The very first goal is to 'eradication poverty in all its manifestations worldwide by 2030'. This implies that extreme poverty must no longer be a reality for everyone. Extreme poverty as it is now defined is $1.25 per day. 17 objectives, 169 targets, and 304 indicators have been proposed by the Open Working Group on Sustainable Development Objectives for 2030 of the United Nations General Assembly. The Transforming Our World: The United Nations Sustainable Development Summit's debates led to the adoption of the 30 Agenda for Sustainable Development. The SDGs were created during the 2012 Rio+20 meeting in Rio de Janeiro and are not legally enforceable.

Literature Review and Data

Eliminating poverty is a top objective for researchers in all areas of the social sciences, including management, entrepreneurship and economics (Ahlin & Jiang, 2008). This is a response to the severe poverty problem's seriousness and the measures to tackle its obviously variable results (Easterly, 2006). These actions include of bottom of the pyramid efforts, microfinance, and property rights promotion programmes, among others, These programmes have not had much of an influence on extreme poverty, and they might even be responsible for some new issues (Easterly, 2006). Whether economic progress has reduced poverty in India has been heavily disputed. Some experts believed that the agricultural growth process sparked by the green revolution gave little to no benefit to the rural poor, while others argued that farm-output expansion was the key to reducing rural poverty. This debate is old but influential. Social poverty is a new issue that has emerged. While some impoverished people are able to transcend poverty economically, many are unable to do so socially (Si et al., 2021). Their population is growing, they are prosperous materially but impoverished socially, and there are still a lot of mental and behavioural anomalies that contribute to this situation (Si et al., 2021).

India saw a greater than halving of poverty between 2005 (PL 35%) and 2020 (PL 15%). Except for the recessionary years of 2008, 2009 and 2020, annual GDP growth averaged 7%–8%. The ARDL model's correlation coefficient revealed a strong association between GINI (0.76) and PL (0.32) and the GDP, as well as between GINI (1.5) and PL (0.5) and FDI (Sukhadolets et al., 2021).53.7% of Indians, according to the 'official' international MPI, resided in multidimensionally poor families in the years 2005–06. Only 48.5% of the population is identified as multidimensionally poor in the same year using the MPI-I approximation, which maintains comparability with earlier (weaker) NFHS dataset (Alkire & Seth, 2015). The headcount ratio (H), which is usually reported because the MPI includes it as a partial index, should be used to communicate vital information that is missing from the MPI, such as the number of people who moved out of poverty (Alkire et al., 2021).

Economic growth is frequently a goal of development policy. The relationship between growth and poverty is complex, though, and various growth periods have quite diverse effects on poverty, according to a substantial corpus of research (Aggarwal & Kumar, 2015). In contrast to agglomeration in megacities, this has no statistically significant impact on the pace of reducing poverty; the empirical data show a link between a drop in poverty and the transition from rural agriculture to rural nonfarm enterprises and secondary towns (Christiaensen & Todo, 2014).

Poverty and Growth in India 2004–20

The data (Table 3.1) serve as a reference for the poverty estimates in Table 3.2. Five different periods – 2004–11, 2011–14, 2011–17, 2017–19 and 2014–19 – are represented by the data. The data during these times reflect a number of macroeconomic phenomena in India. The highest GDP growth (the foundation for traditional back of the envelope projections concerning poverty trends) occurred between 2004 and 2011 (6.4% annually), above the 5.4% annual increase seen between 2014 and 2019.

Following are the outcomes of Table 3.1.

Real per capita consumption growth in national accounts has remained largely stable at 6.2% annually (as deflated by the PFCE deflator). From 2017 to 2019, the growth in per capita consumption, deflated by the CPI, climbed at a pace of 5.7% annually, which is greater than the 4.0% growth observed from 2004 to 2011, when GDP growth was at its highest. This expenditure rise must be taken into consideration when estimating headcount poverty and inequality. Because of

Table 3.1. Inflation Pattern With the Growth Rate of Economy.

CAGR (in %)

	2005–12	2012–15	2013–17	2018–20	2019–21
GDP (nominal)	12.7	10.7	10.0	7.7	2.7
GDP (real)	6.4	5.0	5.7	4.1	1.4
Deflator GDP	6.3	5.7	4.3	3.6	1.3
PFCE (nominal)	11.4	11.8	10.8	8.1	8.5
(Deflator) PFCE	5.2	6.1	6.4	5.5	5.2
Poverty line	5.0	4.9	3.7	3.4	2.9
PFCE (deflator)	6.3	5.6	4.4	2.6	3.3
Poverty line	8.4	7.9	6.1	3.6	3.6
$1.9 (PPP)	−14.1	−16.6	−24.0	−35.2	−32.9
$3.2 (PPP)	−4.6	−7.1	−10.2	−22.4	

Source: Ministry of Statistics and Programme Implementation.

Table 3.2. List of Major Schemes for Poverty Eradication by the Government of India.

S. No	Poverty Eradication Scheme Government of India	Objective of Scheme
1	Integrated Rural Development Programme (IRDP)	IRDP's major goal is to eliminate poverty, hunger, and unemployment in rural India.
2	Jawahar Gram Samridhi Yojana	JGSY public awareness campaign in towns, particularly those with a large BPL population. This entails rethinking the arrangement at a higher (public) level in order to assess its natural value.
3	Rural Housing – Indira Awaas Yojana	By the end of March 2022, provide a house with basic facilities to all rural families who are homeless or living in dilapidated structures.
4	Food for Work Programme	The National Food for Work Initiative is a pay employment programme aimed at alleviating rural poverty.

(Continued)

Table 3.2. *(Continued)*

S. No	Poverty Eradication Scheme Government of India	Objective of Scheme
5	National Old Age Pension Scheme (NOAPS)	National Old Age Pension Schemes (NOAPS) – providing social security to senior citizens below BPL.
6	Sampoorna Gramin Rozgar Yojana (SGRY)	The initiative is self-targeting in nature, with the goal of providing jobs and food to those living in rural areas who are poor.
7	NRLM – National Rural Livelihood Mission (Deendayal Antyodaya Yojana)	The Ministry of Rural Development created DAY-NRLM with the goal of reducing rural poverty by giving residents access to work possibilities.
8	Mahatma Gandhi National Rural Employment Guarantee Act (MGNREGA) 2005	It provides 100 days of guaranteed paid work to rural unskilled labourers.
9	National Urban Livelihood Mission	It will cover all district's headquarter towns and all the other towns with a population of 1 lakh or more as per the Census 2011.
10	Pradhan Mantri Kaushal Vikas Yojana	This scheme targets 10 million youth (2016–20) who will get the desired skill set so that they can earn their livelihood.
11	Pradhan Mantri Jan Dhan Yojana	Every qualified adult would receive a basic savings bank account with Rs. 10,000 overdraft limits.
12	Pradhan Mantri Awas Yojana – Gramin	To provide a complete grant to rural inhabitants living below the poverty line (BPL).
13	Pradhan Mantri Awas Yojana – Urban (Housing For All)	Government offers financial assistance for housing in collaboration with the public and private sectors.
14	National Food Security Act	Under two categories, Antyodaya Anna Yojana (AAY) families and

Table 3.2. *(Continued)*

S. No	Poverty Eradication Scheme Government of India	Objective of Scheme
		Priority Households, 50% of urban residents and 75% of rural residents are entitled to get heavily subsidised food grains (PHH)).
15	Gram Swaraj Abhiyan	Its main objectives are to advance social harmony, increase public knowledge of government programmes that help the poor, contact low-income households to enrol them, and get feedback on various welfare efforts.
16	Pradhan Mantri Adarsh Gram Yojana	Main objective of PMAGY is to construct village roads, community halls/meeting places, community restrooms, drainage works, hand pump installation.

the sharp decrease in inflation, which went from a compound annual growth rate of 8.4% during the time of strong GDP growth to just 3.6% from 2014 to 2019, there has been a drop in poverty during the period (2014–19 vs. 2004–11). Deflator inflation decreases as well, but not as much (instead of declining by 4.8% points, the rate fell by 3% points).

For the years 2004–20, the estimates for poverty are shown in Table 3.2. The most important conclusion from these figures may be that, depending on the method used, extreme poverty in India ranged from 1.4% (official MMRP method), to 5.4%, in the year before the epidemic, 2019 pre-pandemic 2019 poverty was barely 1.4 ppt, down 10.8 ppt from 2011 to 2012, under the 'official' MMRP methodology. Although it is no longer valid for India13, the PPP$1.9 poverty level continues to be recognised as the worldwide threshold for severe poverty and is used as a standard for statements regarding the eradication of extreme poverty. This issue needs to be made explicit. Using this measure, India may credibly assert that before the epidemic, the country was just about to end severe poverty.

The poverty headcount ratio decreased from 37.2% to 21.9% between 2004–05 and 2011–12, according to an assessment by the Indian government's NITI Aayog. According to Global Multidimensional Poverty Index 2020, 640 million people in India experienced multidimensional poverty in 2005–06. Social protection programmes were successfully implemented during a 10-year period, enabling 273 million people to transcend multidimensional poverty.

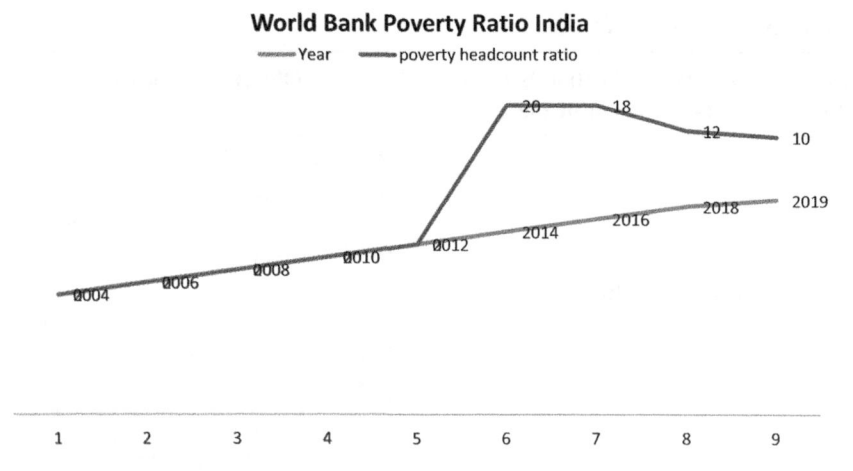

World Bank Poverty Ratio India

10% Population Living in Poverty at $2.15 a Day (2019 PPP) – India. *Source:* World Bank.

Using the updated $2.15 per day poverty criterion, Indian poverty shows that 10% of Indians were poor in 2019, down from 22.5% in 2011. In rural India, there were more poor people than in urban regions: 11.9% in rural and 6.4% in urban areas. According to the estimate posted on the bank website, 'Compared to 2011, extreme poverty has decreased by 12.3 percentage points in 2019, with rural areas seeing the largest decreases in poverty.' However, it concludes that, based on consumption data from India's national accounts, the level of poverty was 'considerably higher' than had previously been predicted by other organisations. On the other hand, it claims that 'Consumption disparity in India has moderated since 2011'.

Schemes for Poverty Eradication by Government of India

The Indian Government has started, maintained and improved a number of planning initiatives from the early 1950s to aid the underprivileged in becoming self-sufficient in food acquisition and overcoming hunger and poverty. Researchers, academics, several national institutions and international organisations have all given the IRDP a thorough evaluation. They have all identified a number of conceptual and organisational issues with it.

Impact of Poverty Eradication Schemes

By giving families and households who are below the poverty line adequate access to food, financial help and basic necessities, poverty alleviation programmes seek to lower the rate of poverty in the nation. By giving homes to the needy in rural and urban areas, programmes like the Pradhan Mantri Awas Yojana and

Housing for All by 2022 have played a significant part in lowering the poverty rate. All the schemes for the poor have a positive impact on reducing the poverty level in India. Table 3.3 below shows the latest schemes and their impact on poverty.

Table 3.3. List of major impacts of Poverty eradication schemes.

Schemes	Effectiveness (Elements of Schemes)	Effectiveness (Elements of Schemes)
Cash transfers	500 rupees per month for 3 months for women holders of Jan Dhan Accounts	Total amount of Rs. 30,000 crore released to 20 crore women who get benefited by this scheme.
	1,000 rupees to vulnerable areas (widows, Divyangs, elderly)	Released funds of Rs. 2,814 crore will benefit 2.82 crore people.
	6,000 rupees per year in three instalments are paid under the Pradhan Mantri Kisan Samman Nidhi (PM-KISAN).	In this scheme, 10 crore farmer families received transfers totaling Rs. 1.8 lakh crore as of 1 January 2022.
Food security	Prime Minister Garib Kalyan in addition to the standard monthly NFSA food grains, 80 million participants of the Anna Yojana programme will receive an additional 5 kg of free food every month.	(1) Launched in March 2020 and continued under Phase-V till March 2022. (2) The 600 LMT food grains granted to states and UTs from March 2020 to November 2021 are equal to 2.07 lakh crore in food subsidies.
	LPG gas for cooking to poor family	Under Ujjwala 2.0's (released 10.8.2021) streamlined processes, the initial refill and hotplate are free.
Employment	Prime minister Garib Kalyan Rojgar Abhiyaan (PM-GKRA) seeks to provide returnee migrant workers with urgent job and livelihood possibilities.	As of 27 July 2021, generated 50.8 crore man-days of employment while spending 39,293 crore.
	Mahatma Gandhi National Rural Employment Guarantee Scheme (MGNREGS)	11.2 core people will have jobs in 2020–21, producing 389.2 crore person days. 111,171

(Continued)

Table 3.3. *(Continued)*

Schemes	Effectiveness (Elements of Schemes)	Effectiveness (Elements of Schemes)
		crore in funds were released. As of 25 November 2021, 8.85 crore people had jobs, producing 240.4 crore person days. Release of 68,233 crore in funds.
Skill development	Deen Dayal Upadhyaya Grameen Kaushalya Yojana	2020–21: Training for 38,289 candidates and employment for 49,563 candidates. 2021–22 (until October 21): 14,568 candidates were trained and 21,369 were hired.

Source: Economic survey of India 2021–22.

Conclusion

The government's initiatives to combat poverty in the nation have been quite effective in helping those who fall into the category of those who live below the poverty line establish solid financial foundations. These programmes also significantly increase employment levels in the society. The changes also place a strong emphasis on openness, making programme information available to the general public at the village level, and emphasising the value of physical, financial and social audits. The government should mandate the introduction of better programmes with zero balance rates in the future to reduce poverty in society.

The poverty headcount ratio decreased from 37.2% to 21.9% between 2004–05 and 2011–12, according to an assessment by the Indian Government's NITI Aayog. According to the UNDP Global Multidimensional Poverty Index 2020, 640 million people in India were living in multidimensional poverty in 2005–06. Because social protection programmes were implemented successfully, 273 million people were able to overcome multidimensional poverty over a 10-year period. Around 35% (265 million individuals) of the rural population were considered to be poor prior to COVID. For the FY2021–22, this figure is anticipated to increase to anywhere between 381 and 418 million. In India, an additional 150–199 million people would experience poverty as a result of the COVID-19 problem, and those who are already impoverished will be pushed even deeper into it.

The government unveiled the AtmaNirbhar Bharat unique economic and comprehensive package to tackle the COVID-19 pandemic's effects and promote economic growth. The RBI's measures in this package accounted for around Rs. 27.1 lakh crore, or more than 13% of India's GDP. In addition to other things, the package included relief measures for households in the form of cash and in-kind transfers, employment provision measures under the Pradhan Mantri Garib Kalyan Rojgar Abhiyaan and increased MGNREGS allocation, relief measures for MSMEs and NBFCs based on credit guarantees and equity infusions, and regulatory and compliance measures.

References

Aggarwal, A., & Kumar, N. (2015). Structural change, industrialization, and poverty reduction. In *Structural change and industrial development in the BRICS* (p. 199). Oxford University Press.

Ahlin, C., & Jiang, N. (2008). Can micro-credit bring development? *Journal of Development Economics, 86*(1), 1–21. https://doi.org/10.1016/j.jdeveco.2007.08.002

Alkire, S., Oldiges, C., & Kanagaratnam, U. (2021). Examining multidimensional poverty reduction in India 2005/6–2015/16: Insights and oversights of the headcount ratio. *World Development, 142*, 105454.

Alkire, S., & Santos, M. E. (2010). *Acute multidimensional poverty: A new index for developing countries.*

Alkire, S., & Seth, S. (2015). Multidimensional poverty reduction in India between 1999 and 2006: Where and how? *World Development, 72*, 93–108.

Christiaensen, L., & Todo, Y. (2014). Poverty reduction during the rural–urban transformation–the role of the missing middle. *World Development, 63*, 43–58.

Easterly, W. (2006). *The white man's burden: Why the west's efforts to aid the rest have done so much ill and so little good.* Penguin Press.

Godinot, X., & Walker, R. (2020). Poverty in all its forms: Determining the dimensions of poverty through merging knowledge. *Dimensions of Poverty: Measurement, Epistemic Injustices, Activism*, 263–279.

Jha, R., Gaitha, R., & Shankar, S. (2008). Reviewing the national rural employment guarantee programme. *Economic and Political Weekly, 43*(11), 44–48.

Lo, K. (2021). Can authoritarian regimes achieve just energy transition? Evidence from China's solar photovoltaic poverty alleviation initiative. *Energy Research & Social Science, 82*, 102315.

Poddar, S., Bharti, S., & Sharma, K. S. An empirical study on impact of microfinance on poverty alleviation in rural India.

Ravallion, M. (2011). A comparative perspective on poverty reduction in Brazil, China, and India. *The World Bank Research Observer, 26*(1), 71–104.

Ravillion, M., & Datt, G. (1995). *Growth and poverty in rural India.* World Bank Policy Research Working Paper. World Bank.

Reddy, V., Shekhar, M., Rao, P., & Gillispie, S. (1992). *Nutrition in India.* UN ACC/SCN Country case study prepared for the 15th International congress of Nutrition, Australia.

Poverty report of UNDP. (2010). https://hdr.undp.org/content/human-development-report-2010

Si, S., Ahlstrom, D., Wei, J., & Cullen, J. (2021). Introduction: Business, entrepreneurship and innovation toward poverty reduction. *Business, Entrepreneurship and Innovation Toward Poverty Reduction*, 1–20.

Sukhadolets, T., Stupnikova, E., Fomenko, N., Kapustina, N., & Kuznetsov, Y. (2021). Foreign direct investment (FDI), investment in construction and poverty in economic crises (Denmark, Italy, Germany, Romania, China, India and Russia). *Economies, 9*(4), 152.

Tendulkar, S. D., Sundaram, K., & Jain, L. R. (1993). *Poverty in India*. 1970–71 to 1988–99, ARTEP working papers. ILO-ARTEP.

Yadava, R. N., & Sinha, B. (2021). Poverty assessment for reorienting poverty alleviation programmes in the Forest Fringe Area of Madhya Pradesh, India. *Indian Journal of Public Administration, 67*(2), 214–236.

Yesudian, C. A. K. (2007, October). Poverty alleviation programmes in India: A social audit. *Indian Journal of Medical Research, 126*, 364–373.

Zuo, C. V. (2022). Integrating devolution with centralization: A comparison of poverty alleviation programs in India, Mexico, and China. *Journal of Chinese Political Science, 27*(2), 247–270.

Chapter 4

Climate Change Adaptation Challenges Require Technical Expertise and Data Management

N. Yogeesh

Government First Grade College, India

Abstract

Climate change, sometimes known as global warming, affects society and the economy. Recently, media and public interest to this problem has increased. This chapter, 'Technical Area and Data Management on Climatic Changes Adaptation Challenges of the 21st Century', provides a detailed overview of global warming and how society recognises and confronts it locally and worldwide (Kriegler et al., 2014). This chapter examines non-climate modelling approaches to quantify and anticipate complicated climate change effects on populations and ecosystems. It examines how to measure ecosystem vulnerability and how to adapt to climate change. This knowledge also impacts worldwide sustainable development debates. The chapter discusses how social, economic and ecological systems are all impacted by climate change in a variety of ways, leading to significant economic losses that will probably get worse the longer we wait to take action. Because of this, the main goal of this chapter is to encourage planning and capacity building at the local, regional, national and international levels to deal with the effects of climate change at the local, regional, national and international levels. This is done by using a unified approach to improve coordination and develop climate resilience in nations that are more likely to be affected by climate change. Overall, this chapter shows how hard climate change is by looking at both the problems and the chances of adapting to and reducing the effects of climate change.

Keywords: Global warming; climate change; global climate; data loses; communication breakdowns

Creating Pathways for Prosperity, 45–65
Copyright © 2025 Yogeesh N
Published under exclusive licence by Emerald Publishing Limited
doi:10.1108/978-1-83549-121-820241005

Introduction

The number of warmer days and nights each year has grown due to rising average world temperatures since the 19th century. In turn, this results in an increase in the frequency of wild and forestry fires as well as heatwaves and other extreme weather conditions, temperatures that are greater than normal for the time and place (Clark et al., 2016). Heatwaves are periods of very hot and humid weather that are uncharacteristic of the area and season.

A place's climate is defined as its average weather over a long period of time. The Herculean challenge of combating global climate change depends on worldwide agreement as well as the efforts of local governments, businesses, and individuals (Global Climate Observing System (GCOS), 2003).

Climate change is occurring, and it is anticipated that this trend will last for some time. The amount of greenhouse (warming) gases generated globally and the degree of uncertainty inside the earth's climate responsiveness will be the main determinants of how severe climate change will be in the future decades. If greenhouse gas (GHG) emissions are significantly reduced, the average annual increase in global temperature may be kept at 2°C or below. However, the average annual global temperature increase in relation to pre-industrial periods may reach 5°C or greater by the end of the century if significant reductions in such emissions are not made (Kriegler et al., 2014; O'Neill et al., 2020; Phillips et al., 2020).

Seasonal climatic swings cause severe natural catastrophes, resulting in enormous losses to private and public property, as well as mortality, starvation, loss of livelihood, sicknesses, and population relocation at their worst. These disasters are brought on by droughts, floods, and storms. Additionally, the Climate Science Panel's Fourth Evaluation Report summarises the widespread consensus among trustworthy scientists that the climate is changing and will continue to alter substantially. The construction sector nations with both the least ability to adapt – will likely suffer the worst effects of these developments, which will generally be negative.

The great news would be that scientific advancements have provided humans with instruments that may be able to reduce negative affects by providing some capacity to predict what will occur in the future so that, at the very least, some sort of preemptive measures may be done. In theory, a higher likelihood of drought could prompt a number of immediate mitigation actions, such as more careful flood control, agricultural responses such as increased planting of agricultural failure crop varieties, and government-level recognition that affected communities could require financial or other assistance. Finally, the information obtained from analysing past climate data would help humanity in future climate management (World Climate Data Monitoring Programme (WCDMP), 2005).

'The climatic record of the past' is the key term here. A trustworthy record of the past and present climate is vitally necessary in order to create successful adaptation plans for the future. Because climate has unique requirements that forecasting does not, this is typically more difficult than just compiling and recycling those observations made to enable operational weather forecasting. In particular, extended observational records devoid of severe gaps, significant errors and in homogeneities are needed by climate scientists including service providers. Networks designed primarily towards weather forecasting may or may not meet these requirements.

Objectives

- This chapter provides a comprehensive overview of the issue of climate change and the efforts to mitigate its effects.
- The focus is on understanding the complex impacts of climate change on ecosystems, communities, and socio-economic systems, as well as the need for adaptation.
- The chapter emphasises the importance of interdisciplinary collaboration and global coordination in addressing climate change.
- The economic costs of inaction are high, and there is a need to prioritise resilience building and preparedness at all levels.
- Overall, the goal is to foster a sustainable future that balances the needs of the planet and its inhabitants.

Greenhouse Effect on Climate Change

Carbon dioxide and other GHGs blanket the earth when they build up in the atmosphere. Directly passing through this blanket, sunlight, which is predominantly short-wave radiation, continues until it approaches the planet's surface.

The earth emits longer wave infrared back into space after absorbing solar energy. The GHG cloak is struck by infrared radiation as it leaves the atmosphere. A fraction of it is absorbed and returned to the earth, but the bulk of it just flows through. This absorbs infrared radiation, which heats the surface, leading to the 'greenhouse effect'.

It's critical to comprehend how crucial the greenhouse effect is to life on Earth. Without GHGs' ability to trap heat, it would be exceedingly cold and difficult for humans to survive. However, by producing additional GHGs, humans have exacerbated the greenhouse effect.

The denser GHG layer is now more efficient at absorbing infrared radiation. In other terms, the warming tendency is stronger and causing the globe to warm faster rather than keeping its temperature constant.

Global Warming

The phenomenon of rising average air temperatures close to the surface of the Earth during the previous century or two is referred to as global warming. Since the middle of the 20th century, researchers studying climate change have gathered enormous amounts of data on a variety of weather phenomena, including temperature, precipitation, and even storms, as well as on factors that influence the climate, like ocean circulation and atmospheric composition. These findings show that although the Earth's temperature has fluctuated practically constantly from the start of geological timescales, human activity has been largely responsible for the current climate change since the start of the Industrial Revolution. Many climate experts concur that if the average global temperature climbed by even more than 2°C (3.6°F) within such a short period of time, significant societal, economic, and ecological destruction would result. A few instances of this form of devastation are rising sea levels, altered farming practices and enhanced extinction rates of various animal and plant species. Many data-supported scenarios mostly depend on future concentrations of that, so GHGs, which have progressively been introduced further into lowest environment as a result of the burning of fossil fuels for use in transportation, industry and home usage. This greenhouse effect, which is the root of current global warming, has intensified as a result of the existence of gases including CO_2, methane, nitrous oxide, and water vapour. This event caused the Earth's surface and lower atmosphere to warm. The average worldwide temperature, as seen in Fig. 4.1, is derived from many datasets including various regions throughout the globe and is measured in degrees Celsius (Riahi et al., 2017; Yogeesh, 2019).

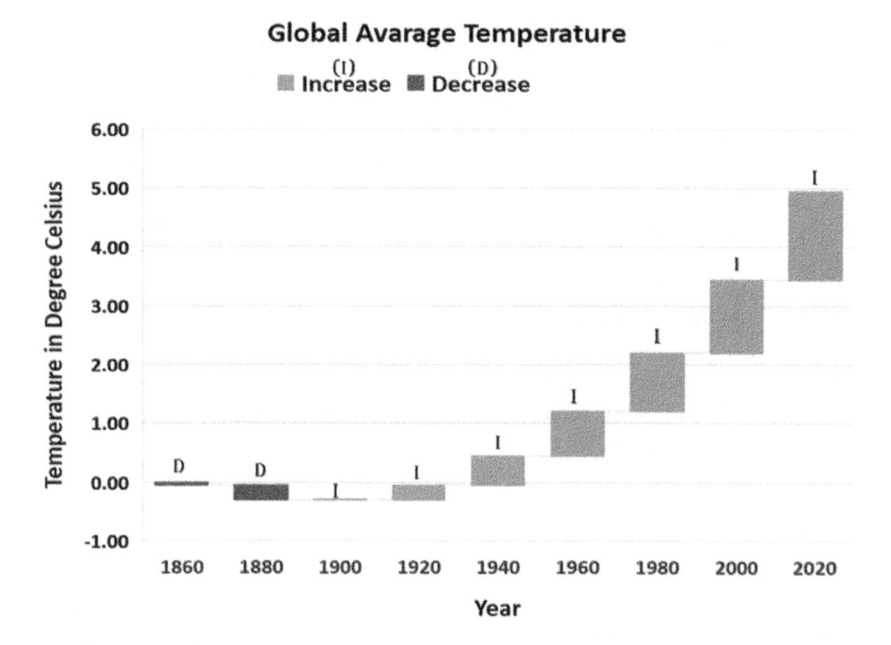

Fig. 4.1.   Using a Number of Global Temperature Data Sets, the Average World Temperature in Degrees Celsius.

Climate Hazards and Climate Change Impacts

Temperatures are greater than normal for the time and place. Heatwaves are periods of very hot and humid weather that are uncharacteristic of the area and season. Fires are raging in rural places where there are lots of trees or grass or bushes, and which spread swiftly and uncontrollably. A stretch of unusually dry weather that is lengthy enough to produce major supply problems due to the lack of water. Periods of unusually heavy rainfall are above average for the area and the season, which can cause floods and the unanticipated falling down of a mountain and cliff of a pile of rock or soil.

Soil, silt and rock are frozen under permafrost. It is present in locations that are always cold and is always frozen. But as a result of climate change, permafrost has begun to gradually melt, raising the danger of ice and rock falls. The process by which sea water gradually separates land from a coast. A rise in the ocean's average depth. It could be brought on by local land movements or a change in the global ocean's volume. Other climate change effects like greater temperatures or excessive precipitation might make it easier for non-native species to spread and endanger ecosystems, habitats, or other species. Other climate change effects like greater temperatures, excessive precipitation, or harm to vital infrastructure can

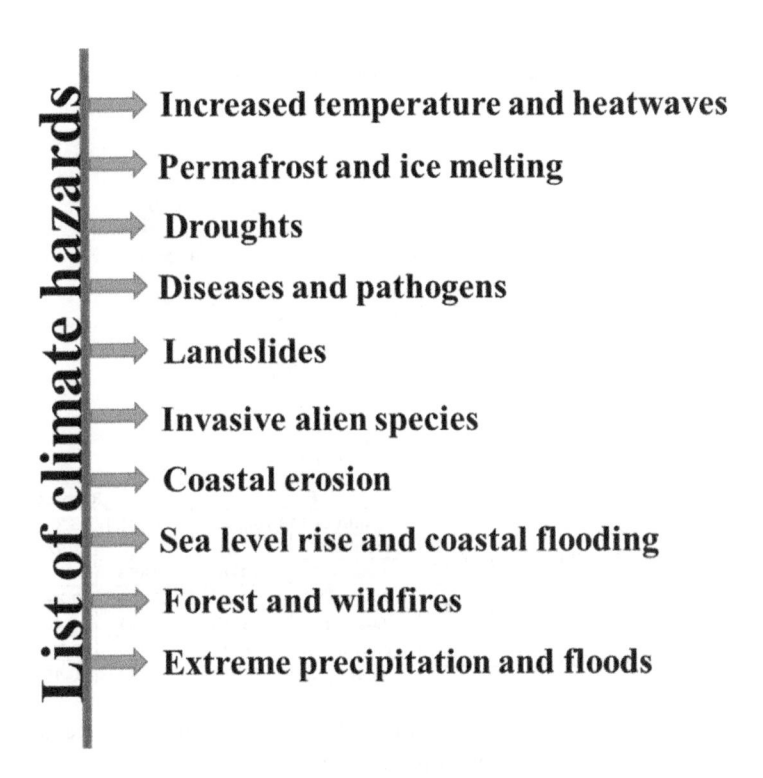

Fig. 4.2.   List of Global Climate Hazards.

promote the spread of transmissible or vector-borne illnesses. The visualisations shown in Fig. 4.2 illustrate a comprehensive compilation of global climate hazards.

List of Desired Climate Records

One may argue that at least 30 years of such data records are necessary at enough stations to capture all of a country's main climatic zones and sensitive regions, even though generalisations regarding the duration of an adequate record are difficult to draw. These data would need to be collected at least daily in order to effectively capture climatic extremes. The data should also be coherent and supported by credible sources (metadata). It will be more difficult to discern and attribute trends of rainfall of similar sized time series to climate change when there is a 15% rainfall discontinuity. The endeavour would be extremely difficult if no data were provided that established the time and source of the gap.

Every month's worldwide surface temperature in 2022 was among the 10 hottest for that particular month. The year's biggest worldwide temperature departure was recorded in the month of March, at +0.94°C (+1.69°F), whereas the year's lowest was recorded in the month of November, at +0.75°C (+1.35°F).

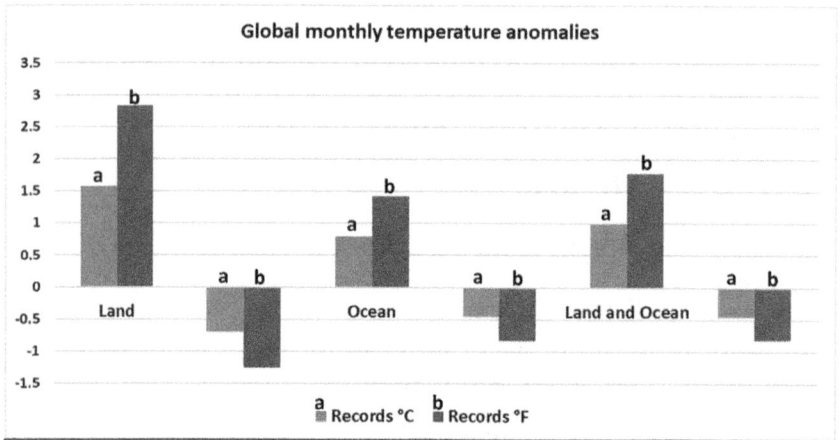

January–	Anomaly		Rank		Records		
December	°C	°F	(out of 143 years)	Year(s)	°C	°F
Land	+1.29 ± 0.14	+2.32 ± 0.25	Warmest	7th	2020	1.57	2.83
			Coolest	137th	1884	-0.7	-1.26
Ocean	+0.69 ± 0.16	+1.24 ± 0.29	Warmest	6th	2016	0.79	1.42
			Coolest	138th	1904	-0.46	-0.83
Land and Ocean	+0.86 ± 0.15	+1.55 ± 0.27	Warmest	6th	2016	0.99	1.78
			Coolest	138th	1904	-0.45	-0.81

Fig. 4.3.   Global Monthly January–December Ranks and Records Temperature Anomalies.

The temperature change worldwide with respect to months recorded in various scenarios can be expressed in the following Fig. 4.3.

Additionally, the series of time must not have any substantial gaps in the data because they might have a disastrous effect on statistical correlations in particular. Finally, it is possible to monitor global climate more effectively the more variables that are recorded. Knowing an area's average and extreme rainfall, temperature ranges as well as the frequency of thunderstorm, hailstorms and frosts is helpful for a variety of reasons (Yogeesh, 2019; Yogeesh et al., 2023).

Unfortunately, economic reasons are acting in the other direction just when high-quality networks are most necessary for climate observation and forecast purposes – and this reality is becoming more acknowledged.

Impacts of Automatic Weather Stations

Budgets funding National Meteorological and Hydrological Services are getting more and more restrictive, which is a reality in almost all nations. In this setting, automated instrumentation as well as remote-sensing techniques are progressively replacing somewhat resource-intensive manned observational networks.

There has been a trend towards automating parts of an observational network during the last 10–15 years. As of late 2006, automatic weather stations (AWSs), which are expanding, accounted for an estimated 23% among all province basic synoptic network stations. There is no doubt that AWSs have had some desired qualities for climate science, including such cost-effectiveness, greater data, a better capability to recognise radical views, the ability to deploy through remote as well as hostile climates, methods of allowing access to data, measurement continuity and objectivity, and more. They can also be used for many forms of quality control (Abbott, 1986).

On the other hand, AWSs may have a negative impact on the climatic record, as evidenced by experience in a number of nations. The following effects have been noted:

- Data loses, communication breakdowns and insufficient data backups, which result in large gaps in database continuity.
- Time-series have become inhomogeneous, sometimes as a result of poor maintenance and sometimes as a result of improper change management for example, not allowing enough time for traditional observations to overlap with those from AWSs. A change to the wind sensor in certain nations caused discontinuities for peak wind speeds, infuriating the national standards organisation; maintenance methods may cause misleading data spikes.
- There are times when accuracy and precision are questioned, particularly when it comes to rainfall. Once more, this can cause homogeneity problems and have a negative impact on choices that have a major financial impact.
- Due to the intricate electronics with AWSs, maintenance calls for more specialist expertise than could be easily accessible in some nations.

- Unless outfitted with specialised sensors, AWS deployment typically leads to a loss of visual assessment, making it challenging to build certain climate improve track setting with respect to harmony.

Hence, many of the aforementioned consequences could be avoided if AWS is implemented with strong deployment and change management practices, as well as frequent maintenance. As technology advances, additional mitigation of the aforementioned issues should be expected; for example, improved data loggers can reduce data loss while optical sensors can capture certain types of occurrences. The problem is that cutting-edge administration and new technology usually result in expense increases.

The potential to deliver far higher observation density than is achievable with traditional networks makes remote-sensing systems appealing. Overseas or sparsely inhabited areas, they are very useful. One of the disadvantages is that it might be challenging to correctly monitor or understand some variables. Additionally, a limited amount of surface station is required to 'ground truth' the data derived from the satellite or from radar, etc. This will necessitate not just the construction of an ideal combination of observation systems but also a cautious change-management approach as observational systems develop (Rashmi et al., 2023). The latter represents an important scientific project.

Observational Data Management and Stewardship

An operational network that can routinely collect and record climatic observations must exist in order to guarantee that the global climate history can very much adequately supporting climate surveillance with service supply. However, this is not a sufficient prerequisite. Additionally, the data have to be freely accessible, preserved and subject to rigorous quality control. It is challenging to use the climate record to build climatologist, create statistical prediction schemes or incorporate it into climate models if it only exists in significant portions or only in physical manuscript form. Unfortunately, proper management for observational data continues to be a significant issue in many, especially developing, nations.

The necessary steps for data management are outlined below to guarantee that the data from the observations are accessible and ready for usage. The need that nations continue to be open to sharing their data in order for the rest of the globe to have access to it must be added to these.

Data Rescue and Digitisation

Large volumes of data are often stored in paper formats that are entirely inaccessible, like logbooks or record-sheets. The amount of risk of irreversible damage or loss through dangerous fire, water, decay, thefting and bug or vermin assault is increased in such configurations, which is much worse. Due to this, WMO has been increasingly concerned with data recovery and digitalisation initiatives, particularly in poorer nations. It has received helpful support from government organisations in several nations to aid in these efforts. Activities often include protecting sensitive data from loss or damage very once, digitising or imaging them, and/or moving them to safer places (even abroad). Training NMHS employees in efficient record-management and archiving practices is also crucial.

Database Technology and Archiving

Effective data access in the present-day entails having the data stored electronically and preferably in ways that make it possible for it to be quickly fed into spreadsheets, analytical tools and climate models. CCl encourages and supports different data management efforts to help with these objectives. The suggestion and use of non-proprietary software for data management in developing and least developed nations, created with those countries' NMHSs' unique demands and constraints in mind, is one recent example. The Caribbean, African, and Pacific regions have so far used the Producers and suppliers Clim-Soft software suite. Training sessions, unique report formats, as well as a discussion boards forum support it. The Australian Meteorology Bureau has provided support for the Oceanic 'arm' of this project since they have found that in-country coaching is much more effective than workshops, which can only be attended through one person per nation.

There is still a requirement to make sure paper documents are kept safely and in accordance with recognised archiving standards in cases where digitising data has not been possible.

Quality Assurance/Control (QA/QC)

For information to be really trustworthy, it needs to be capable of being identified, fixed, removed or at the least flagged. In other words, QC must be applied to every piece of data. In the past, QC was a very physical procedure that required NMHS employees to physically compare each item of data put into logbooks of having valid information against a series of tests as well as use their extensive observational and frequently qualitative operator experience. This approach limits the role of the manual operator, if there is one, to looking at and making judgements on circumstances that are brought up by the automatic testing method. Effective quality control procedures include giving the data a quality flag and keeping an auditing trail to guarantee that the original relevant data can be recreated if necessary.

In terms of the degree and kind of QC, the number of stations, the variable type, the frequency of the data and, of course, the manpower and computing resources, all play a part. Additionally, certain facilities test for homogeneity. The EPA is updating the policies based on the quality assurance for surface related to climate data in collaboration with the Team of experts for Observation Standards and Guidelines for Climate. Ensuring that recurrent or systemic mistakes are recognised and sent back to observing management for investigation and correction is a crucial step in the QC/QA process. It is a given that the ideal type of quality control is to make sure that the source document is as near to faultless as possible.

Initiatives on a Global Scale to Digitise

To understand better, detect, anticipate and adapt to global climate variability, comprehensive and consistent assessments must be conducted using long-term, high-quality and trustworthy climatic instrumental time series. Regional climate research and forecasts, satellite data calibration, the creation of climatic quality reanalysis data and the ability to translate climate proxy findings into instrumental terms are just a few of the advantages.

Particular Challenges Exist in Developing Nations

In a previous section, it is discussed that collecting and maintaining climate data might be difficult for developing and least developed countries. In addition to severe resource limitations, there may be high staff turnover, little opportunity for new hire training, poor or limited equipment and storage facilities, frequent remote locations and difficult access due to inadequate infrastructure, poor communications and a low priority given to meteorology by the government.

However, without data from these nations, it becomes more challenging to not only deliver the level of climatic services needed locally to control climate-related risk but also to create a genuinely world picture of the weather, its fluctuations and their changes.

It will make an effort to offer recommendations on how to handle some of the endemic issues mentioned in the preceding paragraphs. There will also be some recommendations for resource mobilisation, such as using aid and climate change financing organisations, employing private money whenever possible and increasing the visibility of the NMHS in its own nation.

Repercussions of Climatic Change on Society With Economy

The socio-economic effects of climate change are quite complex and vary by sector and area. The same global climate consequences can be felt significantly differently across industries and socio-economic groups even within a local area or region (Yogeesh, 2023a). While it is challenging to precisely map all potential socio-economic effects of climate change, illustrations of consequences in significant industries that are pertinent to several European and Asian countries are including.

Social and Public Health Vulnerability

Impacts on public social and health vulnerability are one of the key ways that climate change will influence economic systems. Climate change will exacerbate a number of dangers to people's well-being with safeties, in such a way as: deaths due to illness caused by heat or hot waves or colder snaps; loss of life, chemical exposure, and poisoning resulting from floods or wildfires; emergence of new diseases as well as the spread of transmitted diseases as a result of based on the scenario in pathogen, virus, and parasite behaviour.

Heatwaves, for illustration, will cause due to heat fatigue, dehydration, even heat or hot strokes, while colder snaps can always cause trauma and also hypothermia. Both these types of extremes will have the potential to aggravate pre-existing conditions, in addition to respiratory and cardiovascular disorders. Asthma and allergy complaints are on the rise, and higher temperatures are predicted to change the length, beginning, and severity of the pollen season (Yogeesh, 2023b).

An increased risk of infectious disease outbreaks may result from a rising climate and shifting land use practices. The global climate change will be an influence or affect the distribution as well as transmission of infectious illnesses, while it is not the only factor in this process; for instance, human behaviour and international trade are frequently more significant factors. This influence could be felt directly by changing the behaviour underlying pathogens and vectors, or it might be felt more subtly by changing how humans behave and are exposed to infectious illnesses. For instance, warmer weather may encourage individuals to spend more time outside in tick-infested areas.

Finally, there is mounting evidence that the danger of future pandemics will rise as a result of climate change and other human actions that have an influence on biodiversity. Rising temperatures and other climatic changes are anticipated to cause certain animal species' spatial patterns to shift, which will enhance the possibility of interacting with them. This raises the possibility of novel viruses spreading from animal populations to human ones. Recent studies indicate a substantial rise in the probability of animal-to-human virus transmission even under more hopeful climate change scenarios, emphasising the significance of adaptive measures like emergency preparation.

Forestry, Aquaculture and Agriculture

Climate change is projected to have an impact on crop yield, species reproductive and grottiness, water source, the development of species of invasive alien, illnesses, infections within the agricultural, forestry and aquaculture sectors. While some locations may benefit from these alterations due to the development of new species or longer sustainable seasons, others might experience a decline in yield. Changes in costs, agriculture revenue, and total food security on a regional, national, or even worldwide level are all economic ramifications of these transformations. As a result, the poll found that agricultural losses are the second most often stated socio-economic impact of climate change.

Transport Industry

Extreme events also may cause physical infrastructure damage, which may have an impact on the transportation business. Increased temperatures and heatwaves would make rail buckling and concrete deterioration issues worse. The movement of people and goods may be restricted as a result of such damage to the infrastructure of the road, rail, river, and air transport networks, with consequent economic repercussions across sectors and nations, particularly if logistical service networks are jeopardised.

Production With Services

Although the impacts of global warming on industries like production or services, especially some apart from tourism, in addition to health care are not fully understood, they are now almost certainly the result of changes in the major driving forces of the economy, such as changes in work performance, changes in energy requirements, or disruptions throughout transportation systems. These modifications may lead to changes in the cost and quality of manufacturing inputs, an increase in production costs, the disruption of supply networks, or the cessation of services. Technological advancements in the manufacturing industry may be able to counteract anticipated reductions in labour productivity brought on by increasing temperatures, greater humidity, or the development of pathogenic and vector borne illnesses. For the services sector, this may not be feasible.

Energy (Power) Sector

One of the primary effects of climate change in an energy or power sector is probably a shifting huge demand for energy or power. The volume and duration of the demand for cooling and heating energy can be impacted by temperature extremes. The quantity of electricity generated by thermal power generating might be impacted by decreased water availability. For instance, the fossil-fuel or with biomass, or some nuclear energy plants all will depends heavily on water for the cooling, and output at these facilities might be halted by a water crisis. When these varying patterns of energy supply and demand are combined, there may be dangers to the general stability of power networks at moments of peak demand.

Extreme weather events may also physically harm energy infrastructure, leading to blackouts or other safety risks that might endanger business operations in other areas of the economy.

Infrastructure, Housing and Construction

The growth of local infrastructures and land usage are among the challenging primary competencies. Due to changing weather patterns and catastrophic occurrences like floods and landslides, development is likely to experience delays and higher expenses. In addition, since the need for reconstruction and repair work may increase as a result of new patterns for natural catastrophes and damages, construction material specifications and with construction rules are always expected to change to accommodate with the change in relevant weather conditions. The occurrence of severe events can also physically harm vital infrastructure, such as that related to electricity, transportation, and education.

Tourism Sector

Climate change is quite likely to have an effect on tourism. The amount of beach tourism in renowned European locations like the Mediterranean might decline because of rising temperatures, increased temperatures, sea level rise, and coastline erosion. Similar to how increased temperatures and changes in snow supply might result in less ski tourists in popular locations like the Alps. Existing effects could cause these varieties of tourism to move to new areas or various times of the year, or they might pave the way for new kinds of tourism. For instance, lower-elevation alpine regions with shorter ski seasons are increasing the opportunity for alternative tourist pursuits like camping, mountaineering or hiking.

Services and Management of Water

Risks are created by climate change for the efficient delivery of required water utilities to the various industry/sectors and the overall utility of water source. Changes in precipitation can have immediate effects like floods or droughts, but there is also a chance that the water infrastructure will sustain damage. The latter might prevent the community from receiving water for irrigation or for watering plants. Climate change-related service interruptions or quality declines might endanger the public's health by facilitating the spread of illness. Additionally, climate change may exacerbate rivalry among industries for vital resources like water. For instance, the competition among agricultural and aquaculture, energy, tourism, and water supply could be made worse by a strain on water resources brought on either directly by climate change, such as droughts, or indirectly by the change in the environment, such as losses to critical infrastructure brought on by floods, wildfires, or storms. Long-term water shortages could thus necessitate setting priorities for requirements and utilisation among industries/sectors at the municipal or regional or local level.

List of Technical Areas Under Climatic Changes Adaption

This part covers a number of important technical topics, such as increasing societal political will and ownership, aligning goals with important national policies, evaluating costs and investment possibilities and putting up methods for tracking and reporting success. A varied collection of experts in governance and policy, finance, global warming, energy and development are consulted for our Climate Promise work. The following graphic clearly illustrates this idea in Fig. 4.4.

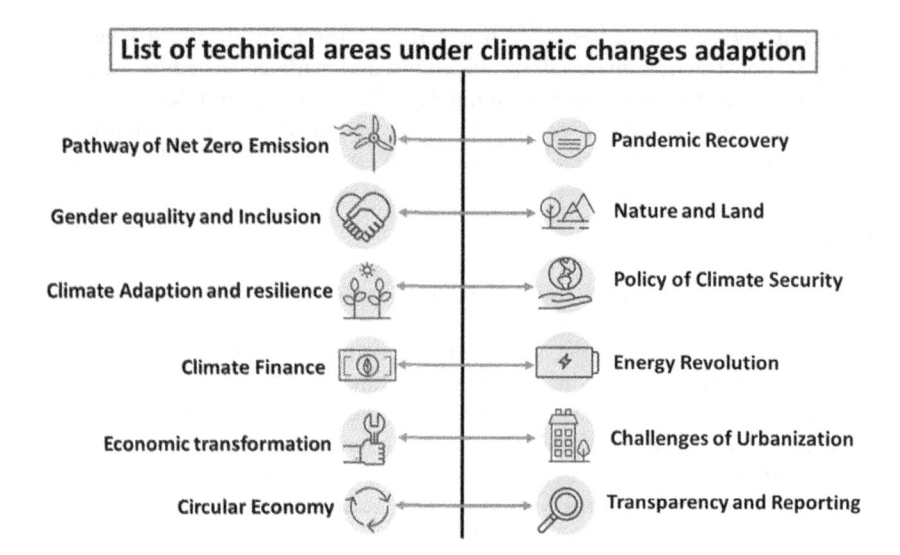

Fig. 4.4.   A Ladder List of Technical Areas Under Climatic Changes Adaption.

Pathway of Net Zero Emission

We urgently need to shift towards low-emission economic development if we want to achieve the goals of the Paris Agreement and stop catastrophic climate catastrophe. The science says that in order to do this, net zero emissions must be reached in the second part of this century. When the quantities of GHGs created and those removed from the atmosphere are balanced, zero net emissions are attained. To do this, we must drastically alter how we generate energy, cultivate and travel, as well as remove carbon dioxide from the environment.

Gender Equality and Inclusion

Evidence suggests that the burden of global warming is borne disproportionately by women, young people, indigenous peoples, communities, individuals who have disabilities and the poor.

We must acknowledge the disparities and inequities in how we are coping with the changes, especially between those women and men, if we are to successfully address the difficulties posed by a world that is quickly warming.

But we must go farther; in order to prevail in this battle, we must draw on all of the information, abilities and viewpoints at our disposal while also drawing on the expertise of those who have served on the front lines.

The goal of inclusion is the result. But it also pertains to having the freedom and authority to choose and participate. The right to participate in shaping one's own destiny for individuals of all ages, genders and backgrounds.

Particularly young people are rising up. They have led projects in their nations and communities and have inspired a worldwide movement calling on their governments to take drastic climate action.

In the meanwhile, women throughout the world are increasingly taking the lead in planning and decision-making processes, as well as in identifying and developing solutions to achieve transformational climate action.

Local communities and indigenous peoples keep speaking up to demand that our rights and customs be upheld.

Climate Adaption and Resilience

Governments are required to both scale up and achieve their adaptation goals under the Climate Promise. Devastating floods that claim lives. Crops destroyed by severe droughts. Homes were damaged by wildfires. New headlines warning of the impending climate calamity appear every week. The race to create resilience is now just as critical as the race to achieve zero emissions since more warming is now certain and extreme weather is increasing.

Climate Finance

The phrase 'climate finance' can be used in a variety of contexts. In its broadest meaning, it denotes a business that use financial institutions or technological advancements to promote environmental sustainability, like in the case of creating or implementing new solar energy systems or other renewable energy sources. Developing nations are already investing valuable resources in mitigation and adaptation due to their awareness of the serious risks associated with combating climate change. The security and prosperity for their population for next generations will be greatly enhanced by this investment.

However, governments cannot cover the expenditures on their own. Especially those who are working to alleviate poverty among their inhabitants. A lot more is required. Financing often comes from a variety of public and commercial sources and is typically provided at the local, state or international level.

Economic Transformation

Although the transition to low-carbon economy would clearly benefit the environment, what about people? What societal repercussions result from the largest economic revolution the world ever has experienced?

Evidence suggests that, if well managed, the transition may be a tremendous force in promoting social justice, green jobs and the eradication of poverty.

The statistics are convincing. 1 in 3 of the 11.5 million jobs in renewable energy that were anticipated to be held globally in 2019 were held by women.

The International Renewable Energies Agency predicts that over 40 million people might be employed by renewables by 2050, and the numbers are rising according to International Renewable Energy Agency (IRENA) or the World Energy Outlook by the International Energy Agency (IEA).

Circular Economy

We should be concerned about the effects of our present production and consumption habits on the environment. We are already in 'ecological overshoot', using more natural resources than are necessary to support us. If we continue on our current track, it is predicted that we will need the natural capital equivalent of approximately three planets.

Circular economy techniques may be used by countries to accomplish short-to-medium-term environmental and essential objective, as well as relatively long-term net zero targets and other closely connected developmental and environmental concerns. The formulation of climate policy plans, as well as nationally set contributions, make this potential feasible.

Simply said, continuing as normal is not an option. Fortunately, a change from conventional 'take, make, dispose' models of industry towards regenerative and circular ones is already taking place. Reduced emissions of GHGs and other types of pollution is one advantage of the transition for both humans and the environment. Approaches based on the circular economy can aid nations in accelerating the transition to more accessible, resilient, and low-carbon economies. They can help natural systems regenerate while also addressing the climate and biodiversity challenges and generating new green employment. Degradation of the ecosystem, loss of biodiversity and pollution.

Pandemic Recovery

But no one anticipated the spread of COVID-19. A once-in-a-lifetime epidemic that claimed and over 4.5 million lives and devastated national economies in 2020 threatened would derail the attempt. The COVID-19 epidemic has brought attention to the importance of making investments in robust, equitable and sustainable recovery (Phillips et al., 2020).

The decisions and investments made now need to be leveraged again for future as governments throughout the world continue to deal with the effects of COVID-19. We also need to consider the world after the epidemic. This is our chance to move society and the environment forward more effectively (Yogeesh, 2020).

The good news is that nationally determined contributions may serve as a foundation for a smart, green recovery by providing a road map for climate action that can promote economic development, technological advancement, job creation and the eradication of significant social inequities.

Nature and Land

The life support system of our planet is its healthy ecosystems. They also support our development and prosperity, as nature as well as its services total account for just more than half of world GDP. Forests, fisheries and with agriculture support the livelihoods of more than two billion people.

Despite its enormous worth, human activities are contributing to nature's fast decline. While the destruction of the world's forests continues at a rate of about 10 million hectares annually, costing the world economy close to US$10 trillion, species of animals and plants are vanishing at a rate not seen in 10 million years (O'Neill et al., 2020).

While the degradation of ecosystems increases, our susceptibility to temperature increases; climate change is dramatically accelerating the loss of species.

Policy of Climate Security

Conflicts have spread, gotten more complicated and lasted longer all over the world. Today, two billion people are thought to reside in unstable and conflict-affected regions. It's anticipated that the number will rise.

Simultaneously, the frequency and severity of climatic stresses and shocks have grown, disrupting lives and livelihoods, escalating competition for environmental assets, causing relocation and fostering food insecurity. More nations are recognising the threat the climate issue poses to world peace and security.

Although violent conflict is not directly caused by climate change, its effects can worsen the drivers.

In unstable and conflict-affected environments where people already face a humanitarian crisis and have inadequate coping mechanisms, the unusual negative cause of change in climate is always exacerbated. Children and women are also disproportionately impacted.

Action on climate change can also be hampered by conflict and insecurity. The capacity of nations and territories dealing with violent conflict to develop and execute climate policy is lowered. Climate action can fall to the wayside during the post-conflict rebuilding process as more pressing issues are dealt with.

Energy Revolution

Changes to clean, renewables are essential to addressing the climate catastrophe since the energy sector is responsible for over three-quarters of human-caused emissions of GHGs.

Beyond tackling climate change, switching from fossil fuels has many other advantages. Millions of employments for men and women might be created as a result of the energy transition. In addition, time, renewable energy sources have the ability to provide everyone with access to electricity, which helps to realise almost all other SDGs.

Several countries are attentively examining how they might embrace the opportunity as we are on the verge of an energy revolution.

The key will be to enable the massive renewable energy expenditures required to fuel a fair transformation.

Challenges of Urbanisation

By 2050, it is expected that about 75% of the global population are resident in the area of urban, making urbanisation one of the century's defining trends. The numerous advantages of urban living, including better employment prospects, higher earnings, easier availability of services and wider access to cultural areas, are the reason why city migration is currently on the rise.

Our cities are enormous engines for growth, contributing to around 70% of the global GDP thanks to their enormous human capital. However, this economic growth also brings about high energy consumption, and cities also account for more than 70% of global GHG emissions (Riahi et al., 2017).

Cities may play a revolutionary role in creating growth routes that are cleaner and much more resilient because of their environmental impact. Urbanisation may reduce inequality as well as the growth of slums and informal settlements if it is managed properly, laying the groundwork for a more equitable and sustainable future.

In reality, if we want to keep global warming below 1.5°C, we need to start tackling climate change in urban areas. Enabling leadership and key players in cities will be essential to fulfilling these commitments as nations transition from defining ambitious objectives to achieving them.

Transparency and Reporting

The Paris Agreement prioritises transparency. We cannot proceed from planning through action and defeat climate change if nations do not make an effort to be honest about their contributions to climate change.

In a variety of respects, transparency and reporting about climate action are essential. First, it enables the international community to evaluate overall development and contributes to the growth of confidence that everyone is contributing. By creating a foundation for increased ambition, it is also essential for realising the full promise of the Paris Agreement.

The difficulties that nations and communities experience are shown through communicating climate action, which may elevate the voices of those who require the most help.

Furthermore, giving governments access to current and trustworthy emissions of GHGs data, reactions and climate-related policies aids in the development of fact-based policies. Additionally, it advances our scientific knowledge of climate change, including the steps and regulations required to lessen it and prepare for its effects.

The promotion of collaboration, capacity-building and knowledge transfer necessary to improve the international response to climate change is furthered through reporting on activity and the assistance mobilised and needed.

Exposure to Risk and Requirement of Adaptation

Nowadays, as discovered by the current findings, changing global climate will always have a wide range of physical and socio-economic effects in both industrialised and developing nations. These effects may differ depending on a number of different countries and geographical microregions, as well as unique physical traits like coastlines, height, flora, or microclimate. These effects might vary, even among the same nations or regions, putting different strains on regional and local socio-economic systems and local populations. Furthermore, local communities can face new difficulties as a result of the price of loss including economically get loss linked to disrupted source of economic activity across industry/sectors.

Significant financial losses and expenses may be incurred as an outcome of the socio-economic effects of changes in climate. Current estimates suggest that the consequences of inactivity are expected to increase exponentially in the future, despite the fact that the precise forecasts depend on the sector evaluated and the models employed. Last but just not least, the cumulative consequences of climate change may have an influence on local communities' economic success and wellbeing, particularly those of its most vulnerable people. Through commerce, international financial flows and migration, regions and nations in Europe and Asia are also susceptible to the effects of climate change outside their boundaries, which might worsen the effects they currently suffer.

Conclusion

It is widely acknowledged that global climate change will always pose one of the greatest threats to both the environment and mankind. The meteorological community, and notably the environmental community, will have to play a crucial role in supporting major global initiatives that will be required to mitigate the effects. The basis for this assistance will thus need to be an operational system designed with the useful requirements of the specific climatic plan in the minds of people. The competence of an authority to design and implement the best solutions will determine the success of adaptation measures. Continued expenditures in climate adaptation research should address the shortage of data needed to scale down climate forecasts to the local level. At every level of government, but especially at the local level, adequate resources should be made available to realise the investments needed for adaptation measures. The multiple level global unusual climate and energy or power dialogues advocated in the Regulation of Governance may provide appropriate forums to address the problems that various stakeholders are facing as well as their specific assistance requirements, especially to the degree that these problems are cross-sectoral.

Implications

The content highlights the critical need to address climate change in a comprehensive and coordinated manner across different levels – local, regional, national, and international. It emphasises the urgent need for increased preparedness and capacity-building to respond to the far-reaching impacts of climate change on both socio-economic and ecological systems. The content emphasises the importance of adopting a cohesive and interdisciplinary approach to understanding and quantifying the complex effects of climate change on different communities and ecosystems.

Additionally, the content notes that adapting to the impacts of climate change will likely be expensive, and delaying action could result in significant economic losses. Therefore, the content underscores the importance of investing in climate resilience to mitigate the negative consequences of climate change.

Overall, the implication of the content is that climate change is a multifaceted issue that requires a coordinated effort at different levels to effectively address and mitigate its impacts on both human and natural systems.

References

Abbott, P. F. (1986). Guidelines on the quality control of surface climatological data (WMO/TD No. 111). WMO.

Clark, P., Shakun, J., Marcott, S., Mix, A., Eby, M., Kulp, S., Levermann, A., Archer, D., Bitz, C., Weaver, A., Clark, J., Kotthoff, U., Schmittner, A., van der Wal, R., Min, S.-H., Sanchez Goñi, M. F., Bloch-Johnson, J., Tamburini, F., Wright, A., & Grießinger, J. (2016). Consequences of twenty-first-century policy for multi-millennial climate and sea-level change. *Nature Climate Change, 6,* 360–369. https://doi.org/10.1038/nclimate2923

Global Climate Observing System (GCOS). (2003). Second report on the adequacy of the global observing system for climate (GCOS Report No. 82, WMO/TD No. 1143). WMO.

Kriegler, E., Edmonds, J., Hallegatte, S., Ebi, K., Kram, T., Riahi, K., Winkler, H., van Vuuren, D., Smolka, A., Giddens, A., Jakob, M., Harnisch, J., Krey, V., Morton, J., Kriegler, H., Wilson, R., Sheehan, P., Fujimori, S., & Tavoni, M. (2014). A new scenario framework for climate change research: The concept of shared climate policy assumptions. *Climatic Change, 122*(3), 401–414. https://doi.org/10.1007/s10584-013-0971-5

O'Neill, B., Carter, T., Ebi, K., Harrison, P., Kemp-Benedict, E., Kriegler, E., Kok, K., Preston, B., Riahi, K., Seneviratne, S., van Ruijven, B., Bijl, D., Bréchet, T., Fisher-Vanden, K., Fujimori, S., Rothman, D., Wada, K., Weyant, J., & Xu, L. (2020). Achievements and needs for the climate change scenario framework. *Nature Climate Change, 10,* 1074–1084. https://doi.org/10.1038/s41558-020-00952-0

Phillips, C. A., Caldas, A., Cleetus, R., Dahl, K., Declet-Barreto, J., Dominguez, R., Licker, R., Merner, L. D., Ortiz-Partida, J. P., Phelan, A. L., Spanger-Siegfried, E., Talati, S., Trisos, C. H., Carlson, C. J., Vicente-Serrano, S. M., Wilkinson, E., Wolf, S., & Yarwood, Z. (2020). Compound climate risks in the COVID-19 pandemic. *Nature Climate Change, 10,* 583–586. https://doi.org/10.1038/s41558-020-0804-2

Rashmi, M., Girija, D. K., & Yogeesh, N. (2023). Fusion of blockchain with internet of things and artificial intelligence for keener healthcare solutions. In G. Karthick & S. Karupusamy (Eds.), *Contemporary applications of data fusion for advanced healthcare informatics* (pp. 112–136). IGI Global. https://doi.org/10.4018/978-1-6684-8913-0.ch005

Riahi, K., van Vuuren, D., Kriegler, E., Edmonds, J., O'Neill, B., Fujimori, S., Bauer, N., Calvin, K., Dellink, R., Fricko, O., Lutz, W., Popp, A., Cuaresma, J. C., Samir, K., Leimbach, M., Andrijevic, M., Arnell, N., Gidden, M., Lawrence, P., O'Brien, K., & Takahashi, K. (2017). The shared socioeconomic pathways and their energy, land use, and greenhouse gas emissions implications: An overview. *Global Environmental Change, 42*, 153–168. https://doi.org/10.1016/j.gloenvcha.2016.05.009

World Climate Data Monitoring Programme (WCDMP). (2005). Report of the RA V Data Management Workshop. WMO. 28 November–3 December 2004 (WCDMP-No. 57, WMO/TD No. 1263).

Yogeesh, N. (2019). Graphical representation of mathematical equations using open-source software. *Journal of Advances in Scholarly Researches and Allied Education, 16*(5), 2204–2209.

Yogeesh, N. (2020). Mathematical maxima program to show Corona (COVID-19) disease spread over a period. *TUMBE Group of International Journals, 3*(1), 14–16.

Yogeesh, N. (2023a). Fuzzy clustering for classification of metamaterial properties. In S. Mehta & A. Abougreen (Eds.), *Metamaterial technology and intelligent metasurfaces for wireless communication systems* (pp. 200–229). IGI Global. https://doi.org/10.4018/978-1-6684-8287-2.ch009

Yogeesh, N. (2023b). Fuzzy logic modelling of nonlinear metamaterials. In S. Mehta & A. Abougreen (Eds.), *Metamaterial technology and intelligent metasurfaces for wireless communication systems* (pp. 230–269). IGI Global. https://doi.org/10.4018/978-1-6684-8287-2.ch010

Yogeesh, N., Girija, D. K., Rashmi, M., & Divyashree, J. (2023). Enhancing diagnostic accuracy in pathology using fuzzy set theory. *Journal of Population Therapeutics and Clinical Pharmacology, 30*(16), 695–704. https://doi.org/10.53555/jptcp.v30i16.2533

Chapter 5

Revisiting Microfinance as an Instrument of Sustainable Development

Rajeev Sengupta[a], Ameya Patil[a] and Shahid Lone[b]

[a]Dr. Vishwanath Karad MIT World Peace University, India
[b]National Institute of Technology, Srinagar, India

Abstract

Today, financial viability and the creation of social value form the main axis for the operation of inclusive firms. However, depending on who offers the ideas for inclusive enterprises, there can be questionable presumptions regarding what is promised in relation to poverty. One dubious premise is that all poverty can be solved by the market. Markets may be a prerequisite but not sufficient condition for resolving social problems. Financial inclusion through microfinance is a crucial facet of social inclusion. At the World Summit for Social Development (WSSD) in March 1995, governments made a commitment to eradicate poverty on a global scale, citing it as a moral, social, political and economic imperative. One of the three main objectives of the WSSD was the eradication of poverty. Microfinance provides financial services for persons living below the poverty line and for small businesses that lack access to traditional banking services and related products. Microcredit is the lending of small amounts of money to underserved consumers. Microfinance succeeded where institutional financing failed, but its viability is in question. An all-encompassing approach is required to support the growth of the new microfinance sector and manage the balance that must be struck between outreach and sustainability. It is well known that only efficient institutions can greatly lower the long-term expense of serving irregular and low revenues.

Keywords: Poverty; microfinance; financial inclusion; sustainability; e-inclusiveness

Creating Pathways for Prosperity, 67–84
Copyright © 2025 Rajeev Sengupta, Ameya Patil and Shahid Lone
Published under exclusive licence by Emerald Publishing Limited
doi:10.1108/978-1-83549-121-820241006

Introduction

The general equilibrium continues to perplex us when global poverty and inequality has exponentially widened the gulf. Global poverty is one of the world's most urgent issues in contemporary times, and governments are mired in developing and rolling out sustainable poverty alleviation programmes to bridge this gulf. The world's poorest people remain undernourished, frequently go without access to basic necessities like power, education (both basic and higher education) and have limited or no access to health facilities. The multidimensional nature of poverty allows it to be not compartmentalised into one single fit definition. It depends on the context of a particular country. In the United States, a person earning less than $ 24.55 is considered to be living in abject poverty, whereas a person in Ethiopia, it's almost 10 times lower at $ 2.04 per day. According to the World Bank, for the last three decades, economically weaker section people earning less than $ 2.15 per day at 2017 purchasing power parity formed a major chunk and showed a declining trend, but the same was interrupted and impacted by the pandemic which hit the world. There has been a consistent rise in relation to people who are been left in abject poverty pre- and post-pandemic, i.e. from 70 to 700 million between 1970 and 2015. Extreme poverty now affects 9.3% of the total world population, up from 8.4% in 2019. During the pandemic, it was the poor who suffered the most, while the rich got richer. And it is one of many firsts in decades, global inequality rose as a result of their losses in income being double those of the world's richest people. The policy makers, due to explosion in technology, have rethought as to how people could be brought under financial inclusion frameworks by making use of digitalisation processes, which is to say how to integrate ways and means and harness digital technologies for the benefit of those who the current financial system has not catered before and would be left in even more vulnerable position if not tended. This paper reimagines how inclusive businesses with the help of election mechanisms could be envisaged under microfinance framework, exploring its benefits, challenges and potential implications for reducing poverty and development. For businesses and financial systems in relation to e-inclusiveness, microfinance has numerous benefits, primarily in reduction of poverty and then the trickle-down effect in upward mobility. There are huge swathes of areas and households where e-inclusiveness is still a distant dream and microfinance has the potential to enable businesses and households to access financial services through digital channels such as unified payment services powered by digital technologies. This will ensure economic mobility for households and also usher in a new phase of growth for small businesses that early had no access to formal financial services.

Since technology is changing and informing business in an immense way, using it to harness benefits of microfinance could prove tremendously helpful in poverty alleviation. This is particularly critical for low-income households, who may have limited knowledge and skills in financial management. Digital financial inclusion promotes financial stability by reducing reliance on cash, which is often associated with money laundering, corruption and other illicit activities. By promoting digital payments, individuals and businesses can transact more securely and transparently, thereby enhancing financial stability. Despite its benefits, digital financial inclusion also faces numerous challenges.

The unjust divide and subsequent distribution of digitally driven technologies is the greatest and a tremendous challenge across different regions and populations. This means that individuals in low-income areas may not have access to digital technologies, thereby limiting their ability to benefit from digital financial inclusion. It also faces regulatory challenges, particularly in areas where digital financial services are not well regulated. This may expose users to fraud and other risks, limiting their ability to benefit from microfinance-based services. It may be limited by a loss of confidence and distrust in digitally driven services, particularly among low-income households. This is because many individuals may not be familiar with the benefits that electronic enabled services offer and may be reluctant to adopt them due to perceived risks and uncertainties. Also, it has significant implications for economic growth and development. It promotes digitally rendered services related to microfinance which are also essential to financial inclusion, a critical lever of alleviating poverty and ensuring economic mobility. By enabling households and businesses access microfinance related services, it can increase financial intermediation, thereby promoting investment and entrepreneurship. Digital financial inclusion can enhance financial stability by reducing reliance on cash and promoting transparency in financial transactions. It can markedly integrate financial processes, augment investor confidence, and promote economic growth and development.

Due to financial interconnectedness, it can promote financial innovation by ensuring that microfinance as a financial instrument serves the economically weaker sections of society by alleviating poverty in a sustainable way. The economic mobility of economically weaker sections and marginalised population can be attained by tailoring context situated microfinance policies. Using digital channels for offering credit and other services, digital financial inclusion can promote financial inclusion, enhance financial literacy, and promote financial stability. However, it also faces numerous challenges, particularly in areas with limited access to digital technologies and inadequate regulation. Nonetheless, digital financial inclusion has significant implications for economic growth and development, and policymakers should prioritise efforts to promote its adoption and uptake. For the first time in decades, global inequality rose. The staggering reduction primary education and essential healthcare has made poor further exposed and vulnerable to sustainable living and will have lasting repercussions on their ability to earn a living if policymakers do not take corrective measures. The recovery has been erratic ever since. The increased cost of food and energy is partially attributable to the crisis in Ukraine, as well as to climate shocks and violence, all of which have slowed the rate of recovery. By the end of 2022, as many as 685 million people may still be struggling to make ends meet. The world's progress towards the 2030 target of ending extreme poverty has been set back by recent disasters. According to current projections, 6.89% of the global population, or more than 500 million people, will have to make do on less than $2.15 per day by 2030. The fact that abject poverty is especially prevalent in Middle East, North Africa and Asia, violent areas, and backward communities makes the effort even more difficult.

Globally, poverty is a pervasive problem affecting billions of people, particularly females and it is often caused by financial exclusion. Financial exclusion refers to the lack of services and resources which can lead to limited opportunities to participate in economic activities and save money. Sustainable poverty alleviation and financial inclusion have become a critical policy goal for governments, international organisations, and the private sector. This chapter explores the relationship between sustainable poverty alleviation and financial inclusion and explores the various strategies that can be used to foster microfinance as a vehicle for achieving sustainable poverty alleviation. Sustainable poverty alleviation and financial inclusion are interrelated concepts that can support each other. Microfinance can help alleviate poverty by providing people with access to financial services that can enable them venture into formal financial system and imagine economic mobility for themselves. Microfinance as part of financial inclusion can also cater to unbanked and underbanked segments of society, which can help individuals and households to exhibit an appetite for financial shocks and build resilience against poverty. Moreover, sustainable poverty alleviation can promote financial inclusion by creating a more stable economic environment that ensures harnessing financial instruments like microfinance. Sustainable poverty alleviation can also reduce the cost of providing financial services to low-income populations, making it more commercially viable for financial service providers to serve this market segment.

Microfinance involves providing small loans and other financial services to low-income individuals and households. Microfinance can help to build financial inclusion by providing access to credit for people who would otherwise be excluded from formal financial services. Microfinance can also support sustainable poverty alleviation by promoting entrepreneurship and small business development. Digital financial services, such as mobile banking, can provide people with access to financial services without requiring them to physically visit a bank branch. Digital financial services can be particularly useful in rural areas, where physical access to banks can be limited. Moreover, digital financial services can be more cost-effective than traditional banking services, making them more accessible to low-income populations. Financial literacy programs can help individuals and households to understand the benefits of financial services and how to use them effectively. Financial literacy programs can also help people to develop good financial habits, such as saving and budgeting, which can contribute to sustainable poverty alleviation. Social protection programs, such as cash transfers, can provide a safety net for vulnerable populations and help to prevent them from falling into poverty. Social protection programs can also provide access to financial services, such as bank accounts, which can support financial inclusion. Sustainable poverty alleviation and financial inclusion are critical policy goals that can support each other. Financial inclusion can help to alleviate poverty by providing access to financial services, while sustainable poverty alleviation can promote financial inclusion by creating a more stable economic environment. Strategies such as digital financial services, financial literacy programs, microfinance, and social protection programs can be used to promote financial inclusion as a means of achieving sustainable poverty alleviation.

Achieving sustainable poverty alleviation and financial inclusion will require coordinated efforts from governments, international organisations, and the private sector to develop policies and programs that support these goals.

Literature Review

Poverty alleviation, poverty reduction and poverty relief are all umbrella terms for a collection of initiatives whose ultimate goal is to help the poor become economically self-sufficient (Zainal et al., 2019). Several poverty alleviation strategies have been suggested by developmental economists and allied experts, and the Governments of different countries have tries different poverty alleviation programmes suggested by the Governmental committees formed therein to tackle this issue. Different researchers have carried research studies on poverty reduction strategies which mainly includes top bottom impact (Kaldor, 1966; Hoff & Stiglitz, 2001), resettlement for spatial poverty (Merkle, 2003; Yang et al., 2020), financial inclusion (Churchill & Marisetty, 2020; Ozili, 2021), microfinance (Ghosh, 2013), and digital finance including mobile money (Ahmad et al., 2020; Mushtaq & Bruneau, 2019). A rising tide is said to raise all boats. Hence, several research studies, especially around the 1950s, suggested a trickle-down approach to poverty alleviation, which mentions about automatic spill-over of growth onto the poor (Kaldor, 1966; Kuznets, 1955). Supporters of trickle-down economics reason that growth and higher incomes at the top will trickle down to the poor, resulting in a greater number of jobs, higher output, increased income and reduced poverty. This theory posits that if an economy expands, the rewards will have an expansionary impact on economically weaker sections of society and will lead to economic mobility.

An unhealthy fixation on GDP and growth as the best indicators of economic health is reflected in the trickle-down theory. In accordance with this theory, the adage 'One size fit all' holds true. As the theory sees it, growth is the only thing that will ever matter in the fight against poverty. When the economy picks up steam, problems disappear. Growth is a process through which benefits trickle down to the lowest members of society, lifting them up as a whole as time goes on. Growth will definitely accompany some amount of reduction in poverty, though it may be a sufficient circumstance for poverty alleviation (Škare & Družeta, 2016).

However, trickle-down effect does not seem to work, as promulgated by the theory (Fosu, 2010). Today, many economies and the world as a whole are facing the challenges related to alleviating poverty and wealth distribution which is leading to multidimensional inequality. Some researchers laid bare that economic growth will pass in the form of yielding dividends by tweaking the policies but not by ipso facto. The top-down theory (for human development) requires support of inclusionary policies to help reduce sharp inequalities in income and wealth, improve economic mobility and generate jobs (Hoff & Stiglitz, 2001). In relation to reducing poverty, along with the magnitude of economic growth, its composition also matters (Loayza & Raddatz, 2010). The economies whose growth has significant contributions from unskilled labour-intensive sectors such as agriculture (Christiaensen et al., 2011; Dethier & Effenberger, 2012) and manufacturing are better placed to reap the benefit of growth on alleviating poverty.

In Middle East North Africa and Asia, rural communities have a higher concentration of poverty than their urban counterparts. Given this scenario, digital financial inclusion and extension mechanisms will fill the gap to alleviate poverty over the long term, if the right methods are deployed based upon the requirements of the particular households of that geography(Maulu et al., 2021). Since environmental and geographic factors play a significant role in contributing to poverty (Liu et al., 2018), the practice of resettlement as a means of reducing poverty has gained popularity (Merkle, 2003). China has made an attempt to exploit the mode of resettlement through its national programme called Poverty alleviation resettlement (Liu et al., 2018; Yang et al., 2020). Similarly, the concept of urbanisation was seen to be instrumental in reducing poverty by making a move towards non-farm employment avenues. However, ample evidence in developing economies reveal that, workers who are relatively less poor in the rural sector are more likely to migrate and make some money, while remaining relatively poor in the destination urban sector (Ravallion et al., 2007). At the same time, some nations are exploring to move beyond the rural–urban divide and focusing to develop its non-agriculture based rural economy and tertiary townships (Christiaensen et al., 2013). This idea 'RURBAN' has been explored by several nations, which ought to be thought of as urbanisation in rural areas, or creation of modern facilities on rural areas (Kolhe & Dhote, 2016; Revi et al., 2006). In the year 2016, India explicitly went for 'RURBAN', with a focus on creation of a group of households that retain, foster and exhibit the spirit of community driven life in rural areas while putting an emphasis on equity and inclusiveness without sacrificing amenities that are seen as primarily urban in nature.

Objectives

Exploring the connection between microfinance and effective poverty reduction techniques for economic growth and sustainable development.

Ascertaining how businesses and financial systems can benefit by integrating microfinance models in their frameworks.

E-Inclusiveness and Digital Financial Inclusion

People can now access financial services through digital channels like mobile banking and online payments thanks to e-inclusivity. The World Bank reports that the proportion of adults with bank accounts rose from 62% in 2014 to 69% in 2017, with digital financial services being a major factor in this expansion. For example, mobile money accounts have expanded rapidly, with over one billion registered accounts globally in 2020. It has enabled businesses to become more efficient by digitising their processes and transactions. A study by Deloitte found that businesses that fully embraced digital technologies were 26% more profitable than their less digitally savvy peers and increased global connectivity, enabling businesses to expand their reach and enter new markets. For instance, the global internet market is predicted to reach $4.9 trillion in 2021, following years of fast growth. E-inclusiveness has spurred innovation by enabling businesses to develop new products and services that leverage digital technologies. Fintech start-ups, for instance, have emerged and are utilising digital technologies to offer cutting-edge financial services like peer-to-peer lending and digital wallets. They have also played a significant role in enhancing financial inclusion, which refers to how much access people and businesses have to formal financial services. The Global Findex database shows that, as a result of the development of digital financial services, the proportion of adults with bank accounts rose from 51% in 2011 to 69% in 2017.

E-inclusiveness has had a transformative impact on businesses and financial systems, enabling greater access to financial services, improving business efficiency and innovation, enhancing global connectivity and driving financial inclusion. When people are aware of the opportunities and the methods of problem resolution, knowledgeable and are financially included, poverty levels are bound to fall. Financial inclusion entails providing everyone with affordable access to and usage of fundamental formal financial services (Inoue, 2019). These financial services include payments, insurance, credit and savings. Three variables – banking penetration, access to banking services, and use of banking services – are used to gauge financial inclusion. Policymakers in many countries have accepted financial inclusion as the route to economic empowerment and a solution to rising poverty rates (Ozili, 2021). According to Neaime and Gaysset (2018), the degree of financial inclusion can be determined by looking at the number of banks and their branches, financial institutions, or ATMs in relation to the population. Poverty reduction and financial inclusion are positively correlated (Churchill & Marisetty, 2020; Khan et al., 2022; Park & Mercado, 2016). Poverty does reduce as a result of banking depth (Honohan, 2008), which is indicated by the amount of credit (Demirgüç-Kunt et al., 2011). Expanding state-led rural branches has been crucial in bringing down the rate of poverty in rural parts of developing nations like India (Burgess & Pande, 2005). Multidimensional poverty has been shown to be reduced through financial inclusion (Tran et al., 2022). In addition to reducing poverty, financial inclusion also lowers vulnerability to poverty (Koomson et al., 2020). Because it gives people access to finance for business startup, manufacturing investment and other commercial activities that increase their income levels, the process of financial inclusion is crucial for eliminating poverty. Poverty alleviation can be achieved through an increase in the number of small and medium enterprises (Chikwira et al., 2022).

Apart from banks and financial institutions, several national governments are looking to promote financial inclusion through microfinance (Ghosh, 2013), which is meant for provisions of primary financial services to low income individuals or groups, including small businesses and entrepreneurs, devoid of access to conventional banking and financial channels. When Muhammad Younus, the father of microfinance, founded the Grameen Bank of Bangladesh in 1976, the word 'microfinancing' was first used, and the microfinance methods were institutionalised. Micro-credit has been found to be effective in reducing poverty in Southeast Asia (Félix & Belo, 2019). Similarly, financial development effected through provision of more domestic credit to poor has been seen to help in poverty reduction (Abosedra et al., 2016). The microfinance projects have been found to significantly increase participation in rural development activities and social capital in the community (Tahmasebi & Askaribezayeh, 2021).

Information and communication technology development and use have dramatically increased in recent years. Adoption of ICT promotes the development of a variety of non-agricultural economic activities in rural areas, such as women-owned microbusinesses. Better information dissemination through ICT and expertise help microbusiness owners understand and run their operations more effectively. Micro and small businesses will have access to market information more quickly and affordably than print media. Additionally, because of the reduced costs, enhanced infrastructure, and information, service delivery and mobile banking would be more effective. According to Mushtaq and Bruneau (2019) and Gallego-Losada et al. (2022), the emergence of digital financial inclusion through information and communication technology has shown a considerable potential to boost financial inclusion. By removing obstacles like cost, distance, and transparency, digital financial services offer a unique opportunity addressing the financial needs of society's most vulnerable people (Kulkarni & Ghosh, 2021). The advantages of ICT adoption through mobile phone, also referred to as mobile banking or mobile money are larger (Ahmad et al., 2020), especially on geographies having lower penetration of bank branches (Allen et al., 2014). It has the capability to overcome infrastructural issues and improve financial access. Mobile devices can improve decision-making, financial services accessibility, savings motivation and smooth consumption for customers. Low-income people can access affordable savings options thanks to mobile money. Kenya's M-Pesa can be viewed in this regard. The governments, especially of poor nations, must adopt proper economic policies and regulatory frameworks, along with financial institutions to harness digital power for spearheading financial inclusion. ICT and financial inclusion have had a significant role in lowering poverty rates, especially in Sub-Saharan African nations (Alimi & Okunade, 2020).

Another application of internet, e-commerce, in rural regions, has a very favourable impact on rural income (Chao et al., 2021) and can thus be a vital element of rural poverty alleviation. Particularly, rural e-commerce entrepreneurship has been found to be a reliable and efficient way to fight poverty and advance long-term social development (Huang et al., 2021).

Creating human capital through skill development via vocational training institutes has been found to be an effective strategy to overcome poverty (Mohsin et al., 2021). Spending on development, enhancing competitiveness, and embracing globalisation helps to reduce poverty (Hassan et al., 2020). Unemployment has been found to be a contributor to poverty. In this context, creation of jobs or entrepreneurship (Zacharias et al., 2021) can be viewed as a feasible solution to decrease poverty levels. According to Sewell et al. (2019), the improvement of rural infrastructure, such as roads and access to necessary services, helps to combat poverty.

If the corporates direct their CSR activities towards pro-poor initiatives, they can support poverty reduction to some extent (Medina-Muñoz & Medina-Muñoz, 2020).

Global Poverty: List of Poor Nations

Organisations like the United Nations place a strong emphasis on assisting the populace of developing countries to improve their economic situation as a means of improving their level of living. Analysing a nation's natural resources, system of education, governance, and national debt can help determine how prosperous it is. Poor countries are typically the least developed (sometimes known less kindly as underdeveloped countries or Third-World nations).

The economy of the world's poorest nations are categorised as low-income economies under the four-tiered system employed by the World Bank. This ranking is determined by dividing each nation's total income by its population to determine its gross national income (GNI) per capita. Gross National Income (GNI) and GDP per capita are roughly equivalent.

Both estimate the monetary worth of all goods and services generated in the country in question. However, GNP also comprises foreign-source revenue (such as foreign investments or real estate holdings). As a result, gross national product (GNP) is regarded to be a slightly more accurate estimate of a country's economic health.

There are two common techniques to report GNP. The first one is expressed in US dollars and was arrived at by applying the Atlas method to the currencies of each country. The second is US dollars adjusted for 'purchasing power parity' (PPP). Low-income countries as of 1 July 2021 have a per capita gross national product (GNP) of less than $1,046 USD, as per World Bank.

A glance into the regions having countries at the bottom and top of the pyramid with regard to poverty indicates that prosperous countries (top 50) have population less than 35% to that of the bottom 50 countries. Their average GNI is 16 times to that of the average of bottom 50 countries. As reflected in Table 5.1

Table 5.1. Bottom 50 Poor Countries: Region Wise.

Region Wise	Country Count	% Countries	Sum of Population 2023	Average of GNI PPP
Africa	36	72%	1,06,91,83,022	2,456
Asia	11	22%	2,06,78,44,815	4,673
North America	3	6%	2,93,64,871	4,463
Bottom 50	**50**	**100%**	**3,16,63,92,708**	**3,064**

amongst the countries impacted by poverty 72% of the bottom 50 countries are in Africa followed by Asia (22%) and North America (6%).

Among the top 50 wealthy countries by GNI, not a single country hails from Africa. Europe, Asia and North America contribute 96% of the top 50 countries, refer Table 5.2. The average population growth rate of the bottom 50 countries is around 2.21% in contrast to 0.36% for the Top 50 wealthy countries, i.e. population growth is six times more in poorer or developing countries than the developed economies, which is a major cause of strain on the limited resources.

Poverty Alleviation Strategies

Despite poverty being a multifaceted phenomenon, economic measures such as income and consumption are usually used to estimate poverty levels. The UNDP also places a focus on Amartya Sen's capabilities approach to measuring poverty. 'End poverty in all its manifestations worldwide', the first of the United Nations' 17 sustainable development goals, pledges that no one will be left behind in the struggle. Global development initiatives and poverty alleviation programmes, whose main objective is to end poverty for the world's poorest and most vulnerable people, are at their core community-driven and participatory approaches. Economic expansion is a powerful tool for alleviating poverty and providing a path out of poverty for those who lack other means. A large percentage of the poor were able to lift themselves out of poverty between 1970 and 2000, according to studies conducted in Africa, Brazil, China and Indonesia. Microfinance may be a key factor in reducing poverty in emerging nations, according to a growing body of studies. Many studies have shown that microfinance can increase the income, savings, and assets of poor households and communities, and can improve their access to basic services. For example, a study by Khandker (2003) found that microfinance had a significant positive impact on poverty reduction in Bangladesh, by increasing the income and consumption of poor households. Another study by Petrick (2003) discovered that microfinance has an advantageous effect on the creation of assets and the empowerment of underprivileged women in rural India.

Table 5.2. Top 50 Wealthy Countries: Region Wise.

Region Wise	Country Count	% Countries	Sum of Population 2023	Average of GNI PPP
Asia	11	22%	25,31,87,852	59,442
Europe	27	54%	44,38,63,008	50,107
North America	10	20%	38,29,72,808	44,214
Oceania	2	4%	3,16,67,211	47,685
Top 50	**50**	**100%**	**1,11,16,90,879**	**50,918**

Source: https://worldpopulationreview.com/country-rankings/poorest-countries-in-the-world

Community-cantered microfinance, capability and social safety nets, market-based, and effective governance are the four main groups into which approaches to reducing poverty can be divided. As it gives access to financial services and commercial possibilities to those who are generally shut out of traditional financial systems, e-inclusiveness in business and financial systems can be a successful technique for reducing poverty. Low-income groups, people living in rural areas, and people without access to conventional financial services can all fall under this category.

Mobile Banking: Individuals can use their mobile phones to access financial services through mobile banking. Services including transfers, deposits, and loans can be categorised under this. Many nations have adopted mobile banking as a way to broaden financial access and combat poverty.

Digital Financial Services: Low-income people may have access to financial services including savings, loans, and insurance through digital financial products like mobile money and digital wallets. As consumers may utilise digital financial services to receive payments and manage their finances, these services can also give people access to entrepreneurial prospects.

E-Commerce: E-commerce provides individuals with access to business opportunities, as they can sell their products and services online. E-commerce can also open up markets to people who would not otherwise have access to them, boosting their income and lowering poverty.

Financial Technology (Fintech): The abbreviation 'fintech' stands for 'financial technology', which refers to the use of technology in the financial industry. Before the development of fintech, persons with low incomes could not have had access to loans, for instance, as a type of financial service. Financial technology has the potential to make previously inaccessible or prohibitively expensive financial products and services available to the general public.

By giving low-income people more access to financial services and business prospects, e-inclusiveness in the business and financial system can aid in the reduction of poverty. This can raise people's living standards and incomes, eliminating poverty and encouraging economic growth.

The most popular strategy for lowering poverty is microfinance, which tries to assist the underprivileged. After rapidly and widely increasing over the past few decades, it is now in use in a number of developing nations in Africa, Asia, and Latin America. Access to microfinance in developing countries is believed by many academics and politicians to empower the poor, especially women, support income-generating activities, promote entrepreneurship, and lessen vulnerability. There are fewer studies that provide definitive and conclusive proof of the contribution that micro-finance has made to advancements in health, nutrition, and education, though.

Global Poverty Alleviation Models

Several approaches to reducing poverty on a global scale have been put into practice in different nations. Sime of the different global models to poverty alleviation are elucidated below:

- Millennium Development Goals (MDGs):
  In 2000, United Nations approved a set of eight global goals to help alleviate poverty and raise living standards around the globe. MDGs addressed issues such as eradication of poverty, promoting education, advancing gender equality, decreasing infant mortality, enhancing maternal health and combating diseases like malaria and HIV/AIDS.
- Sustainable Development Goals (SDGs):
  The United Nations established a set of 17 global goals in 2015 to end extreme poverty, protect the planet, and ensure that all people live in peace and prosperity. The SDGs target a variety of concerns, which include poverty, hunger, health, education, gender equality, water and sanitation, energy, economic development, and partnerships.
- Microfinance:
  Microfinance is a sort of financial service that provides lending, savings and insurance products to persons who are not served by regular financial institutions. Many nations around the world have used microfinance as a technique for reducing poverty.
- Direct Cash Transfers:
  Direct cash transfers are initiatives that provide direct cash payments to low-income people. These programs have been developed in a number of nations in order to alleviate poverty and improve recipients' level of living.
- Social Safety Nets:
  Social safety nets are programmes that provide targeted transfers or subsidies to vulnerable individuals or communities. These programs have been implemented in many countries to provide a safety net and prevent individuals from falling into poverty.
- Human Development:
  In order to combat poverty, human development models place a strong emphasis on expanding access to fundamental services like water and sanitation, health care, and education. These models have been put into practice in numerous nations in an effort to raise living standards and decrease poverty through funding human development.

There are benefits and drawbacks to each model; selecting the best one for a given situation and demographic is a matter of balance. To maximise results, it is common practice to employ a number of different models in concert.

Microfinance: The Panacea for Sustainable Poverty Alleviation?

Microfinance is the practice of providing small amount of loans to low-income people. Microcredit was formerly offered by traders and moneylenders to the rural poor at excessive interest rates, resulting in significant suffering and impoverishment of borrowers, debt trap, bonded labour and forced transfer of rights to properties. When we talk about microfinance, we don't mean 'lending to the poor at fair but sustainable rates from Government and commercial institutional sources', which is a common misconception. As CGAP states, Microfinance refers to the practice of extending basic financial services such as savings accounts and credit to low-income people. According to ACCION, microfinance is a term used to describe a variety of banking and financial services geared for low and middle-income enterprises and consumers.

Microfinance Models

These financial services can be provided through a variety of microfinance schemes, some of which are as follows:

- *Grameen Bank Model:* This strategy was created in Bangladesh by Muhammad Younus and is predicated on the concept of group-based lending. Peer pressure ensures that borrowers pay back their loans when they band together to guarantee each other's debts.
- *Self-Help Group (SHG) Model:* Individuals form cooperatives to pool their resources and borrow and lend money to one another under this system. Self-help groups (SHGs) are led by their members and based on the tenets of mutual trust and co-operation.
- *Joint Liability Group (JLG) Model:* Lending to groups rather than individuals, this strategy is quite similar to the SHG model. Each individual in the group shares equal responsibility for the debt.
- *Microfinance Institutions (MFI) Model:* MFI's are companies that provide microfinance services to individuals and enterprises with little financial resources. They function independently from conventional banking institutions and may get backing from the government, international organisations and other bodies.
- *Hybrid Model:* This model provides a new perspective on microfinance by incorporating elements from previous models. One possible hybrid strategy can be to combine group lending with individual loan and savings services.

The target population's unique needs and surroundings will influence the model selection. These models each have advantages and drawbacks of their own. Whatever strategy is employed, microfinance's objective is to improve the financial stability of low-income individuals and small enterprises by giving them access to financial services.

Role in Poverty Alleviation

Microfinance is considered a tool for poverty alleviation, since it provides financial services to those who are underserved by traditional banks. Microfinance can assist people in starting or growing a business, managing their money, and reducing their exposure to financial shocks by giving them access to credit, savings, and insurance products. Numerous studies have demonstrated how offering microfinance services can aid in reducing poverty. For instance, having access to funding can assist people in starting or expanding a business, increasing their income and standard of living. Savings can also assist people in creating a safety net and improving their financial management. But it is important to keep in mind that microfinance is not a panacea for eradicating poverty. It must be incorporated within a larger strategy that gives equal weight to issues like infrastructure, healthcare, and education. Additionally, the efficacy of microfinance in decreasing poverty might vary depending on the particular situation and how it is used.

Essential Requirements for Success of Microfinance

The success of microfinance implementation is influenced by several prerequisites, comprising.

- *Adequate demand for financial services:* The target community must have a high enough demand for microfinance services for the programme to be effective. Through market research and community engagement, this can be evaluated.
- *Appropriate delivery channels:* Microfinance organisations must select delivery methods that are suitable for the intended audience. For instance, group-based lending might work better in rural areas whereas individual lending might work better in cities.
- *Financial sustainability:* MFIs must have a stable financial future in order to keep serving their customers. This can be accomplished by broadening their range of products, putting cost-cutting measures in place, and raising enough money.
- *Strong governance and management:* To enable efficient decision-making and risk management, MFIs need to have robust governance and management processes in place. This includes having transparent business practices, consistent monitoring and evaluation, and explicit regulations and processes.
- *Effective outreach and marketing:* MFIs must successfully engage the target demographic and sell their services to them. This entails engaging in community outreach, promoting their goods and services, and offering pertinent financial education.
- *Collaboration with related entities:* Collaboration with other stakeholders, including as local groups, governmental agencies, and the commercial sector, can be advantageous for MFIs. These alliances can assist MFIs in reaching more clients, enhancing operations and having a greater effect.
- *Adequate institutional safeguards:* The growth and sustainability of the microfinance sector depend on a favourable legal and regulatory environment. This includes rules and laws that support financial inclusion and defend the rights of those who receive microloans.

Conclusion

Microfinance in the space of digital financial inclusion being an essential driver of sustainable poverty alleviation has opened spaces, which allows microfinance to be proxied through e-commerce instruments and made available for mass consumption.

This chapter adds conceptual dimensions to the scant literature on e-inclusivity and microfinance in emerging markets, including Middle East, Africa and Asia, while offering further scope for model building in this field. The complete poverty alleviation is an ambitious, yet much needed for fostering sustainable development. Microfinance has the potential to be a significant tool for cauterising inequality and poverty challenges in emerging markets. However, it is important to recognise that microfinance must not be treated as a magic wand, and that it must be implemented with care and attention to its limitations and challenges. To be effective, microfinance must be accompanied by social empowerment, community development, and a focus on the poorest and most vulnerable groups. Furthermore, microfinance must be integrated into a broader framework of poverty reduction, which includes access to basic services, social protection, and economic development. Microfinance has several advantages over traditional forms of aid. It empowers marginally disadvantaged and low-income people by providing them with access to financial resources through which they can lift themselves out of poverty and enables people to become self-reliant, and it promotes entrepreneurship and innovation. It is sustainable as it creates a cycle of repayment and lending that allows Microfinance institutions to continue providing financial services to economically weaker section households while being cost-effective as it has a lower administrative cost than traditional aid programs. In emerging markets, the evidence-based policy making constantly suggests how microfinance is changing the lives of the people and how it can bear economic dividends, in the form of upward mobility, in the long run if implemented diligently. Millions of people in South Asia are unbanked and underbanked with little to no access to credit lines or financial resources to ensure their upliftment from poverty but and it is here that microfinance as a financial instrument can play larger role by connecting the community to financial sector. Microfinance enables economically weaker section households in society to invest in their businesses, which leads to income generation, poverty alleviation, and ultimately to a trickle-down effect. The discourse on microfinance is nuanced, and practices of critique within the mainstream literature ensure that instruments impact on poverty alleviation be quite significant and not a mere cosmetic touch. E-inclusiveness and microfinance when blended is a panacea, particularly for low income developing countries. This chapter helps in broadening the insights for policymakers as well as academic practitioners and the blend of both how financial systems and businesses can be leveraged to the best advantage of poverty reduction.

References

Abosedra, S., Shahbaz, M., & Nawaz, K. (2016). Modeling causality between financial deepening and poverty reduction in Egypt. *Social Indicators Research*, *126*(3), 955–969. https://doi.org/10.1007/s11205-015-0929-2

Ahmad, A. H., Green, C., & Jiang, F. (2020). Mobile money, financial inclusion and development: A review with reference to African experience. *Journal of Economic Surveys*, *34*(4), 753–792. https://doi.org/10.1111/joes.12372

Alimi, A. S., & Okunade, S. O. (2020). Financial inclusion, ICT diffusion and poverty reduction: Evidence from Sub-Sahara African countries. *Asian Journal of Economics and Business*, *1*(2), 139–152.

Allen, F., Carletti, E., Cull, R., Qian, J. Q., Senbet, L., & Valenzuela, P. (2014). The African financial development and financial inclusion gaps. *Journal of African Economies*, *23*(5), 614–642. https://doi.org/10.1093/jae/eju015

Burgess, R., & Pande, R. (2005). Do rural banks matter? Evidence from the Indian social banking experiment. *The American Economic Review*, *95*(3), 780–795.

Chao, P. E. N. G., Biao, M. A., & Zhang, C. (2021). Poverty alleviation through e-commerce: Village involvement and demonstration policies in rural China. *Journal of Integrative Agriculture*, *20*(4), 998–1011. https://doi.org/10.1016/S2095-3119(20)63422-0

Chikwira, C., Vengesai, E., & Mandude, P. (2022). The impact of microfinance institutions on poverty alleviation. *Journal of Risk and Financial Management*, *15*(9), 393.

Christiaensen, L., De Weerdt, J., & Todo, Y. (2013). Urbanization and poverty reduction: The role of rural diversification and secondary towns 1. *Agricultural Economics*, *44*(4–5), 435–447. https://doi.org/10.1111/agec.12028

Christiaensen, L., Demery, L., & Kuhl, J. (2011). The (evolving) role of agriculture in poverty reduction – An empirical perspective. *Journal of Development Economics*, *96*(2), 239–254. https://doi.org/10.1016/j.jdeveco.2010.10.006

Churchill, S. A., & Marisetty, V. B. (2020). Financial inclusion and poverty: A tale of forty-five thousand households. *Applied Economics*, *52*(16), 1777–1788. https://doi.org/10.1080/00036846.2019.1678732

Demirgüç-Kunt, A., Córdova, E. L., Pería, M. S. M., & Woodruff, C. (2011). Remittances and banking sector breadth and depth: Evidence from Mexico. *Journal of Development Economics*, *95*(2), 229–241. https://doi.org/10.1016/j.jdeveco.2010.04.002

Dethier, J. J., & Effenberger, A. (2012). Agriculture and development: A brief review of the literature. *Economic Systems*, *36*(2), 175–205. https://doi.org/10.1016/j.jdeveco.2010.10.006

Félix, E. G. S., & Belo, T. F. (2019). The impact of microcredit on poverty reduction in eleven developing countries in south-east Asia. *Journal of Multinational Financial Management*, *52*, 100590. https://doi.org/10.1016/j.mulfin.2019.07.003

Fosu, A. K. (2010). Does inequality constrain poverty reduction programs? Evidence from Africa. *Journal of Policy Modeling*, *32*(6), 818–827. http://doi.org/10.1016/j.jpolmod.2010.08.007

Gallego-Losada, M. J., Montero-Navarro, A., García-Abajo, E., & Gallego-Losada, R. (2022). Digital financial inclusion. Visualizing the academic literature. *Research in International Business and Finance*, 101862.

Ghosh, J. (2013). Microfinance and the challenge of financial inclusion for development. *Cambridge Journal of Economics*, *37*(6), 1203–1219.

Hassan, M. S., Bukhari, S., & Arshed, N. (2020). Competitiveness, governance and globalization: What matters for poverty alleviation? *Environment, Development and Sustainability*, *22*(4), 3491–3518. https://doi.org/10.1007/s10668-019-00355-y

Hoff, K., & Stiglitz, J., (2001). Modern economic theory and development. In G. Meier & J. Stiglitz (Eds), *Frontiers of development economics: The future in perspective* (pp. 389–459). OUP/World Bank.

Honohan, P. (2008). Cross-country variation in household access to financial services. *Journal of Banking & Finance*, *32*(11), 2493–2500. https://doi.org/10.1016/j.jbankfin.2008.05.004

Huang, L., Xie, G., Huang, R., Li, G., Cai, W., & Apostolidis, C. (2021). Electronic commerce for sustainable rural development: Exploring the factors influencing BoPs' entrepreneurial intention. *Sustainability*, *13*(19), 10604. https://doi.org/10.3390/su131910604

Inoue, T. (2019). Financial inclusion and poverty reduction in India. *Journal of Financial Economic Policy*. https://doi.org/10.1108/JFEP-01-2018-0012

Kaldor, N. (1966). *Causes of the slow rate of economic growth of the United Kingdom: An inaugural lecture*. Cambridge University Press.

Khan, I., Khan, I., Sayal, A. U., & Khan, M. Z. (2022). Does financial inclusion induce poverty, income inequality, and financial stability: Empirical evidence from the 54 African countries? *Journal of Economic Studies*, *49*(2), 303–314. https://doi.org/10.1108/JES-07-2020-0317

Khandker, S. R. (2003, January). Micro-finance and poverty: Evidence using panel data from Bangladesh. SSRN. https://ssrn.com/abstract=636307

Kolhe, N. P., & Dhote, K. K. (2016). Urban centers: The new dimension of urbanism. *Procedia Technology*, *24*, 1699-1705. https://doi.org/10.1016/j.protcy.2016.05.198

Koomson, I., Villano, R. A., & Hadley, D. (2020). Effect of financial inclusion on poverty and vulnerability to poverty: Evidence using a multidimensional measure of financial inclusion. *Social Indicators Research*, *149*(2), 613–639.

Kulkarni, L., & Ghosh, A. (2021). Gender disparity in the digitalization of financial services: Challenges and promises for women's financial inclusion in India. *Gender, Technology and Development*, *25*(2), 233–250. https://doi.org/10.1080/09718524.2021.1911022

Kuznets, S. (1955). Economic growth and income inequality. *The American Economic*, *45*(1), 1–28.

Liu, W., Xu, J., & Li, J. (2018). The influence of poverty alleviation resettlement on rural household livelihood vulnerability in the western mountainous areas, China. *Sustainability*, *10*(8), 2793. https://doi.org/10.3390/su10082793

Loayza, N. V., & Raddatz, C. (2010). The composition of growth matters for poverty alleviation. *Journal of Development Economics*, *93*(1), 137–151. https://doi.org/10.1016/j.jdeveco.2009.03.008

Maulu, S., Hasimuna, O. J., Mutale, B., Mphande, J., & Siankwilimba, E. (2021). Enhancing the role of rural agricultural extension programs in poverty alleviation: A review. *Cogent Food & Agriculture*, *7*(1), 1886663. https://doi.org/10.1080/23311932.2021.1886663

Medina-Muñoz, R. D., & Medina-Muñoz, D. R. (2020). Corporate social responsibility for poverty alleviation: An integrated research framework. *Business Ethics: A European Review*, *29*(1), 3–19. https://doi.org/10.1111/beer.12248

Merkle, R. (2003). Ningxia's third road to rural development: Resettlement schemes as a last means to poverty reduction? *Journal of Peasant Studies*, *30*(3–4), 160–191.

Mohsin, M., Iqbal, N., Taghizadeh-Hesary, F., & Iram, R. (2021). Measuring the performance of poverty reduction programs in rural Pakistan. In *Poverty reduction for inclusive sustainable growth in developing Asia* (pp. 165–182). Springer.

Mushtaq, R., & Bruneau, C. (2019). Microfinance, financial inclusion and ICT: Implications for poverty and inequality. *Technology in Society, 59*, 101154. https://doi.org/10.1016/j.techsoc.2019.101154

Neaime, S., & Gaysset, I. (2018). Financial inclusion and stability in MENA: Evidence from poverty and inequality. *Finance Research Letters, 24*, 230–237. https://doi.org/10.1016/j.frl.2017.09.007

Ozili, P. K. (2021, October). Financial inclusion research around the world: A review. *Forum for Social Economics, 50*(4), 457–479. Routledge. https://doi.org/10.1080/07360932.2020.1715238.

Park, C. Y., & Mercado, R. V. (2016). Does financial inclusion reduce poverty and income inequality in developing Asia? In *Financial inclusion in Asia* (pp. 61–92). Palgrave Macmillan.

Petrick, M. (2003). M. Zeller and R. L. Meyer (Eds.) The triangle of microfinance: Financial sustainability, outreach, and impact. The Johns Hopkins University Press, Baltimore, MD, USA, 2003. ISBN: 0-8018-7226-X, 399 pp., Price: US$35 (paperback).

Ravallion, M., Chen, S., & Sangraula, P. (2007). New evidence on the urbanization of global poverty. *Population and Development Review, 33*(4), 667–701. https://doi.org/10.1111/j.1728- 4457.2007.00193.x

Revi, A., Prakash, S., Mehrotra, R., Bhat, G. K., Gupta, K., & Gore, R. (2006). Goa 2100: The transition to a sustainable urban design. *Environment and Urbanization, 18*(1), 51–65. https://doi.org/10.1177/0956247806063941

Sewell, S. J., Desai, S. A., Mutsaa, E., & Lottering, R. T. (2019). A comparative study of community perceptions regarding the role of roads as a poverty alleviation strategy in rural areas. *Journal of Rural Studies, 71*, 73–84. https://doi.org/10.1016/j.jrurstud.2019.09.001

Škare, M., & Družeta, R. P. (2016). Poverty and economic growth: A review. *Technological and Economic Development of Economy, 22*(1), 156–175.

Tahmasebi, A., & Askaribezayeh, F. (2021). Microfinance and social capital formation-a social network analysis approach. *Socio-Economic Planning Sciences, 76*, 100978. https://doi.org/10.1016/j.seps.2020.100978

Tran, H. T. T., Le, H. T. T., Nguyen, N. T., Pham, T. T. M., & Hoang, H. T. (2022). The effect of financial inclusion on multidimensional poverty: The case of Vietnam. *Cogent Economics & Finance, 10*(1), 2132643.https://worldpopulationreview.com/country-rankings/poorest-countries-in-the-world

Yang, Y., de Sherbinin, A., & Liu, Y. (2020). China's poverty alleviation resettlement: Progress, problems and solutions. *Habitat International, 98*, 102135. https://doi.org/10.1016/j.habitatint.2020.102135

Zacharias, T., Yusriadi, Y., Firman, H., & Rianti, M. (2021). Poverty alleviation through entrepreneurship. *Journal of Legal, Ethical and Regulatory Issues, 24*, 1–5.

Zainal, N., Nassir, A. M., Kamarudin, F., Law, S. H., Sufian, F., & Hussain, H. I. (2019). The social role of microfinance institutions in poverty eradication: Evidence from ASEAN-5 countries. *International Journal of Innovation, Creativity and Change, 5*(2), 1551–1576.

Chapter 6

E-Governance as a Strategy Towards Poverty Alleviation: An Analysis From Indian Perspective

Rajshree Dutta

Fakir Mohan University, India

Abstract

E-governance is the term used to describe the use of communication and information technologies for government. It guarantees information flow transparency, aiding in the improvement and redefinition of social, environmental and economic values. The implementation of numerous central and state initiatives is the responsibility of the Rural Development Department. The execution of almost all systems makes use of Management Information Systems (MIS) software. The state government's policy aims to provide top-notch internet services with a focus on the needs of the citizenry. A number of programmes, including CRISP, NEGP, NIC, E-choupal, Gyandoot, etc. have already been put into use, and more e-government initiatives are in the operation. In a country like India, where demand is high owing to a huge population, alleviating poverty is more crucial and infrastructure is a significant determinant for faster economic growth. By providing improved access to essential commodities like roads, water, drainage, energy, transportation, infrastructure would raise inhabitants' quality of life. One thing is certain: the development of the Indian economy will be fuelled by technologically driven e-Governance solutions as it strives to become a global superpower. The initiatives made in the field of e-Governance that can hasten economic development are therefore the main emphasis of this chapter, which is based on secondary sources. E-governance initiatives can aid in advancing good governance. E-promotion of governance can be of more inclusive governance and can aid in resolving the enormous global issues associated with poverty alleviation. The chapter will go on to outline how e-governance software enables stakeholders to not only monitor quality, cost, and schedule but also regulate deviations through

Creating Pathways for Prosperity, 85–97

Copyright © 2025 Rajshree Dutta

Published under exclusive licence by Emerald Publishing Limited

doi:10.1108/978-1-83549-121-820241007

ongoing automated monitoring, escalations, and transparency. The anticipated problems and limitations of e-governance initiatives are also described.

Keywords: E-governance; poverty alleviation; good governance; infrastructure; development

Introduction

In the present day, information and communication technology (ICT) have
greatly enhanced people's lives in every aspect. Additionally, they have enabled
the government to offer better services even in the most isolated regions of the
country. For those who live in rural sections of the nation, several ICT apps have
been created. The Ministry of Rural Development has taken a number of actions
at various levels to improve the ICT infrastructure in order to offer all rural
Indian inhabitants opportunity, information, and simple access to rural development programmes. Such advances have made it easier to access a wide range of
services and information in a very affordable way. The adoption of numerous
e-governance initiatives through ICT has finally shown to be a significant
contribution to rural development and a way of reducing poverty.

E-promotion for governance can promote more inclusive governance that can
aid in resolving the enormous global issues associated with poverty alleviation.
'We have discovered that people's involvement is central to the accomplishment
of anti-poverty programmes', writes Gurcharan Das in 2002. The 'capacity
approach' of Amartya Sen is used in the argument (Sen, 2000). Sen believes that
poverty encompasses more than just a lack of income. It also entails loss of
fundamental skills. People can act and make decisions when they are free from
things like disease, early mortality, avoidable morbidity, unemployment, and
illiteracy. Lack of these liberties results in incapacity. Sen argues that in order to
increase people's skills, admittance to information through ICT combined with
involvement and empowerment is required. ICT interventions are essential to
development policy. Globalisation is significantly facilitated by ICT. ICT has
consistently shown that it has the ability to reduce poverty in underdeveloped
nations (APDIP-UNDP, 2003).

Objectives and Methodology

The objectives of this chapter are to explore various e-governance efforts in India
and to determine the fundamentals for reducing poverty using ICT. The study is
mostly analytical and descriptive in character. It is based on secondary information acquired from open sources including newspaper reports, journal articles,
books as well as the website of the Ministry of Rural Development. This chapter
outlines about the e-governance efforts that can hasten economic growth and
boost citizens' sense of empowerment. E-governance initiatives can achieve this
by promoting good governance.

E-Governance: The Conceptual Understanding

Since the country of India made e-governance a component of its strategy, it has made significant strides. Information and communication technologies are used in e-governance to enhance communication across government agencies and between the public and government. The electronic interchange of information and transactions between the government, the general public (citizens and other stakeholders) and employees is referred to as e-governance. The World Bank claims that e-governance, or the use of information technology by various government departments and agencies, can change how people, businesses, and the government engage with one another. These technology developments could have a number of positive effects. The idea of e-governance is not just employed in India but is widely adopted worldwide and the credit is towards the abundance of open source software solutions. Individuals have profited from the economic market information offered by e-governance initiatives, but it has also improved the educational standards of kids in rural areas through a number of educational projects (Bhatia & Kiran, 2016).

E-governance makes extensive use of this approach in the application of objective development through ICT. Additionally, creative ICT use may bridge the gap between government, business, and civil society and promote development that is people-centred (Rogers, 2002). A new paradigm for reforming the public sector may be offered through electronic governance. Governments may streamline bureaucratic processes, pay attention to citizens and service users, and strengthen ties with private sector and neighbourhood organisations by using ICT. Undoubtedly, a flexible method for increasing citizen abilities is the nation's National Information Infrastructure (NII), which may be considered as a part of the evolving Global Information Infrastructure (GII). The success of the global information infrastructure depends on the concept of flexible regulation. At each level of the communication process,[1] the aim of regulation should, in the broadest sense, be to uphold a number of core democratic ideals (Rogers, 2002).

Poverty: Conceptual Analysis at the Global Level

The predicted fall in poverty levels over the past few decades has not occurred as much, especially in emerging countries, despite the efforts of international organisations. This has risen the issue of what type of governmental policies globally are best to support the elimination of poverty. There are particular worries regarding the quantity of resources devoted to eradicating poverty and the methods through which they are implemented. It is believed that the outdated paradigm of a technocratic administration financed by donors is insufficient and ineffectual.

The private sector and civil society are just two of the many contributors to effective public policy and global governance, along with the smooth operation of

---

[1]Liberty, equity, community, efficiency, participatory access and universal access are some of the essential democratic values of the communication process.

the institutional and socio-cultural frameworks in which they operate (Collier & Dollar, 1999). This belief is shared by public policy practitioners more and more (Collier & Dollar, 1999). The eight Millennium Development Goals (MDGs)[2] were set by world leaders in 2000, and they made an unusual pledge to raise living standards by accomplishing all of them by 2015. These goals were especially focused on addressing hunger, poverty, and the environment. The majority of the MDGs are still obstinately out of reach for most countries, despite progress being made on several fronts.

According to Wallace (2007), the global effort to reduce poverty by half from its 1990 level by 2015 is progressing as planned. Sub-Saharan Africa, which is home to 30% of the world's extreme poor, is still headed in the wrong direction. East Asia, the Pacific, and South Asia are the regions with the best possibilities of attaining the overall MDG aim because they have implemented dynamic, transformative public policy measures. However, the international community must deal with much more than just problems with financial governance. New job opportunities are created when trade barriers are removed, but this also brings up difficult issues with labour standards and other social issues that are closely related to poverty. Transformational public policy approaches are required in order to identify whose well-being, which rights, and what objectives are most important. As a result, one of the most important and challenging issues facing the modern world is global governance in different areas like health, transportation, finance or trade among others.

According to Mboho and Inyang (2011), the idea of poverty is broad and includes both overt and covert deficiency, inadequacy, and a scarcity in various areas of human existence. The World Development Report (2001) states that poverty has a wide range of characteristics, including a lack of opportunities, restricted capabilities, insufficient levels of security, and a lack of empowerment. Poverty is not merely defined by low income levels. According to the Report (2001), there are largely favourable empirical connections between these many characteristics of poverty. There is a growing understanding that countries will be better able to reduce poverty sustainably with the help of development partners and transformational public policy solutions. Such policy choices must be infused with enough political will to modify the crucial facets of the political system in the interests of the vast majority of the populace.

Social safety nets are created to defend against any negative consequences of reform measures on the poor, which is a major component of transformative public policy. These tools include e-governance systems as well as current social protection policies that have been adopted for this purpose, such as those that create jobs, provide food subsidies, services in healthcare sectors, provide reasonable education for all, establish plans for social security, etc. which aimed at promoting the common good (Ugoani, 2015).

---

[2]The eight MDGs, which have a target year of 2015 and vary from eradicating extreme poverty to stopping the spread of HIV/AIDS and ensuring access to elementary education. All of the nations and top development organisations in the world endorsed it as a model. They have inspired previously unheard-of attempts to help the world's poorest people.

Governments all around the world are putting more and more e-governance technologies into place as a part of public sector reforms to improve good governance and service delivery. The country's many problems like inequality, poverty, service delivery, human rights, corruption, etc. are all thought to be solved via e-governance. The administration is aware of the pressing need to combat poverty and enhance service delivery to the vast majority of its population. The idea of public service for everyone informs many programmes. Some e-governance initiatives have been successful in empowering people to address development challenges, combating poverty, and raising socio-economic and living conditions for citizens. The expensive access to broadband, the multiplicity of languages that is required to be translated into the language of internet, red-tapism, bureaucratic systems, sustainable use of financial resources and the use of top-down approaches in projects with less or no initial user involvement, are some of the challenges that are faced by the project relating to e-governance (Harris & Rajora, 2006).

Seven Foundational Elements of Pro-poor E-Governance

There are seven components to the pro-poor e-governance strategy that the United Nation Development Programme (UNDP) suggests in order to improve services for the rural poor. The following is a list of the blocks:

As part of the government's obligation to provide equal chances for everyone, especially the poor and marginalised, the first building block is concentrated on adopting e-government policies and practices with a pro-poor and socially inclusive perspective. A United Nations assessment of e-government readiness found an increasing need for enhanced citizen participation in civic activities of the government because these activities have an impact on citizens' rights, incomes and social values.

The second building block answers the following queries: What are the many pro-poor e-governance services and activities that have a significant impact on the provision of local services and can persuade people to regularly use e-governance services? The appropriate applications differ depending on the circumstance, but determining which one local governments and beneficiaries will benefit from most will be crucial to pro-poor e-governance's success and long-term viability. Local governance processes can be aided by e-governance applications that make it feasible to access budgets and development plans. They may be designed to deliver direct information services to those who would not otherwise have access to them. Alternately, they could be provided to middlemen like corporations and groups of civil society.

The third building block emphasises that providing high-impact information services requires a complicated organisational transformation process in many circumstances and goes beyond merely allowing government and citizens to engage online.

The fourth building block underlines the significance of participatory planning and capacity building initiatives for local governments, communities and public employees in the planning, implementation and utilisation of pro-poor e-governance services. The success of e-governance efforts depends on prioritising participatory planning that includes all significant stakeholders, including the users and receivers of the services. Pro-poor e-governance should include methods for incorporating underprivileged women and men in the development and implementation of ICT-based service delivery.

To deliver local services based on ICT, the fifth pillar includes forming public–private and civil society partnerships. Experience suggests that in addition to public–private partnerships, civil society organisations, including academia, which frequently have crucial knowledge of communities and their aspirations, must also be taken into account in the delivery of services in order to ensure that services are meeting the needs of the poor.

The subject of the sixth building block is the choice of the suitable technological combination. Numerous technologies can be utilised to encourage people to become active in governmental issues, according to research and experience. Therefore, policies must be in support of a balanced mix of information sharing and community empowerment. In addition to the most contemporary technologies like the internet and SMS communicated via mobile phones, this may also include local radio and television.

The seventh and final building block focuses on the necessity of an extensive monitoring and evaluation system for ongoing initiatives and programmes as well as the creation of new interventions that take into account how they will affect the weak and disadvantaged. The provision of a way for project stakeholders and recipients to submit feedback is another useful feature.

Since there are no set guidelines for action, each nation must approach e-governance differently based on the particular circumstances, requirements and opportunities. To provide examples for long-term reproduction and enhancement of effective practices at the national level, pilot projects should be developed (UNDP, 2007).

E-Governance Initiatives for Rural India

India has been independent for 75 years, but according to the 2011 Census Report, 69.84% of the country's population still resides in rural regions. Roads, nutrition, education and government services are just a few of the services and infrastructure that rural areas continue to lag behind in comparison to urban areas. Given these pervasive characteristics of rural India, e-governance has shown to be effective as a portal for information flow and to speed up the successful implementation of rural India's development programmes for poverty reduction. The Indian Government has unquestionably made substantial efforts to close the digital gap and support e-governance, which has been proven to be a successful implementation method. This includes the launch of the Digital India campaign in 2015.

Through the use of a rural development strategy, people can better their and their families' lives by obtaining more of the things they require. It is a method that helps poor people living in rural areas improve their quality of life over the long term. However, due to limited rural infrastructure and a lack of knowledge among rural populations, India's adoption of e-governance in the area of rural development has been somewhat slow. Despite the slow acceptance, there are various e-governance initiatives striving to develop the rural area. Implementing various e-governance technologies or approaches in rural India will encourage quick, open, responsible, efficient and effective communication among rural communities, supporting rural development while also saving the government time and transaction costs.

Governance is now regularly brought up while talking about poverty. By ensuring the poor's participation in decisions that affect them, governance affords the underprivileged the ability to influence policy agendas and voice their thoughts (Adejumobi, 2006). In its 'Poverty Report' for 2000, the UNDP referred to governance as 'the missing link' in the fight against poverty. Governments may come up with good plans for decreasing poverty, obtain financing to put those plans into operation, and even set objectives, but they still fail to reduce poverty in any appreciable way. The 'missing link' between anti-poverty programmes and poverty reduction are institutions that are responsive and accountable. Good governance is required to increase the government's capacity to deliver and hold itself accountable for the resources at its disposal in order to fully place eradicating poverty on the agenda of public policy (Nyong'o, 2001).

Poverty Alleviation Through E-Governance

Computerised Rural Information System Project (CRISP): Even though the Indian Government has implemented numerous measures to combat poverty, a significant number of people continue to live in poverty. The Rural Soft 2000 was the most recent of the four CRISP application software package versions that the government has created so far. Common people can have admittance to all information on government portals through Rural Soft 2000, and it also enables the government keep tabs on the actions and progress of many agencies. It has been put into practice in 15 areas around the nation that the ministry wired with a cutting-edge VSAT (satellite-based) network.

NeGP: To give the general people access to public information and services in their neighbourhood through open, well-known channels, the National e-Government Plan was developed. It contributes to ensuring that all citizens of India have access to trustworthy, affordable government services. NeGP, which is overseen by the Department of Administrative Reforms and Public Grievances (DAR&PG) and the Department of Electronics and Information Technology (DEIT), was introduced on 18 May 2006, and it consists of 8 components and 27 Mission Mode Projects. It was developed especially for rural areas so that locals could easily use the Common Service Centre (CSC) and State-Wide Area Network (SWAN) services.

NIC: It is a part of the 1976-founded Department of the Indian Ministry of Communications and Information Technology. It is an effort to house all government e-governance efforts and programmes centrally. It lends assistance to the smooth execution of the Indian Government's Digital India plans as well as government IT services. Blocks, districts, the state government and the federal government are all included.

Projects for E-Government in Rural India

E-choupal: Agriculture still contributes significantly to India's economy despite the country's recent tremendous industrialisation. Farmers are taken advantage of by middlemen in rural India at every step of the consumer sales process. These intermediaries or agents work to keep farmers from getting market information while increasing their profit margin. In order to solve these difficulties among rural farmers, the Indian Tobacco Company's International Business Division (ITC-IBD) created a strategy called e-Choupal (i.e. a village gathering place that tremendously helps the farmer). By the year 2012, several e-Choupals had been established as a result of this project, and each one had received a computer, connectivity of printer and internet, uninterruptible power supply. As a result, the supervisors were able to purchase raw materials at the lowest possible price straight from the farmers, and the farmers also benefited greatly from the lack of a middleman. By 2020, Indian Tobacco Company Limited targeted to expand 20,000 e-Choupals, which will serve 15 million farmers and encompass a total of 100,000 villages throughout 15 states.

Gyandoot: Its aim is to establish direct communication with the rural populace. In Dhar district, the Madhya Pradesh government initiated the Gyandoot initiative in January 2000. The state's civil workers frequently interacted with numerous gram panchayats as part of this programme, which helped them better grasp the issues, ambitions, and goals of the rural populace. A rural internet system was established by the district's educated unemployed youngsters. All of the programmes under the Gyandoot projects are being carried out by Sooch-nalaya. Due to its economic benefits and assistance to the poor rural population, it is particularly advantageous. They offer a variety of services and information about women's issues, markets, user fees, health, education and agriculture. They also assist in services relating to land ownership. This network covers more than 600 communities and almost half of a district's population.

Jagriti E-Sewa: Jagriti E-Sewa should be utilised by all citizens of a growing country like India because it contributes to the creation of a number of pro-grammes that target individuals in rural and semi-urban areas of the nation with information and communication. It makes all kinds of information and data easily accessible to everyone at the lowest cost through ICT and e-governance efforts. In this project, dial-up telephone connections are frequently used to deliver information to the public using outdated computers. Any type of change, including language changes and others, generally takes less time to do. These kinds of projects are frequently set up in the village centre or other well-known locations so that they can reach at least 25,000–30,000 residents.

Tata Kishan Kendra (TKK): TATA Chemical Limited created Tata Kishan Kendra (TKK) in certain agriculturally focused areas in Northern India, such as Punjab, Uttar Pradesh, and Haryana, with the intention of providing farmers with some important information. Geographic Information Systems (GIS) are used by TKK to collect fundamental data about soil, groundwater, weather, etc. that is thought to be important for crops. Additionally, it provides information on the socioeconomic, governmental, and physical environments to clients in the form of digital maps such as rivers, buildings, roads and the availability of energy connections. It also helps farmers and boosts their productivity in rural areas by employing satellites to take pictures of insects.

Kissan Call Centres: The majority of Indian farmers are uneducated, and they are unaware of the contemporary technologies applied to the agricultural industry. As a result, they have a lot of issues to deal with and many unanswered questions. In order to address all of these difficulties, the Ministry of Agriculture's Department of Agriculture and Cooperation established Kissan Call Centres in April 2002. These call centres were established specifically to respond to questions from farmers in their own languages. Attempts are being made to raise farmer awareness because most villages are unconcerned with the usage of technology in their agricultural sector. Farmers gain from this because they may access a range of information for free via toll-free phones.

Managerial Implications: From 1990–1991 to 2006–2007, it has been observed that e-governance or ICT efforts have grown significantly in India. E-government initiatives, a crucial tool of the modern day, aim to better inform and serve the public about the government and its numerous programmes and projects that are focused on the needs of the people. It brings the general public and the government closer together so they can benefit from numerous development programmes. Initiatives in e-governance have altered the administrative hierarchy, which is largely to blame for the prevalence of red tape in practically all government departments. The administration and its policies are open to everybody due to the accessibility of all types of information and services for the general public. As a result, the government or administration becomes more citizen-focused.

Indiaagriline: With this project, it is expected to boost e-commerce and also thereby aiming to enhance the economic security of rural communities.

Amul Dairy Portal: By integration and cooperation, it provides connectivity and represents the cooperative values that give the Amul organisation its democratic energy.

Technology and Action for Rural Advancement (TARA): The goal of this social enterprise is to enhance people's well-being and that of their communities. It runs on a commercial model.

ICT or e-governance applications were first deployed in India in the 1990s, but compared to other developed nations, their growth pace is still quite modest, especially in rural areas. Due to its restricted internet access, low levels of digital literacy, and other factors, India is placed at a lowest rank. But in the 21st century, the success of a number of development programmes depends on a sound e-governance strategy. In order to reduce gaps in the digital platform, the government should place more emphasis on the successful execution of e-governance programmes and projects (Chetia, 2020).

The IT tools will help expand the network of the agriculture business on a national and worldwide level, according to the Central Department of Agriculture and Cooperation's (DAC) vision paper 2020. Additionally, IT will create 'agriculture online' by establishing communication channels between farmers, researchers, scientists, and administrators. According to Madaswamy (2004), the proliferation of ICT has a wide range of potential applications that may have an impact on all levels of organisation, who are essential indicators for reducing poverty.

Many ICT projects[3] were designed to be based on the suggestions of the ISDA (Information for Sustainable Agricultural Development)-95 Conference in order to assist farmers in increasing labour productivity, increasing yields, and realising a greater price for their food. The purpose of the conference was to give rural areas useful agricultural information (Madaswamy, 2004). Furthermore, programmes like Video Doctors in Tamil Nadu and Narayan Hrudayalaya in Karnataka use telemedicine to help the poor and rural population. As a result, computers and websites act as e-commerce hubs as well as social gathering spots for knowledge sharing.

Challenges

The following are some of the difficulties faced by e-governance projects implemented for poverty alleviation in India:

- Levels of implementation, which includes the intended beneficiaries conditions as well as the structure of the organisations involved. Both the demographic and geographical distribution should be taken into account.
- The implementation period includes the number of organisations participating, the kinds of inter-organisational networks that would emerge, and the nature, timing and delivery of benefits.
- The degree to which each participant in the implementation process is involved, as well as their skill levels and room for improvement.
- Utilise ICT infrastructure currently in place as efficiently as possible.
- Establish efficient ties to current government sponsored programmes for reducing poverty and accelerating their implementation.
- Recognise the chance to increase marketplaces that the underprivileged in rural areas may access.

---

[3]Agrisnet, Agmarknet, Arisnet (Agricultural Research Information System Network), Seednet, Coopnet, Hortnet, Fertnet, Vistarnet, PPIN (Plant Protection Informatics Network), APHnet (Animal Production and Health Informatics Network), Fishnet, LISnet (Land Information System Network), AFPInet (Agricultural and Food Processing Industries Informatics Network) are a few examples of ICT projects.

- Recognise the opportunity for communication-based motivating improvement made possible by e-governance.
- Include more information about the efforts being made by large corporations like ITC, Hindustan Lever Limited and Mahindra Finance to expand their businesses among rural and underserved communities.
- Expand the network and technical infrastructure.
- Increase the scope of non-governmental organisations' objectives, such as the Self Employed Women's Association (SEWA).
- Encourage the growth of rural and low-income people's businesses through public or private microfinance.

Recommendations

Initiatives in e-governance offer the comprehensive range of effectiveness that attempts to reduce poverty. E-governance activities inside government and in society at large can:

- Complement efforts and programmes to reduce poverty carried out by various government departments and agencies.
- By reducing duplication and enhancing efficacy, assist in the integration of these exercises.
- To achieve larger levels of substantive freedom, encourage market expansion and the corporate activities of multinational corporations. Sen (2000) claimed that 'Freedom of one kind will empower the other' as the intended result.
- Pick market and business development options as shown in the e-choupal project. There is the need for inspection of locations where physical implementation can be done in stages and choose regions based on the beneficiaries potential adaptation and the types of restrictions.
- E-governance's interactive features can be used to promote education, health, and cleanliness.
- Establish a network of microfinance organisations and business development consultancies to aid in the growth of businesses and markets.
- Promote specialised industries and endeavours.
- Encourage governments to adopt market-liberalising measures both domestically and internationally (Pathak & Husain, 2006).

Way Forward

The route to progress and the eradication of poverty lacks effective governance. A national anti-poverty plan would address how the political system should be set up to increase participation, accountability, citizenship rights (both political and economic) and political inclusion in addition to policy documents outlining what the government intends to do to combat poverty. Governments should adopt a proactive stance to combat poverty by improving the underprivileged access to basic necessities including food, shelter, medical care and social security.

Programmes to reduce poverty must be directed towards the poor; they cannot be charitable. Through informed participation politics, the poor should be involved in deciding their own fate. Poor people must have a say in the decisions that affect their lives for achieving sustainable economic progress. In particular, empowering women's political participation fosters social independence and increases the policy community's attention to gender issues. In order to establish an environment for the poor's empowerment, accountability must be ensured.

The opportunity to restructure their life, utilise the resources and opportunities provided by the state framework and take part in development will be provided to the poor by empowerment. It is crucial to use resources properly, which is made feasible by encouraging democracy and public participation. The government must provide more job options for recent graduates because many young people turn to crime as a method of subsisting. Additionally, this will aid in lowering crime rates. Businesses should encourage sustainable development. Those in charge of the bureaucracy should have high moral standards and be trustworthy.

Conclusion

A tool for achieving good governance objectives is e-governance. Due to initiatives to close the digital divide in developing countries like India, it is the most significant phenomenon in contemporary society. The Indian Government has already started a number of projects, including ICT, E-governance and Digital India. The e-government tool supports, among other things, the growth of social networking sites, rural emancipation and citizen participation in governance.

E-government is urgently required in order to deliver essential services to rural residents at the lowest possible cost, which can be a good strategy for reducing poverty in rural India. For the Panchayatiraj institution to effectively meet the needs of the rural poor, they should have access to enough technological resources. Increasing digital literacy through technology improvements has been and will continue to be an important part of India's rural development; it can be stated in conclusion. Because it offers a one-stop solution to issues like poverty, which are more prevalent in rural regions, ICT in e-government is successful. Pro-poor e-governance provides chances to meet the MDGs through improving local assistance to the less fortunate. Governments are urged to build e-governance for the underprivileged and include it in their overall plan to fight poverty.

References

Adejumobi, S. (2006). Governance and poverty reduction in Africa: A critique of the poverty reduction strategy papers (PRSPs). http://www.lanic.utexas.edu/project/etext/llilas/cpa/spring06/welfare/adejumobi.pdf, Accessed on 15 January 2023.

APDIP-UNDP Report. (2003). *Information and communication technologies for governance and poverty alleviation: Scaling up the successes.*

Bhatia, A., & Kiran, C. (2016). Rural development through E-governance initiatives in India. *IOSR Journal of Business and Management (IOSR-JBM), Special Issue*, 61–69.

Census Report of India. (2011). *Office of the Registrar General and Census Commissioner.*

Chetia, K. (2020). E-governance for rural development: Assessing the impact of E-governance initiatives and projects in rural India. *Journal of Critical Reviews*, 7(4), 3852–3857.

Collier, P., & Dollar, D. (1999). *Can the world cut poverty in half? How policy reform and effective aid can meet the DAC targets. International monetary fund seminar series* (Vol. 49, pp. 1–44).

Das, G. (2002). *The elephant paradigm.* Penguin Books.

Harris, R., & Rajora, R. (2006). *Empowering the poor: Information and communications technology for governance and poverty reduction-a study of rural development projects in India.* UNDP- APDIP ICT4D Series. http://www.apdip.net/publications/ict4d/EmpoweringThePoor.pdf. Accessed on 14 January 2023.

Madaswamy, M. (2004). Digital inclusion to foster rural enterprise: A government's digital initiatives and agenda for small and marginalized farmers in India. In *Regional workshop on implementing e-government.* UN Conference Center.

Mboho, K. S., & Inyang, A. I. (2011). Poverty Alleviation Programme in Nigeria: A study of the United Nations Development Programme (UNDP) Micro-Credit Scheme in Uyo LGA of Akwa-Ibom state. *International Journal of Social and Policy Issues*, 8(1), 162–174.

Nyong'o, P. A. (2001). *Governance and poverty reduction in Africa.* Economic Research Paper, No. 68, Africa Development Bank.

Pathak, R. D., & Husain, Z. (2006). E-governance for poverty alleviation: Indian cases and prospects for poverty alleviation in Uttar Pradesh. *Chinese Public Administration Review*, 3(3–4), 51–61.

Rogers, W. (2002). *Electronic governance: Abridged definitive conceptual framework.* Commonwealth Secretariat.

Sen, A. (2000). *Development as freedom.* Oxford University Press.

Ugoani, J. N. N. (2015). Global governance and poverty reduction through millennium development goals: Some regional experiences. *Independent Journal of Management & Production*, 6(4), 991–1017.

UNDP. (2007). Pro-poor public service delivery with ICTs: Making local E-governance work towards achieving the millennium development goals. APDIP e-Note 11/2007, 1–4.

Wallace, L. (2007). Elusive MDGs: Missing by a long shot. *Finance & Development*, 44(2), 4.

World Bank. (2000/2001). World development report: Attacking poverty. http://www.worldbank.org/poverty/wdrpoverty/index.htm, Accessed on 12 January 2023.

World Bank. (2001). *Issue note.* E-Government and the World Bank.

Chapter 7

E-Inclusiveness in Business and Financial System: An Economic Perspective

Arti Yadav, Parul Yadav and K. Latha

Department of Commerce, Ramanujan College, University of Delhi, India

Abstract

According to G20, 'Inclusiveness basically signifies the accessibility of the various resources (goods, services, and livelihoods) on a commercially viable basis to the economically vulnerable section of the society through making them part of the organizations' value chain as customers, retailers, distributors, and suppliers'. With the increased application of digital technology in every sphere of life, the concept of inclusiveness has moved to e-inclusiveness. So, the present chapter tried to investigate the conceptual journey from inclusiveness to e-inclusiveness from business and financial system aspects. Further, it presents an insight into how the e-inclusiveness aspect impacts the poverty level mainly from the developing country's perspective. The study also suggests that from the perspective of developed as well as developing economies, the public and private sector players strive to develop an effective financial system incorporating an inclusiveness aspect.

Keywords: E-inclusiveness; developing countries; financial system; financial inclusion; sustainable development goals

Introduction

In the present world, the concept of e-inclusion is mostly associated with digital technologies impeding the blocks of class, sexuality, age, race and gender, supporting the identity, agency and culture aspects (OECD, 2018a, 2018b). The participation in the information society from every segment of society in terms of affordable access to the tools and techniques of Information Communication and Technology (ICT), along with the skill set to apply these tools is to be assessed over time (United Nations, 2003). Opportunities offered in the form of digital

Creating Pathways for Prosperity, 99–116

Copyright © 2025 Arti Yadav, Parul Yadav and K. Latha

Published under exclusive licence by Emerald Publishing Limited

doi:10.1108/978-1-83549-121-820241008

platforms, digital financial services, the internet, and mobile phones developed the possibility in terms of additional employment opportunities, increased information and knowledge and additional income. If fostered properly, will surely boost economic growth along with growth in the labour market, gender equality and a high level of digital and inclusive world (The World Bank, 2014). People's capability to use the digital product and services and at the same time using the information generated by both public and private entities can increase inclusivity (Zdjelar & Hrustek, 2021).

From the individual as well as the business perspective, financial inclusion assists in making better asset-building, savings and investment decisions. Around the world, it has been seen that low-income people mostly depend on cash for most of their transactions which is quite difficult and insecure to handle (Draboo, 2020). The emergence of digital platform in the form of various financial services such as the opening of accounts in banks, payments through digital mode, and investments in business, healthcare, and education has helped low-income people to come above the poverty line (World Bank Group, 2020). Even the U.N. Sustainable Development Goals has included the goal of financial inclusion as part of seven of the 17 goals for developing economies together with economic growth, decent work, zero poverty and reduced inequality (United Nations Foundation, 2022). According to studies by the World Bank and World Economic Forum, in the reduction of poverty, it has been found that mobile money services such as store and transfer of funds through using mobiles, provided opportunities for higher income earnings (Pazarbasioglu & Mora, 2020; Pomeroy, 2022). Each country has a different ecosystem that enables or prohibits the country to create an inclusive financial system. It includes factors like state of an economy, financial sector and innovation, poverty levels, financial literacy, and regulatory framework (Ozili, 2021).

However, since 1990, the recent COVID-19 pandemic and the war in Ukraine have been the biggest impediment to the effort towards reduction in the level of poverty as there is an increase of about 70 million in the number of people in extreme poverty to around 719 million. The crisis has been seen mostly in terms of health, food, and energy crises along with the negative impact of climate change. It has become indeed very difficult to eradicate extreme poverty. It has become very crucial to dedicatedly strategise in order to eradicate poverty (The World Bank, 2022a, 2022b, 2022c). The challenge however is the concentration of poverty in parts like Sab Sahara Africa, conflict-prone areas and rural regions, where it becomes all the more difficult to reach. It has been reported in 2018 that 43 countries in the world with an extreme level of poverty are prevailing in fragile and conflict-affected situations (FCS) and sub-Saharan Africa. It is estimated that by 2030 the people living in extreme poverty in FCS shall contribute to two third of the global poor (The World Bank, 2020). In light of the above considerations, the present chapter intents to study the conceptual aspect of inclusiveness in the business and financial system in the era of digitalisation. Further, it will examine the impact of how e-inclusiveness in business and financial system affects the level of poverty from the perspective of developed and developing economies. Finally, the study will try to explore the opportunities for poverty reduction through the digital business and financial system inclusiveness mainly for the developing countries.

Literature Review

The World Summit on the Information Society (2003) has shown different perspectives on the use of ICT, as many of them have doubts that this will bypass low-income communities and will create a digital divide. On the other hand, some were looking for programs and opportunities that promote usage and decrease the level of the digital divide (Ye & Yang, 2020). The concept of the digital divide was originally propounded in the United States in its second falling through the net report entitled Falling Through The Net II: New Data on the Digital Divide, whose main focus was to examine the impact of computer penetration rates and telephone on different groups in the society including elderly, low-income groups, women and minorities (National Telecommunications and Information Administration, 1998).

However, in the 20th century, the concept of the digital divide has been seen as a gap between the reach of ICT and its effective use through tools by the people and those people who didn't have this reach. The advent of internet and the World Wide Web is a breakthrough innovation of technology, without which smooth and effective functioning of various businesses is quite impossible (Hynes, 2021, pp. 103–120; OECD, 1998). Not only the availability of internet infrastructure but also state and national institutions, accessibility and affordability of Internet Services, and knowledge of the users all play an important role and become essential elements of the digital divide (Chakravorti, 2021). Also, the way people used to communicate has changed over the years. Recently communication mostly take place in the form of voice-over-internet protocol, blogs, emails, instant messaging, social media sites and wireless communication devices. All these have made the access, distribution and communication of information very fast and effective (Rogers, 2019).

Though the reach of ICT in terms of its penetration is not what was expected, as it failed to reach the most vulnerable and disadvantaged groups (Perez-Escolar & Canet, 2022). Other new trends like augmented reality and the emergence of the metaverse have led to an increase in the divide (Dodhia, 2022). It has been found by Persaud (2001), that the digital disparity was seen mostly in terms of the knowledge gap, compared to the income gap. To bridge this gap, the concept of inclusiveness in financial aspects holds a key place, which means having a responsible and sustainable way of access of financial products and services such as payments, transactions, credit, insurance and savings in an affordable form for individuals and businesses (Omar & Inaba, 2020). Affordability of the broadband across various income groups can also help in achieving inclusivity besides other strategies taken by the government (Chakravorti, 2021). In the present digital world as said by President Jim Yong Kim, World Bank Group

> Universal access to financial services is within reach – thanks to new technologies, transformative business models and ambitious reforms... As early as 2020, such instruments as e-money accounts, along with debit cards and low-cost regular bank accounts, can significantly increase financial access for those who are now

excluded signified the essence for both individuals as well as businesses (The World Bank, 2014). Perez-Escolar and Canet (2022) further added that disabled people and older adults are the ones who are mostly excluded from the concept of digital inclusion along with the gender divide, rural-urban, rich and poor, which are also showing increasing concern regarding internet accessibility. Businesses especially, the startup owners would want to expand their reach and therefore access to the internet becomes crucial. For example, in order to increase sales digital access to the local community is more favourable than a physical location. A business can become successful if the owners are able to bridge the divide and maximise their audience reach successfully (Dodhia, 2022).

The association between development and financial inclusion is an ongoing topic in most developing countries (Cicchiello et al., 2021). Financial inclusion is an important element for financial development which can be seen more in developing economies (Lenka, 2022). Nevertheless, for regions like Africa and Asia, financial inclusion is a vital issue; the fruits of the digital age are not shared in equal terms as the gaps can easily be seen between rural and urban populations, poorer and richer households and men and women (Demirgüç-Kunt & Klapper, 2013). In addition to that, Le et al. (2019) showed in their study that in the developing region of Asia, around one billion people didn't have access to formal financial services. From the developing countries' perspective, efforts are being made mostly at the level of government to provide easy access to affordable digital technology and financial services to low-income and vulnerable groups (Ozili, 2018). Therefore, in the following sections, the study will explicate the concept of e-inclusiveness in the business and financial system, followed by the conceptual aspect of poverty, and a discussion of how this provides an opportunity to reduce the level of poverty mainly from the perspective of developing countries.

E-Inclusiveness in Business and Financial System: A Synopsis

E-Inclusiveness in Business

Inclusiveness in business emerged in the 1990s. Inclusive business measures become important and can't be ignored as they can help in removing social ills (Likoko & Kini, 2017). Inclusive business aims to integrate low-income communities into a business model or ecosystem. The companies strategically orient themselves to make a product that can assist these people to find a place in the value chain (Golja & Pozega, 2012). The demand side includes people from low-income groups as customers and clients. On the supply side, low-income groups can be included as producers, employees etc. (UNDP, 2010). If given the opportunity, they can emerge as entrepreneurs and create a societal impact. It is not easy to engage society at all levels, and therefore, innovation in institutions becomes fundamental. Market mechanisms can help in becoming businesses inclusive in their approach and contribute towards resolving social problems (de Sousa Teodósio & Comini, 2012). Inclusive business models if focused specifically on involving women who come from low-income families can not only solve the goal of inclusivity but also make women economically empowered (Bank, 2016). Businesses gain as they achieve a competitive advantage by winning customers, making the workforce inclusive and at the same strengthening their supply chain. A number of stakeholders can contribute towards making the business models inclusive like companies by including low-income groups on the demand and supply side; governments by providing necessary incentives to businesses promoting inclusivity; inspiring inclusive business models; create a hassle-free and enabling environment for such businesses to function; development partners by advocacy and awareness for inclusivity; funding and establishing community-based business models encouraging inclusivity (UNDP, 2010).

The increase in digital transformation has created an aspect of digital inclusion which can also be called e-inclusiveness. As per the definition by The Institute of Museum and Library Services, digital inclusion is 'the ability of individuals and groups to access and use information and communications technologies'. It addresses aspects related to access to ICT and digital literacy (Bureau of Internet Accessibility, 2017). The concept of digital inclusion has expanded because of the increase in e-commerce, and digitisation of delivery which has led to more opportunities for inclusion (Leveraging Digital Technologies for Social Inclusion | DISD, n.d.). One of the ways in which businesses create inclusivity is by reducing the digital skills divide (Closing the Digital Skills Gap – KPMG Global, 2022).

E-Inclusiveness in Financial System

There is an increasing need to include all sections of society in the financial system through upgraded and contemporary means. Financial inclusion is universal access to the financial services offered by sustainable institutions which are reasonably priced (Patwardhan, 2018). It may be interpreted as access and use of financial services to meet the user's needs (Sun, 2018). One such method of inclusion is related to the digital platforms and applications that aid in doing so. Digital financial inclusion aids in reaching out to the underserved and financially excluded population by providing digital means at an affordable cost (Sun, 2018). It has been one of the crucial issues especially in emerging and developing economies where the financial ecosystem is either underbanked or unbanked (Patwardhan, 2018). Greater inclusion leads to greater access to information and at the same time the quality of life is improved (Zdjelar & Hrustek, 2021). New technology and capabilities developed in the area of finance reflect digital convergence and new forms of money like bitcoin and ethereum extend and leads to expansion of financial services. Many Financial Services are undergoing changes which are fundamental and their impact can be seen in areas like payment methods, financing international trade, stakeholder informedness, global portfolio management and many more (Gomber et al., 2018). A person engaged in such services feels empowered and part of the digital world.

UN sustainable development goals also highlight the problem of inclusion and aim to achieve the financial inclusion of poorer households with a mainstream financial system. UN aims to build a resilient infrastructure so that inclusion is promoted through sustainable industrialisation and innovation (Goal 9 | Department of Economic and Social Affairs, n.d.). Corporate houses have contributed to it by innovating and developing digital financial services. This leads not just to financial inclusion but at the same time creates new opportunities for innovation and improvement of corporation value (Yang et al., 2022). Innovative ICT tools lead to e-inclusion and e-social work (Raya Diez, 2018). Digital financial inclusion can be used as a development intervention wherein networks of fintech companies, state and international organisations can work together and build a network (Gabor & Brooks, 2017).

However, the digital divide is evident in the social ecosystem, leading to the marginalisation of certain segments of society (Zdjelar & Hrustek, 2021). E-inclusion can be viewed as a tool for social inclusion and a means to reduce the digital divide (Raya Diez, 2018). Sizeable welfare benefits can be witnessed when poor households are integrated into the financial system (Radcliffe & Voorhies, 2012). The Global Findex database provides data on global access to financial services. World Bank also highlights that financial inclusion is a cornerstone of the economy's development. The index has indicators on access and use of financial services and digital payments (both formal and informal) and offers insights on financial resilience and behaviours enabling them (The Global Findex Database 2021, n.d.). The database displays wide differences in adult banking account penetration rate, banking sectors' infrastructure development stage, and the use of technology in the banking sector (Koh et al., 2018). Though the number of adults holding account has increased in wake of the corona pandemic and lead to adoption digital financial services (The World Bank, 2021). Another financial inclusion index like NAMPUS (normality, anonymity, monotonicity, proximity, uniformity, and signalling) have also been developed which are flexible and applicable to developing countries (Ambarkhane et al., 2016). The reserve bank of India for instance, uses a composite index for financial inclusion (FI- index) that aims to capture the extent to which financial inclusion has been achieved across the country (Reserve Bank of India, 2022).

Several individual and macro factors have been considered to understand the nature and characteristics of e-inclusion. Individual factors include age, gender, income, and education and macro-level factors include public policies, welfare, and inclusion measures by the society (Silva et al., 2017). A positive impact has been seen in developed and developing economies when greater financial inclusion is present. It stimulates the economic growth of a country (Nizam et al., 2020). Greater outreach has also been associated with measures of financial development and economic development (Beck et al., 2007).

Poverty: An Overview

There are several ways in which the meaning of poverty can be understood. Different clusters of meanings for poverty include income poverty, material lack of wealth or other assets or want, capability deprivation which means what we can do or be and what we cannot do or be and a multidimensional view of deprivation (Chambers, 2002). Poverty has been one of the social issues which have to be addressed through proper measures and continuous evaluation. Several countries have measured poverty on the basis of the minimum amount required to buy a basket of essentials. However, poverty is not only about measurement through a monetary lens but should also consider the aspect of well-being which is generally ignored in traditional measures (World Bank, 2023; World Bank et al., 2021). United Nations has developed an agenda of sustainable development goals wherein one of the important goals is the eradication of poverty. The impact of poverty is all-encompassing. Poverty can be a barrier to the implementation of these sustainable development goals (Wei et al., 2023). The World Bank Group also aims to end extreme poverty which can lead to the promotion of shared prosperity. It is seen that millions of people are living in extreme poverty but this number is slowly and gradually declining (World Bank, 2022).

The income gap not only affects residents but also affects their happiness and creates a negative impact with respect to economic development (Ji et al., 2021). The international poverty line is 2.5 dollars per person per day with 2017 prices. This implies that anyone who lives on a lesser amount then will be considered as living in extreme poverty (World Bank, 2022).

Poverty is measured differently in different countries. The United States for example measures poverty by comparing a person's or family's income with a pre-set poverty threshold or a minimum income needed for basic needs. Anyone whose income falls below the threshold is considered poor. It uses the official poverty measure as well as a supplemental poverty measure. These are implemented by the US census bureau to measure poverty (Institute for Research on Poverty – UW–Madison, n.d.).

The Canadian Government also uses a number of income-based measures which facilitate inter-country and intra-country comparisons. In Canada, The Angus Reid Institute, however, examines poverty by viewing lived experiences of people rather than income. The Angus Reid Institute tries to study poverty by capturing the personal experiences and attitudes of people and then quantifying the economic struggle of Canadians to define poverty (Reid, 2018).

In India, poverty means a socially perceived deprivation of basic human needs consisting of both materials as well as non-material dimensions. Poverty is measured through a specified threshold level of Expenditure. This threshold expenditure is labelled as the poverty line. The limit has minimum amount needed to purchase a basket of goods and services needed to satisfy basic human needs. This should be a socially acceptable level (NITI Aayog, 2016).

Besides poverty being measured in monetary terms, it has become imperative to understand the multidimensional aspect of poverty. A global multidimensional poverty index has been framed. This Global multidimensional poverty index (MPI) identifies multiple deprivations for three dimensions i.e., health including household and individual level, education and standard of living. On the basis of an individual's experience in their household, each is classified as multidimensionally poor and non-poor depending upon a weighted number of deprivations.

These are then aggregated into a national measure of poverty. This measure complements and adds values to poverty measures that are income-based (UNDP, 2021).

It has been found that the economy can reduce poverty by ensuring that digital development is encouraged and new techniques and technology are promoted (Spulbar et al., 2022). In the context of developing economies, it has also been seen that the disadvantaged population is not included in the financial system, thereby creating incoming equality. This further curbs the goal of overall social welfare (Banerjee, 2020). Measures taken by the government create a positive impact when it comes to poverty reduction for both developing and developed Nations. However, a difference is seen when we compare developing and developed economies as developing economies spend less because of fewer resources. The impact related to poverty reduction was a little less in developing economies than the developed economy. Both monetary and non-monetary measures to reduce poverty can be employed. If coupled with foreign aid, a positive relationship exists between poverty reduction and foreign aid (Mahembe & Odhiambo, 2019). The fiscal policy of a government can provide an opportunity and impetus for developing economies specifically to fight against poverty. If aid is directed towards pro poor schemes and disbursed in areas of production, infrastructure development and economic advancement can result in poverty reduction (Mahembe & Odhiambo, 2019). It is being recommended by the World Bank that in order to keep track of the level of poverty and to and extreme poverty countries master regularly measure the progress and come up with measures which can help in measuring poverty accurately and frequently (World Bank, 2022).

E-Inclusiveness in Business and Financial System Leads to Poverty Reduction: Perspective From Developed and Developing Countries

As per the data based on 2017 prices (Fig. 7.1), if anyone is living on less than $2.15 a day, they will be regarded as in extreme poverty, and in 2019, globally around 648 million people were in this zone (The World Bank, 2022a, 2022b, 2022c). In addition to that, around 2.9 billion people didn't have opportunities to associate with the digital economy and access to the internet. From healthcare to banking, media, communication and education, every aspect is affecting life as the digital divide continues even after a higher level of technological advancements (Jasser, 2022). It's quite an interesting fact that the concept of the digital divide still has a significant impact on developed, developing and underdeveloped economies. It is quite substantial in rural areas and disproportionate for some groups as impacting more women compared to men (Antonio & Tuffley, 2014; Reddick et al., 2020). As per Harvard Business School, around half of the population in the United States is unable to have broadband speed access due to the lack of skills or coverage (Chakravorti, 2022). In the digital world, it is quite visible in the last decade for developing economies that e-money has helped millions of people join the formal financial system in areas such as health insurance and agriculture (Asian Development Bank, 2017).

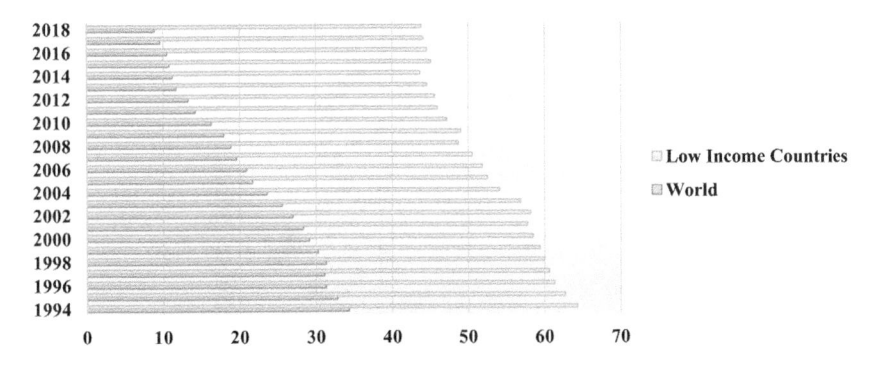

Fig. 7.1.   Poverty Headcount Ratio at $2.15 a Day (2017 PPP) (% of Population) of Low-Income Countries and World Level. *Source:* Authors presentation based on World Bank Database.

The importance of technological advancement as a fundamental global issue along with its inclusiveness has been recently recognised by world leaders on the 75th anniversary of the United Nations (2020a, 2020b, 2020c). Although the concept of digital inclusion is not only about handling issues, it basically provides opportunities to shape an impartial and equitable society and a booming economy (United Nations, 2021). E-inclusiveness of the business and financial system provides numerous benefits to society including of saving money to enhance job prospects along with to work in a flexible mode (Cingano, 2014; OECD, 2018a, 2018b).

The outcome of various studies over time has shown that in inclusive economic growth and a decrease in the level of inequality, financial systems have played a very significant role and that too in a sustainable manner (Norris et al., 2015; United Nations, 2020a, 2020b, 2020c). As per the result of a study, over the long term, there is a 2–3% GDP growth between financially inclusive countries and their less inclusive peers. Additionally, inclusion mainly through bank accounts and increasing participation of women lead to the largest reductions in the level of income inequality (Georgieva, 2020). Affordability of financial products facilitates financial stability and growth of wealth from both individuals as well as business perspectives which will ultimately lead to economic growth (Carbó-Valverde & Sánchez, 2013). It has been also clearly seen in the recent pandemic situation of COVID-19, where in around 200 countries or territories governments trusted the financial system to provide social support benefits (United Nations, 2020a, 2020b, 2020c). Fig. 7.2 clearly shows the rising trend of broadband connections in countries around the world including the OECD countries having a share of around 27% by June 2019. Further, the United Nations and World Bank mentioned that even if looked beyond the COVID crisis, inclusive financial services are an integral part of the achievement of 13 of the 17 Sustainable Goals and hence will be a vital aspect of human development (United Nations, 2022a, 2022b).

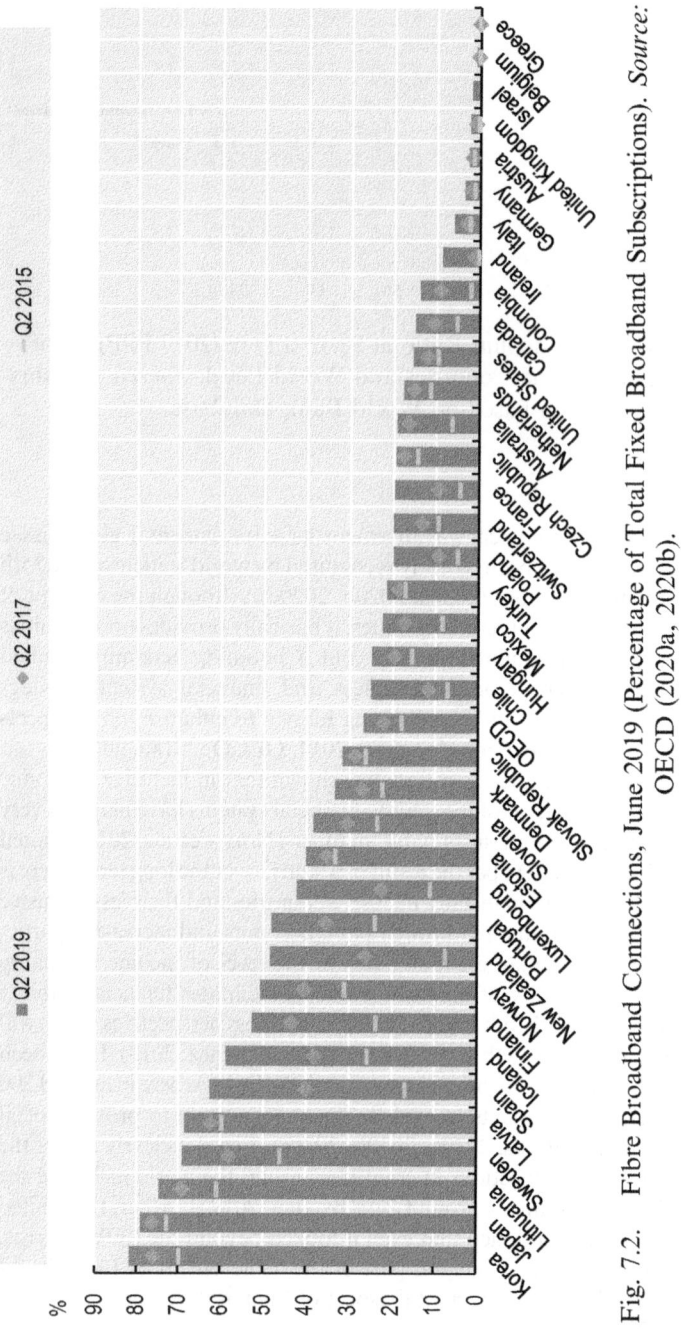

Fig. 7.2. Fibre Broadband Connections, June 2019 (Percentage of Total Fixed Broadband Subscriptions). *Source:* OECD (2020a, 2020b).

Moreover, e-technology was there, but the crisis of COVID-19 has enhanced the need for digital financial inclusion for both developed and developing economies (Tay et al., 2022). In more than 80 countries, digital financial services including services through mobile phones have been launched and already picked up good growth (Agur et al., 2020). So, by using digital technology and mobile phone to access financial services resulted in a shift from cash-based transactions to formal financial services is a big move for millions of formerly excluded and undeserved poor customers (The World Bank, 2014).

Global account ownership has increased up to 76% of the population at the global level and around 71% in developing economies (Fig. 7.3). Fig. 7.3 shows a rising trend in the case of most of the regions. From 2011 to 2021, around the globe, account ownership has increased by 50%, out of which the adult participation level has increased from 51% to 76%. In developing economies, the average rate of account ownership increased from 2017 to 2021 among adults from 63% to 71% (Global Findex Database, 2021). Countries such as China, Thailand, Kenya and India are those where around 80% have moved from access to usage of accounts (The World Bank, 2022a, 2022b, 2022c). The share of adults making or receiving digital payments is nearly 95% in high-income economies, while in developing economies it has increased from 2014 to 2021 from 35% to 55% (Global Findex Database, 2021). The strategies adopted in these economies are mainly in the form of innovation and reforms at the private and government levels respectively, along with the opening of low-cost accounts and easy payment options through digital mode and mobile (World Bank Group, 2020).

Digital financial inclusion has increased in recent years because of the swift adoption of digital technology in businesses and financial system (Mavlutova et al., 2022). Some of the issues associated with traditional financial services like information asymmetry, geographical barriers and cost are overcome by digital financial

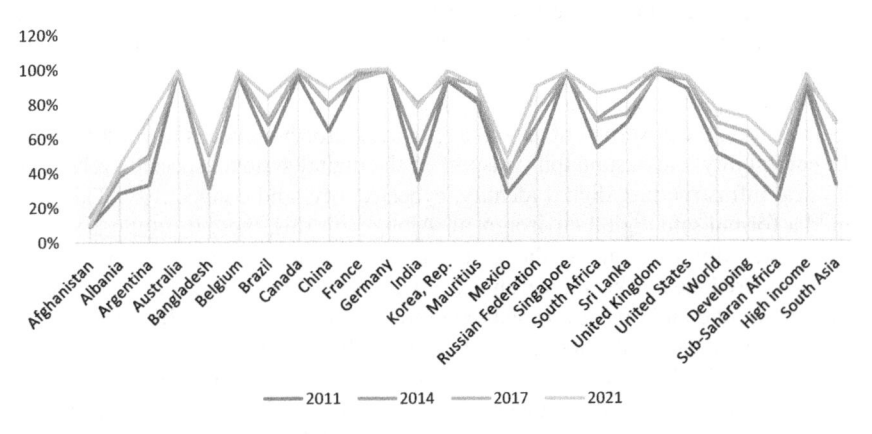

Fig. 7.3. Global Account Ownership (Adults With an Account (%), 2011–2021). *Source:* The World Bank Group, Global Findex Index.

services enabled by fintech (Feyen et al., 2021). Studies in Kenya and Nepal also supported the concept of inclusiveness as they found out that where the households are headed by women, extreme poverty is reduced by 22% due to access to mobile money and able to invest an average of 60% more in businesses respectively (Matheson, 2016; The World Bank, 2022a, 2022b, 2022c).

The intersection of information and technology is changing how we perceive poverty and financial access around the world (Mirza et al., 2019). Also, the situation of the pandemic has made it realise that in such times though the pace and requirement of digital transformation used to accelerate, it has not been without issues (McKinsey and Company, 2020). This situation is highly evident in the Asia-Pacific region where more than two billion people are not able to access the digital world (Fernandez, 2022). Most of the issues can be categorised into four aspects for people to be called digitally included as access, confidence, motivation, and skills (Soomro et al., 2020). In addition to that, the emergence of Internet of Things and 5G will lead to more challenges such as security, privacy, and high-level data production (Attaran, 2021). Irrespective of the ongoing and upcoming issues, digital technologies surely have made life easy for everyone and will continue to change the way people work and live.

Discussion and Conclusion

The efforts for e-inclusiveness in business and financial system through the adoption of new technology in both developed and developing countries is mostly associated with the measures taken by regulators and policymakers. Moreover, efforts are also made to provide convenient and low-cost financial services through digital finance, fintech and mobile phones, along with confirming some of the vital aspects such as the integrity and stability of the financial sector, consumer protection and promotion of fair competition. From the business perspective, innovation is the key to harnessing the opportunities available in the business environment based on tech-enabled solutions. The government is also encouraging the same through promoting responsible finance, knowledge of e-platforms, partnership and innovation.

Therefore, the government as well as private sector both needs to work towards the equitability and sustainability aspect of the digital system especially related to physical infrastructure, digital identity, cybersecurity, and connectivity. This is to build a formal safe digital environment. Along with this, these institutions should also make efforts to narrow the gender gap as women's financial inclusion will provide incredible market opportunities as well as empower them. The high level of importance of e-inclusiveness is realised more recently due to COVID-19 and other climate-related issues like flooding and draughts, having an impact on the financial and economic health of economies around the world. The impact of such events is not only associated with the vulnerable section of society but also with the non-vulnerable section, in a manner as to make available financial services for their benefit. So, to seize new economic opportunities along with inclusiveness, individuals, government as well as businesses should work towards financial health keeping in check the technological advancements mainly digital technology. Further, efforts can be made by financial leaders (both public as well as private) around the world to develop a financial system that is kind of more inclusive in terms of mobility, resilience, long-term security and financial stability.

References

Agur, I., Martinez, P. S., & Rochon, C. (2020). *Digital financial services and the pandemic: Opportunities and risks for emerging and developing economies.* International Monetary Fund (IMF).

Ambarkhane, D., Singh, A. S., & Venkataramani, B. (2016). Developing a comprehensive financial inclusion index. *Management and Labour Studies.* https://doi.org/10.1177/0258042X16666579

Antonio, A., & Tuffley, D. (2014). The gender digital divide in developing countries. *Future Internet, 6*(4), 673–687. https://doi.org/10.3390/fi6040673

Asian Development Bank. (2017). *Accelerating financial inclusion in south-east Asia with digital finance.* Asian Development Bank. https://www.adb.org/sites/default/files/publication/222061/financial-inclusion-se-asia.pdf

Attaran, M. (2021). The impact of 5G on the evolution of intelligent automation and industry digitization. Journal of Ambient Intelligence and Humanized Computing. https://doi.org/10.1007/s12652-020-02521-x

Banerjee, S. (2020). Effect of financial inclusion and stability on equality, poverty, and human development: An empirical analysis in the context of South Asia. *DLSU Business and Economics Review, 30*(1), 130–142.

Bank, A. D. (2016). *How inclusive is inclusive business for women? Examples from Asia and Latin America.* Asian Development Bank. https://www.adb.org/publications/inclusive-business-women-asia-and-latin-america

Beck, T., Demirguc-Kunt, A., & Martinez Peria, M. S. (2007). Reaching out: Access to and use of banking services across countries. *Journal of Financial Economics, 85*(1), 234–266. https://doi.org/10.1016/j.jfineco.2006.07.002

Bureau of Internet Accessibility. (2017). What is digital inclusion? https://www.boia.org/blog/what-is-digital-inclusion

Carbó-Valverde, S., & Sánchez, L. P. (2013). Financial stability and economic growth. In J. F. de Guevara Radoselovics & J. M. P. Monsálvez (Eds.), *Crisis, risk and stability in financial markets. Palgrave Macmillan studies in banking and financial institutions.* Palgrave Macmillan. https://doi.org/10.1057/9781137001832_2

Chakravorti, B. (2021). How to close the digital divide in the U.S. *Harvard Business Review.* https://hbr.org/2021/07/how-to-close-the-digital-divide-in-the-u-s

Chakravorti, B. (2022). How Biden's "internet for all" initiative can actually fulfill its mission. *Harvard Business Review.* https://hbr.org/2022/07/how-bidens-internet-for-all-initiative-can-actually-fulfill-its-mission

Chambers, R. (2002). Power, knowledge and policy influence: Reflections on an experience. In K. Brock & R. McGee (Eds.), *Knowing poverty: Critical reflections on participatory research and policy.*

Cicchiello, A. F., Kazemikhasragh, A., Monferrá, S., & Giron, A. (2021). Financial inclusion and development in the least developed countries in Asia and Africa. *Journal of Innovation and Entrepreneurship, 10*, 49. https://doi.org/10.1186/s13731-021-00190-4

Cingano, F. (2014). *Trends in income inequality and its impact on economic growth. OECD social, employment and migration working papers* (Vol. 163). OECD Publishing. http://doi.org/10.1787/5jxrjncwxv6j-en

Demirgüç-Kunt, A., & Klapper, L. (2013). Measuring financial inclusion, explaining variation in use of financial services across and within countries. *Brookings Papers on Economic Activity*, *2013*(1), 279–340.

DISD. (n.d.). *Leveraging digital technologies for social inclusion.* https://www.un.org/development/desa/dspd/2021/02/digital-technologies-for-social-inclusion/

Dodhia, Z. (2022). Council post: The digital divide: Where does your business stand? *Forbes.* https://www.forbes.com/sites/forbesbusinesscouncil/2022/02/03/the-digital-divide-where-does-your-business-stand/

Draboo, S. (2020). Financial inclusion and digital India: A critical assessment. *Engage*, *55*(17). https://epw.in/engage/article/financial-inclusion-and-digital-india-critical

Fernandez, R. (2022). *The opportunities of digital inclusion and the tech behind it.* TechRepublic. https://www.techrepublic.com/article/the-opportunities-of-digital-inclusion-and-the-tech-behind-it/

Feyen, E., Frost, J., Gambacorta, L., Natarajan, H., & Saal, M. (2021). *Fintech and digital transformation of financial services: Implications for market structure and public policy.* Bank of International Settlements papers no., 117. Monetary and Economic Department. https://www.bis.org/publ/bppdf/bispap117.pdf

Gabor, D., & Brooks, S. (2017). The digital revolution in financial inclusion: International development in the fintech era. *New Political Economy*, *22*(4), 423–436. https://doi.org/10.1080/13563467.2017.1259298

Georgieva, K. (2020). *The financial sector in the 2020s: Building a more inclusive system in the new decade.* International Monetary Fund. https://www.imf.org/en/News/Articles/2020/01/17/sp01172019-the-financial-sector-in-the-2020s

Global Findex Database. (2021). *Financial inclusion, digital payments and resilience in the age of COVID-19.* World Bank Group. https://www.worldbank.org/en/publication/globalfindex/Report

Goal 9. (n.d.). Department of Economic and Social Affairs. https://sdgs.un.org/goals/goal9

Golja, T., & Pozega, S. (2012). Inclusive business – What it is all about? Managing inclusive companies. *International Review of Management and Marketing*, *2*(1), 22–42.

Gomber, P., Kauffman, R. J., Parker, C., & Weber, B. W. (2018). Special issue: Financial information systems and the fintech revolution. *Journal of Management Information Systems*, *35*(1), 12–18. https://doi.org/10.1080/07421222.2018.1440778

Hynes, M. (2021). Digital divides. *The social, cultural and environmental costs of hyper-connectivity: Sleeping through the revolution.* Emerald Publishing Limited. https://doi.org/10.1108/978-1-83909-976-220211007

Institute for Research on Poverty. (n.d.). *How is poverty measured?* Institute for Research on Poverty – UW–Madison. https://www.irp.wisc.edu/resources/how-is-poverty-measured/

Jasser, M. A. (2022). *The digital economy: Bridging the digital divide between developing and developed nations.* World Economic Forum. https://www.weforum.org/agenda/2022/11/bridging-the-digital-divide-to-accelerate-development/

Ji, X., Wang, K., Xu, H., & Li, M. (2021). Has digital financial inclusion narrowed the urban-rural income gap: The role of entrepreneurship in China. *Sustainability*, *13*(15). Article 15. https://doi.org/10.3390/su13158292

Koh, F., Phoon, K. F., & Ha, C. D. (2018). Chapter 15: Digital financial inclusion in South East Asia. In D. Lee Kuo Chuen & R. Deng (Eds.), *Handbook of blockchain, digital finance, and inclusion* (Vol. 2, pp. 387–403). Academic Press. https://doi.org/10.1016/B978-0-12-812282-2.00015-2

KPMG Global. (2022). Closing the digital skills gap. *KPMG*. https://home.kpmg/xx/en/home/insights/2021/08/pulse-of-fintech-h1-21-ant-group-interview.html

Le, T. H., Chuc, A. T., & Taghizadeh-Hesary, F. (2019). Financial inclusion and its impact on financial efficiency and sustainability, empirical evidence from Asia. *Borsa Istanbul Review*, *19*(4), 310–322.

Lenka, S. K. (2022). Relationship between financial inclusion and financial development in India: Is there any link? *Journal of Public Affairs*, *22*(S1), e2722. https://doi.org/10.1002/pa.2722

Likoko, E., & Kini, J. (2017). Inclusive business – A business approach to development. *Current Opinion in Environmental Sustainability*, *24*, 84–88. https://doi.org/10.1016/j.cosust.2017.03.001

Mahembe, E., & Odhiambo, N. M. (2019). Foreign aid and poverty reduction: A review of international literature. *Cogent Social Sciences*, *5*(1), 1625741. https://doi.org/10.1080/23311886.2019.1625741

Matheson, R. (2016). *Study: Mobile-money services lift Kenyans out of poverty*. Massachusetts Institute of Technology. https://news.mit.edu/2016/mobile-money-kenyans-out-poverty-1208

Mavlutova, I., Spilbergs, A., Verdenhofs, A., Natrins, A., Arefjevs, I., & Volkova, T. (2022). Digital transformation as a driver of the financial sector sustainable development: An impact on financial inclusion and operational efficiency. *Sustainability*, *15*, 207. https://doi.org/10.3390/su15010207

McKinsey and Company. (2020). How COVID-19 has pushed companies over the technology tipping point – And transformed business forever. https://www.mckinsey.com/capabilities/strategy-and-corporate-finance/our-insights/how-covid-19-has-pushed-companies-over-the-technology-tipping-point-and-transformed-business-forever

Mirza, M. U., Richter, A., Nes, E. H., & Scheffer, M. (2019). *Ecological Economics*, *160*, 215–226. https://doi.org/10.1016/j.ecolecon.2019.02.015

National Telecommunications and Information Administration. (1998). *Falling through the net II: New data on the digital divide*. United States Department of Commerce. https://ntia.gov/page/falling-through-net-ii-new-data-digital-divide

NITI Aayog. (2016). *Eliminating poverty: Creating jobs and strengthening social programs*. Occasional Paper No. 2. NITI Aayog, Government of India. https://www.niti.gov.in/sites/default/files/2018-12/OccasionalPaper_No2_Poverty.pdf

Nizam, R., Karim, Z. A., Rahman, A. A., & Sarmidi, T. (2020). Financial inclusiveness and economic growth: New evidence using a threshold regression analysis. *Economic Research-Ekonomska Istraživanja*, *33*(1), 1465–1484. https://doi.org/10.1080/1331677X.2020.1748508

Norris, E. D., Kochhar, K., Suphaphiphat, N., Ricks, F., & Tsounta, E. (2015). *Causes and consequences of income inequality: A global perspective*. International Monetary Fund. https://www.imf.org/external/pubs/ft/sdn/2015/sdn1513.pdf

OECD. (1998). 21st century technology: Promises and perils of a dynamic future. https://www.oecd.org/futures/35391210.pdf

OECD. (2018a). Bridging the digital gender divide include, upskill, innovate. https://www.oecd.org/digital/bridging-the-digital-gender-divide.pdf

OECD. (2018b). Preparing our youth for an inclusive sustainable world. The OECD PISA global competence framework. https://www.oecd.org/education/Global-competency-for-an-inclusive-world.pdf

OECD. (2020a). *Advancing the digital financial inclusion of youth.* www.oecd.org/daf/fin/financial-education/advancing-the-digital-financial-inclusionof-youth.htm

OECD. (2020b). Digital transformation in the age of COVID-19: Building resilience and bridging divides. In *Digital Economy Outlook 2020 Supplement, OECD.* https://www.oecd.org/digital/digital-economy-outlook-covid.pdf

Omar, M. A., & Inaba, K. (2020). Does financial inclusion reduce poverty and income inequality in developing countries? A panel data analysis. *Economic Structures, 9*(37). https://doi.org/10.1186/s40008-020-00214-4

Ozili, P. K. (2018). Impact of digital finance on inclusion and stability. *Borsa Istanbul Review, 18*(4), 329–340.

Ozili, P. K. (2021). Financial inclusion research around the world: A review. *Forum for Social Economics, 50*(4), 457–479. https://doi.org/10.1080/07360932.2020.1715238

Patwardhan, A. (2018). Chapter 4: Financial inclusion in the digital age. In D. Lee Kuo Chuen & R. Deng (Eds.), *Handbook of blockchain, digital finance, and inclusion* (Vol. 1, pp. 57–89). Academic Press. https://doi.org/10.1016/B978-0-12-810441-5.00004-X

Pazarbasioglu, C., & Mora, A. G. (2020). *Expanding digital financial services can help developing economies cope with crisis now and boost growth later.* World Bank Blogs. https://blogs.worldbank.org/voices/expanding-digital-financial-services-can-help-developing-economies-cope-crisis-now-and-boost-growth-later

Perez-Escolar, M., & Canet, F. (2022). Research on vulnerable people and digital inclusion: Toward a consolidated taxonomical framework. *Universal Access in the Information Society.* https://doi.org/10.1007/s10209-022-00867-x

Persaud, A. (2001). The knowledge gap. *Foreign Affairs, 80*(2), 107–117.

Pomeroy, R. (2022). *How 'financial inclusion' can help lift millions of people out of poverty – On Radio Davos.* World Economic Forum. https://www.weforum.org/agenda/2022/09/financial-inclusion-findex-radio-davos-world-bank-economist/

Radcliffe, D., & Voorhies, R. (2012). *A digital pathway to financial inclusion.* SSRN Scholarly Paper No. 2186926. https://doi.org/10.2139/ssrn.2186926

Raya Diez, E. (2018). e-Inclusion and e-Social work: New technologies at the service of social intervention. *European Journal of Social Work, 21*(6), 916–929. https://doi.org/10.1080/13691457.2018.1469472

Reddick, C. G., Enriquez, R., Harris, R. J., & Sharma, B. (2020). Determinants of broadband access and affordability: An analysis of a community survey on the digital divide. *Cities, 106,* 102904. https://doi.org/10.1016/j.cities.2020.102904

Reid, A. (2018). *What does poverty look like in Canada? Survey finds one-in-four experience notable economic hardship.* Angus Reid Institute. https://angusreid.org/poverty-in-canada/

Reserve Bank of India. (2022). *Press releases.* Reserve Bank of India. https://www.rbi.org.in/Scripts/BS_PressReleaseDisplay.aspx?prid=54133

Rogers, S. (2019). The role of technology in the evolution of communication. *Forbes.* https://www.forbes.com/sites/solrogers/2019/10/15/the-role-of-technology-in-the-evolution-of-communication/?sh=11f223a2493b

Silva, P., Matos, A. D., & Martinez-Pecino, R. (2017). E-inclusion: Beyond individual socio-demographic characteristics. *PLoS One, 12*(9), e0184545. https://doi.org/10.1371/journal.pone.0184545

Soomro, K. A., Kale, U., Curtis, R., Akcaoglu, M., & Bernstein, M. (2020). Digital divide among higher education faculty. *International Journal of Educational Technology in Higher Education, 17*(1), Article 21. https://doi.org/10.1186/s41239-020-00191-5

de Sousa Teodósio, A. D. S., & Comini, G. (2012). Inclusive business and poverty: Prospects in the Brazilian context. *Revista de Administracao, 47*(3), 410–421. https://doi.org/10.5700/rausp1047

Spulbar, C., Anghel, L. C., Birau, R., Ermiş, S. I., Treapăt, L.-M., & Mitroi, A. T. (2022). Digitalization as a factor in reducing poverty and its implications in the context of the COVID-19 pandemic. *Sustainability, 14*(17). https://doi.org/10.3390/su141710667

Sun, T. (2018). Chapter 2: Balancing innovation and risks in digital financial inclusion – Experiences of ant financial services group. In D. Lee Kuo Chuen & R. Deng (Eds.), *Handbook of blockchain, digital finance, and inclusion* (Vol. 2, pp. 37–43). Academic Press. https://doi.org/10.1016/B978-0-12-812282-2.00002-4

Tay, L. Y., Tai, H. T., & Tan, G.-S. (2022). Digital financial inclusion: A gateway to sustainable development. *Heliyon, 8*(6). https://doi.org/10.1016/j.heliyon.2022.e09766

The Global Findex Database. (2021). *World Bank.* https://www.worldbank.org/en/publication/globalfindex

The World Bank. (2014). Digital financial inclusion. https://www.worldbank.org/en/topic/financialinclusion/publication/digital-financial-inclusion

The World Bank. (2022a). Financial inclusion. https://www.worldbank.org/en/topic/financialinclusion/overview

The World Bank. (2022b). *Global progress in reducing extreme poverty grinds to a halt.* Press Release. https://www.worldbank.org/en/news/press-release/2022/10/05/global-progress-in-reducing-extreme-poverty-grinds-to-a-halt

The World Bank. (2022c). *Measuring poverty.* https://www.worldbank.org/en/topic/measuringpoverty#:~:text=The%20international%20poverty%20line%20is%20set%20at%20%242.15,people%20globally%20were%20in%20this%20situation%20in%202019

UNDP. (2010). *Business solutions to poverty – How inclusive business models create opportunities for all in Emerging Europe and Central Asia.* https://info.undp.org/docs/pdc/Documents/SVK/00057199_GIM%20Report%20Laid%20out2.pdf

UNDP (United Nations Development Programme). (2021). *2021 Global Multidimensional Poverty Index (MPI): Unmasking disparities by ethnicity, caste and gender.* Retrieved from Poverty Overview: Development news, research, data | World Bank.

United Nations. (2003). *Declaration of principles: Building the information society: A global challenge in the new millennium.* World Summit on the Information Society. http://www.un-documents.net/wsis-dop.htm

United Nations. (2020a). *The impact of digital technologies.* https://www.un.org/en/ un75/impact-digital-technologies

United Nations. (2020b). *The social impact of covid-19.* Department of Economic and Social Affairs Social Inclusion. https://desapublications.un.org/publications/ sustainable-development-goals-report-2022

United Nations. (2020c). *World social report 2020 inequality in a rapidly changing world.* Department of Economic and Social Affairs. https://www.un.org/ development/desa/dspd/wp-content/uploads/sites/22/2020/01/World-Social-Report-2020-FullReport.pdf

United Nations. (2021). *Leveraging digital technologies for social inclusion.* Department of Economic and Social Affairs, Social Inclusion. https://www.un.org/ development/desa/dspd/2021/02/digital-technologies-for-social-inclusion/

United Nations. (2022a). *Fragile economic recovery from COVID-19 pandemic upended by war in Ukraine.* Department of Social and Economic Affairs. https://www. un.org/en/desa/fragile-economic-recovery-covid-19-pandemic-upended-war-ukraine

United Nations. (2022b). The sustainable development goals report 2022. https:// unstats.un.org/sdgs/report/2022/The-Sustainable-Development-Goals-Report-2022.pdf

United Nations Foundation. (2022). *Sustainable development goals.* https://www.undp. org/sustainable-development-goals

Wei, Y., Zhong, F., Song, X., & Huang, C. (2023). Exploring the impact of poverty on the sustainable development goals: Inhibiting synergies and magnifying trade-offs. *Sustainable Cities and Society, 89.* https://doi.org/10.1016/j.scs.2022.104367

World Bank. (2021). *The Global Findex Database 2021.* World Bank. https://www. worldbank.org/en/publication/globalfindex

World Bank. (2022). *Poverty and shared prosperity 2022: Correcting course.* The World Bank. https://doi.org/10.1596/978-1-4648-1893-6

World Bank. (2023). *Fragility and conflict: On the front lines of the fight against poverty.* World Bank. https://www.worldbank.org/en/topic/poverty/publication/ fragility-conflict-on-the-front-lines-fight-against-poverty

World Bank Group. (2020). *Digital financial services.* https://pubdocs.worldbank.org/ en/230281588169110691/Digital-Financial-Services.pdf

World Bank, UNDP, & UNICEF. (2021). A roadmap for countries measuring multidimensional poverty. *Equitable Growth, Finance and Institutions Insight.* https://openknowledge.worldbank.org/handle/10986/35808

World Summit on the Information Society. (2003). *Declaration of principles.* UNESCO. https://en.unesco.org/themes/building-knowledge-societies/wsis

Yang, Y., Shi, S., & Wu, J. (2022). Digital financial inclusion to corporation value: The mediating effect of ambidextrous innovation. *Sustainability, 14*(24). Scopus. https://doi.org/10.3390/su142416621

Ye, L., & Yang, H. (2020). From digital divide to social inclusion: A tale of mobile platform empowerment in rural areas. *Sustainability, 12*(6), 2424. https://doi.org/ 10.3390/su12062424

Zdjelar, R., & Hrustek, N. Ž. (2021). Digital divide and E-inclusion as challenges of the information society – Research review. *Journal of Information and Organizational Sciences, 45*(2). Article 2. https://doi.org/10.31341/jios.45.2.14

Chapter 8

Economic and Social Dimensions of Indian Trade Towards Transformation in the 21st Century

Vijay D. Joshi[a], Sukanta Kumar Baral[b] and Manish M. Pitke[c]

[a]Dr. Ambedkar Institute of Management Studies and Research (DAIMSR), India
[b]Indira Gandhi National Tribal University, India
[c]Prin. L. N. Welingkar Institute of Management Development & Research (WeSchool), India

Abstract

India is one of the world's largest exporters of products and services. Given the outstanding contribution of services in India's foreign trade, this study examines the changing international trade pattern for India. It is a nation that is heavily dependent on imports and exports. This study examines the changing international trade pattern for India with the existence of certain global disruptions. The analysis highlights a growing trade surplus in services and an increasing trade deficit (i.e. imports higher than exports) in goods. India needs to have policies in place to emerge as a strong economy in this post-pandemic era. This chapter provides a set of examples based on the research findings. The research suggests that the growing economy and supportive government policies offer greater opportunities for the country in the longer period if urgent policy initiatives and support are extended to existing and potential manufacturing and services sectors. It ultimately seeks to highlight key opportunities, challenges and suggestions to protect and promote India's international trade.

Keywords: Indian trade scenario; social dimensions of Indian trade; social inclusion; the economic aspect of the trade; job creation; impetus to local manufacturing; global trade opportunities

Creating Pathways for Prosperity, 117–134
doi:10.1108/978-1-83549-121-820241009

Introduction

The Covid-19 epidemic has rendered the current state of the world economy unworkable. Because services are interdependent and demand close closeness between the provider and the client, the lockdown mechanism and social distancing have created a dire scenario for international trade in general and services in particular.

Given the outstanding contribution of services in India's foreign trade, this study examines the changing international trade pattern for India. It ultimately seeks to highlight key opportunities, challenges and suggestions to protect and promote India's international trade with the existence of certain global disruptions. This chapter provides a set of examples based on the research findings.

The authors believe that a growing trade surplus in services and an increasing trade deficit (i.e. imports higher than exports) in goods. The growing trade surplus in services for India is not enough to cover the trade deficit in goods. This has taken a toll on the rupee. With the strengthening of the manufacturing sector, India will achieve a comparative edge in the trade of goods with the aim of 'becoming a manufacturing hub of the world'.

The research suggests that the growing economy and supportive government policies offer greater opportunities for the country in the longer period if urgent policy initiatives and support are extended to existing and potential manufacturing and services sectors.

In this context, Drishti (2022) elaborates on the free trade relations between India and the rest of the countries. Let us understand some of the relevant aspects. They are:

- The concept – Free Trade Agreement.
- India and FTAs.
- Other Trade Agreements of India.
- Some points to ponder regarding India's Foreign Trade Policy.

The Concept – Free Trade Agreement

A free trade agreement, sometimes known as an FTA, is an agreement between two or more countries to lower import and export restrictions. These are known as RTAs, or regional trade agreements, in the World Trade Organization (WTO). These are reciprocal trade agreements that liberalise tariffs and services between two or more countries. Free trade zones, customs unions and agreements on economic integration in the service sector are among them.

Under a free trade policy, there are few things to do for (any) government tariffs, quotas, subsidies or prohibitions that prevent the exchange of products and services across international borders. The idea of free trade is therefore against any kind of trade protectionism or economic sanctions.

India and FTAs

- After India decided to leave the Regional Comprehensive Economic Partnership (RCEP), a group of 15 FTA members that also included China, Australia and Japan, FTAs were put on hold.

- Inward arranging is in progress between India and the European Association to move these various work strands ahead. This is stated to have made some progress in the negotiations between India and the European Union in May 2021. Prior, in 2013 they stopped.
- India is right now arranging respective international alliances for certain nations. They are the United Kingdom, Canada, the United Arab Emirates and Australia. The agreement with the United Arab Emirates was 'near to finalisation', while the FTA with Australia was in the 'extremely advanced stage'.

Other Trade Agreements of India Are

- Asia Pacific Economic Deal (APTA): This was previously known as the Bangkok Agreement. A mechanism with a preferential tariff arrangement is this one. Through the exchange of concessions between member nations that have been mutually agreed upon, this aims to increase intra-regional trade.
- Preferential Trade Agreement with South Asia (SAPTA): It is for advancing exchange among the part nations that happened in 1995.
- A Comprehensive Economic Cooperation and Partnership Agreement (CECPA) is agreed upon by India and Mauritius.
- The South Asian Free Trade Area (SAFTA): By 2016, the agreement was signed to eliminate all customs duties on goods traded. It's a kind of goods-only FTA. Information technology services, for example are excluded from this FTA.

Some Points to Ponder regarding India's Foreign Trade Policy

- Unfeasible and Unfavourable FTAs: Over the previous 10 years, India has signed FTAs with some countries. To list a few are Malaysia, the Republic of Korea, Japan and the Association of Southeast Asian Nations (ASEAN). The consensus is that these agreements have benefited India's trading partners more than it has.
- Low contribution from the Manufacturing Sector: Manufacturing accounts for 14% of India's gross domestic product (GDP) in the most recent era. Comparable figures are 11%, 19%, 21% and 25% for advanced and developed countries like the United States, Germany, Japan and South Korea, respectively. The equivalent percentages for emerging and developing nations like Brazil, Russia, Turkey, Indonesia and China are 9%, 13%, 19%, 20% and 27%, respectively, while the share for low-income nations is 8%.
- Protectionism: The Atmanirbhar Bharat campaign has worsened the perception that India is turning into a more protectionist closed market economy.

Literature Review

According to the International Labour Organization (ILO), the social dimension of globalisation refers to how it affects people's personal and professional lives, as well as their families and societies. Issues and difficulties regarding how globalisation is affecting employment, working conditions, income and social protection are frequently brought up. In addition to the world of employment, the social dimension also includes family and community cohesion, security, culture and identity. ILO believes that there are more opportunities for growth and wealth generation arising as a result of international trade. This is resulting in regional economic cooperation and globalisation. In this context, generally, there are different views, opinions and perceptions about international trade and its economic and social effects. These effects have vastly diverse consequences on the possibilities and interests of various sectors of the economy as well as the social/cultural landscape. Some opinions believe that the current model of international trade supports globalisation. This has made issues with unemployment, inequality and poverty worse. On the other hand, some views suggest that international trade and globalisation helped in decreasing the extent of these issues. These issues undoubtedly existed before the start of international trade, but it is obvious that for them to be politically and economically viable, it must help to address them. Therefore, the aim of international trade is regional cooperation which satisfies everyone's needs (ILO, n.d.).

In his article, Akshat Khanduri talks about Indian trade and enlists some of the characteristics of the same. He says that the Indian trade has transformed over the years. In 2020, he estimates that trade in goods and services will total 650 billion US dollars between India and other nations (Khanduri, 2023). This is thought to be a significant characteristic that will propel India to lead the current economic order. He went on to say that in the 21st century, India has become the largest emerging power in the global economy. In a similar vein, India, a rapidly developing South Asian nation, has been compelled to swiftly adjust its trade policies as a result of the dynamic geopolitical environment. A major shift in policy has occurred, transitioning from a reliance on imports to a focus on nationalism and export-oriented values in India's trading system. The country's exchange strategy from 2015 to 2020 aims to maintain its presence in current business markets.

Trade Promotion Council of India says that Indian International Trade is governed and supported by the trade policy.

> India's Foreign Trade Policy also envisages helping exporters leverage benefits of GST (Goods and Service Tax), closely monitoring export performances, improving ease of trading across borders, increasing realization from India's agriculture-based exports and promoting exports from MSMEs (Micro, Small, and Medium Enterprise) and labour-intensive sectors. TPCI (2023)

'India is a good market and offers a good potential (for Australian businesses)', says the Department of Foreign Affairs and Trade, Government of Australia, according to their report. It also cautions that it is not an easy market (to penetrate) as it needs endurance (patience), a broader outlook (perspective) and groundwork (planning and preparation) (DFAT, 2018). The said report says, 'Change in India is often invisible to the naked eye'. Besides this, it is also commenting that the opening of the Indian economy is a good example. Because India's average applied tariff is today one-tenth what it was in 1990, this will offer a good opportunity for Australia to have a strategic partnership with India. Also, it was observed that here in India, the stock of inward foreign direct investment (FDI) has grown by approx. 20% on a year-to-year basis for the last 20 years.

In support of its strong democracy and reliable alliances, India has developed into a major economy with the highest rate of growth in the world, and it is anticipated that within the next 10–15 years, it will rank among the top three economic powers (IBEF). According to the study by the India Brand Equity Foundation (IBEF), exports are crucial for achieving (economic) growth. Exports fared extremely well throughout the pandemic and assisted recovery at a time when all other growth engines were losing steam in terms of their contribution to the GDP. Due to the slowing of some of India's trading partners' economies, future contributions from exports of products may vary. According to Mr Piyush Goyal, Minister of Trade and Industry, Consumer Affairs, Food and Public Distribution, and Textiles, Indian exports are expected to surpass US$ 1 trillion by 2030.

Government rules and regulations including trade policies are crucial in attracting global investments in today's dynamic global trade. Now, global manufacturers seek the stability of the policies in countries of location. It is time for India to learn and implement industry-friendly policies. With China losing the trust and confidence of the developed countries (as their factory), it is a good time for India to explore the opportunities created by the tricky global situations (Panagariya, 2022a).

According to economist Amita Batra, there is much to be prepared as India gradually expands its commercial horizons. According to her, any trade agreement should include features known as 'WTO plus' that go beyond tariff-based market access and take advantage of India's competitive advantage in services. Domestic reform is desperately required for those initiatives to succeed (Batra, 2022). Batra feels that to incorporate more easily 'behind the border' regulatory policies like trade facilitation, rules of origin, intellectual property, investment protection, e-commerce, competition policy, data, labour and the environment, India's trade policy must understand the 'WTO plus' provisions in the newer Free Trade Agreements (FTAs), which go beyond tariff-based market access. Domestic reform is desperately needed in each of these sectors.

Achieving economic growth for India will be an easy task if it follows financial discipline in terms of controlling the current account deficit (CAD) and maintaining a trade surplus periodically (i.e. exports more than imports). In the first quarter of 2022–2023, all the sectors of the economy contributed to the growth, although the services sector growth was particularly strong (Dutta, 2022, p. 15). In this context, the empowered manufacturing sector can provide enhancement to exports. With fiscal discipline, even a 6% rate of growth would put India at ease within the top of the pack of large economies.

Asian Development Bank (ADB) in one of its publications cites the association between poverty (reduction) and (international) trade. According to the publication by ADB, through the liberalisation of international trade, the poor can access a broader range of goods and services at lower prices, which raises real income and reduces poverty. Exchange development reality brings about two victories and failures. Trade can reduce relative poverty, absolute poverty, both or none at all, thereby assisting the poor, but typically to their advantage. By and large, the unfortunate benefit proportionately to the remainder of the populace from financial development is achieved by professional progression and transparency. In addition to affecting overall growth, trade openness has unintended effects on the poor, and there are many differences between countries and historical periods (ADB).

Similar views are echoed by the World Bank and the WTO in their joint publication (World Bank Group and World Trade Organization, 2018). By lowering the cost of the items, they acquire and boosting the cost of the goods they sell, trade can benefit the underprivileged. After trade opening, markets for both products and factors experience relative price shifts. These changes affect the household members who are both purchasers and sellers of products as well as producers of elements (such as labour). Inputs are used by the poor both as consumers and producers. Through commerce, they might have easier access to the labour, materials and technological advancements that boost productivity when producing the goods and services that the less fortunate produce. If trade liberalisation lowers the price of imported goods, it will benefit us as consumers. Salaries and employment as sources of income are both influenced by prices. As producers, the poor can gain by selling their output in overseas markets where they can get a better return.

There is proof that the US-Vietnam FTA has helped to eradicate poverty in Vietnam as an example of how underprivileged firms can benefit from trade. Families in the provinces that witnessed the biggest drops in export costs to the United States also saw the biggest drops in poverty (McCaig, 2011).

Benefits have also been given to those who labour in the informal sector, even though export prospects have promoted the reallocation of personnel from micro-enterprises to the formal sector (McCaig & Pavcnik, 2014).

The Indian economy is undergoing numerous changes. The Indian government is now attempting to establish the rupee as a medium of exchange for both capital and current trades through existing mutual agreements. In summarising this part, we may say that considering its current economic status, India is aiming to establish its supreme legacy not only in Asia but also globally (Khanduri, 2023). To comply with RBI regulations,

> Indian importers undertaking imports through this mechanism shall make payment in INR which shall be credited into the special Vostro account of the correspondent bank of the partner country, against the invoices for the supply of goods or services from the overseas seller/supplier. CNBC (2022)

Objectives

The objective of this research is to provide an overview of India's trade, understand its features and accordingly provide further implications considering the social and economic impact of the same.

Analysis

India is considered an import-sensitive economy with more imports than exports. This has resulted in a trade deficit over the years.

India's Trade Deficit (Import–Export) Scenario for the Last Few Months

Here we are talking about the imports and exports over the last few months for India. Oil prices are one of the key factors that affect imports and exports in the last few months (see Table 8.1).

It is observed that exports increased to US$38.2 billion in April 2022, driven by a surge in international oil prices. This has also impacted imports which have grown to US$ 58.3 billion in April 2022. It may be noted that oil is the main commodity of India's import basket followed by gold. In October 2022, exports contracted and imports grew at their slowest pace in the last 21 months, widening the trade deficit.

India's Imports and Exports Composition (TD, 2022c)

As shown in Table 8.1, it is observed that exports from India fell to US$ 29.8 billion in October 2022 from US$ 35.4 billion in November 2022 (i.e. the previous month).

In recent years, India exported mostly: Jewellery, precious/semi-precious stones and pearls (16% of total shipments); mineral fuels, oils waxes and bituminous substances (12%); vehicles, parts and accessories (5%); nuclear reactors, boilers, machinery and mechanical appliances (5%); pharmaceutical products (5%); and organic chemicals (4%).

Table 8.1. Trade Deficit – Indian Scenario in the Last Few Months (TD, 2022a, 2022b, 2022c).

	In US$ Billion		
Description	**Imports**	**Exports**	**Trade Deficit**
October 2021	53.6	35.7	−17.9
November 2021	52.9	30.0	−22.9
December 2021	59.3	37.3	−22.0
January 2022	52.0	34.1	−17.9
February 2022	55.5	34.6	−20.9
March 2022	60.7	42.2	−18.5
April 2022	58.3	38.2	−20.1
May 2022	60.6	37.3	−23.3
September 2022	61.1	35.4	−25.7
October 2022	56.7	29.8	−26.9

Source: Compiled by the authors.

As shown in Table 8.1, it is observed that imports to India declined to US$ 56.7 billion in October 2022 from US$ 61.1 billion in November 2022 (i.e. the previous month).

In recent years, India mainly imports these commodities: mineral fuels, oils and waxes and bituminous substances (27% of total imports); Jewellery, precious/ semi-precious stones and pearls (14%); electrical machinery and equipment (10%); nuclear reactors, boilers, machinery and mechanical appliances (8%); and organic chemicals (4%).

Yearly, it is observed that India is showing a trend towards increasing oil and gold imports. India's imports of crude (share in total) are shown in Table 8.2 (Crude, 2022).

India's Trade Balance – Merchandise (Goods) and Services

Here we are talking about the trade balance of merchandise (goods) and services. India's trade balance for merchandise and services is shown in Table 8.3 (TBMS, 2022).

Table 8.2. India's Import of Crude (Share in Total) in % (Crude, 2022).

Year	Share in %
2016–2017	26.8%
2017–2018	28.4%
2018–2019	32.7%
2019–2020	32.4%
2020–2021	25.3%
2021–2022	31.8%
2022–2023* *Approx.	40.5%

Source: Compiled by the authors.

Table 8.3. India's Trade Balance – Merchandise and Services (TBMS, 2022).

Year	Net Services Trade (US$ Billion)	Net Merchandise Trade (US$ Billion)
2007–2008	39	−91
2012–2013	65	−196
2016–2017	67	−112
2020–2021	89	−102
2021–2022	108	−189

Source: Compiled by the authors.

India's Trading Partners

International trade is characterised by imports and exports between countries. At present, some of the leading countries among India's top-10 trading partners are the United States, China, the United Arab Emirates, Saudi Arabia and Iraq (Trade, 2022a). Other countries include Singapore, Hong Kong, Indonesia, South Korea and Australia (see Table 8.4).

It will be interesting to note that (after the start of the Russia-Ukraine conflict), India's imports from Russia increased substantially. It is mainly driven by a surge in oil imports. Thus, in this financial year (for the first 6 months, April–September), Russia has emerged as India's fifth-largest trading partner. Its position improved from the 25th place at the end of last financial year (Trade, 2022b) as indicated by the official data (see Table 8.5). This aspect is elaborated subsequently.

India's Trade to Gross Domestic Product (GDP) Ratio

Here we are considering another perspective of international trade from the point of giving a boost to local manufacturing activity. Another aspect here in the context of achieving trade sustainability is the vulnerability of the country to the global recession. This is the trade intensity aspect (which means the trade-to-GDP ratio) and is particularly important for the manufacturing sector. Consider this,

Table 8.4. India's Top-10 Trading Partners in Fiscal Year (FY) 2022 (Trade, 2022a).

Country	Total Merchandise Trade (in US $ Billion)				
	2017–2018	2018–2019	2019–2020	2020–2021	2021–2022
The United States	74.5	88.0	88.9	80.5	119.4
China	89.7	87.1	81.8	86.4	115.5
The United Arab Emirates	49.9	59.9	59.1	43.3	72.9
Saudi Arabia	27.5	34.0	33.1	22.0	42.9
Iraq	19.1	24.2	25.6	15.4	34.3
Singapore	17.7	27.8	23.7	22.0	30.1
Hong Kong	25.4	31.0	27.9	25.3	30.1
Indonesia	20.4	21.2	19.2	17.5	26.2
South Korea	20.8	21.5	20.5	17.5	25.5
Australia	18.0	16.7	12.6	12.3	25.0

Source: Compiled by the authors.

Table 8.5. India's Top Five Trade Partners (April–September) (Trade, 2022b).

April–September	Total Merchandise Trade (in US $ Billion)		
	2021	2022	% Change
The United States	56.4	67.7	20%
China	54.7	60.2	10.1%
The United Arab Emirates	33.4	44.5	33.2%
Saudi Arabia	17.2	28.7	66.9%
Russia	5.8	22.6	289.7%

Source: Compiled by the authors.

Table 8.6. Trade-to-GDP Ratio (TGR) for Select Countries (Thakur, 2022).

Country	Nominal GDP ($ Trillion)	Trade (as % of GDP)
The United States	25.35	23.4%
China	19.91	37.4%
Japan	4.91	31.4%
Germany	4.26	89.4%
India	3.53	43.7%
The United Kingdom	3.38	55.2%
France	2.94	62.0%
Canada	2.22	61.2%
Italy	2.06	63.1%
Brazil	1.83	39.2%

Source: Compiled by the authors.

despite being the largest economy in the world, the United States has a Trade-to-GDP ratio (TGR) of just 23.4% (Thakur, 2022) (see Table 8.6). This is because of its large domestic market.

It is seen that most of the US's goods, including oil, are consumed within the country. This aspect is valid for India too and accordingly, the authorities must take steps to increase the domestic consumption of goods. For this, it requires strengthening the domestic manufacturing sector. Even though currently India has a higher ratio (43.7%), it can achieve trade-related sustainability by achieving a reduction in the same. In the case of China, the reduction in its TGR is attributed to the size of the economy and the large population. However, things are not good for Western European countries, as they remain vulnerable to the global recession due to their higher TGRs.

Findings

India's Trade Deficit Scenario for the Last Few Months

In this context, government sources said that an increasing trade deficit is expected in the coming months of Fiscal Year (FY) 2023 unless the commodity prices are reduced to reasonable levels.

India's Imports and Exports

Oil and gold made up 41% of India's total imports (27% oil, 14% gold) in 2016–2017. This has increased to 45% in 2021–2022, and in April–July this year (in 2022) their combined share may reach 52% (40% oil, 11% gold) (Crude, 2022).

India's Trade Balance – Merchandise (Goods) and Services

India has seen a steady increase in its trade deficit in goods over the past 15 years. Specifically, the trade deficit in goods, which is calculated as imports minus exports, has more than doubled from US$ 91 billion in 2007–2008 to US$ 196 billion in 2012–2013.

India's Trading Partners

Some changes occurred in (International) Trade Relationships between India and other countries (Trade, 2022a). It was observed that during the last 5 years (i.e. from 2017–2018 to 2021–2022), India's merchandise trade partners have consolidated themselves. The United States has beaten China to emerge as India's largest trading partner in 2021–2022. This is the position that the United States has occupied during 3 of the last 5 years.

India's Trade to GDP Ratio

In 1990, total trade as a proportion of the GDP for India was around 13%. Today it is more than 40% (DFAT, 2018).

Indian economy is more dependent on global trade than Chinese and the United States. Despite being the largest trade partners for most of the countries, China and the United States also have high domestic markets to reduce (their) exposure to global tremors. The two largest economies – the United States and China have become less global in the past decade. China's TGR has slipped from over 50% (in 2011) to about 37% (in 2021), according to the data provided by the World Bank. In the case of the United States, it has dropped from 30% to 25% (TGR, 2023).

Conclusion

India's Trade Deficit Scenario for the Last Few Months

India's trade deficit is governed by the extent of imports. Thus, prices of petroleum products or oil commodities will influence the trade balance. There is a need to decrease imports (and increase exports).

In this context, government sources said that an increasing trade deficit is expected in the coming months of FY 2023 unless the commodity prices are reduced to reasonable levels.

India's Imports and Exports Composition

Oil and gold are the major commodities in India's import basket. Price fluctuations in these commodities will have some effect on international trade.

As shown in Table 8.2, oil and gold are the major commodities of import. In this context, India needs to formulate policies for reducing oil imports. Accordingly, India needs to find alternative sources of supply for the same or make arrangements to produce here to be self-reliant (or Atmanirbhar). India can take a step towards becoming a green economy.

India might learn from Kazakhstan how to make the switch to green energy. The oil-rich nation intends to export green hydrogen soon (Lillis, 2022). Western Kazakhstan aspires to take the lead among clean energy exporters worldwide. The area is well known for its oil and gas resources. In this regard, the President's office on 27 October 2022 stated that the government has inked a US$50 billion agreement with the European renewables company Svevind to construct one of the five largest green hydrogen production plants in the world in the Mangystau Region.

The European Union is pressing ahead to establish collaborations with developing economies/nations on hydrogen and clean technology, starting with Kazakhstan (Romano, 2022), as UN climate talks came to an end in the Egyptian resort city of Sharm-El-Sheikh.

India must implement strategic measures to facilitate its shift from a fossil fuel-dependent economy to a more sustainable one. It is crucial to prioritize the adoption of circular economy practices by designating specific areas or zones for environmentally-friendly businesses. 'India can lead the way in accelerating the progress towards a less-competitive, healthier, and prosperous world', says Bill Gates. Gates believes in India's commitment to reducing carbon emissions (Gates, 2022). While it is required (for the world) to have groundbreaking technologies to prevent any climate disaster, (at the same time) (some countries) individuals must step forward to show that climate change is important. Policies should encourage the manufacturing industry as it has a contribution to the GDP besides employment generation. Social inclusion of low-income people should also be considered.

Emphasis on 'Make in India' or local manufacturing aimed at providing products to global markets. This will generate jobs and it will add to the GDP and thereby growth of the economy. Social and financial inclusion are the other goals to meet with the help of this local manufacturing – Make in India campaign. With China losing its trust in the West and other countries, India must look to become the 'Production hub of the World'. Soumya Kanti Ghosh believes that the news is good for India. With the GDP levels reaching the pre-Covid-19 stage, the economy is set to grow and will enter a good phase in the medium term (Manufacturing, 2022). The pandemic has changed the plans and expectations (of some countries) and one of the beneficiaries of that could be India. Just have a look at this – the latest iPhone 14 manufacturing plant is at Chennai – Foxconn facility. The large quantity of orders that it has got is a clear indication that India is finally making its presence felt. It is included in the China plus one manufacturing plans of the multinational corporation (MNCs). There is no dearth of opportunities here if it is nurtured, boosted and supported systematically. India's status as a preferred supplier to the world in the global supply chain can range across commodities – from chips to coal.

With regards to gold imports, it is suggested that the Government of India in association with the Reserve Bank of India (RBI) may work on the 'Gold Monetisation Scheme'. This may involve the common man or citizen of India. The scheme would encourage keeping certain minimum gold deposits with the Government of India and these are backed by the security and bank guarantee. The availability of gold from the domestic market will reduce gold import to some extent, as the scheme achieves more acceptability.

India's Trade Balance – Merchandise (Goods) and Services

India's trade deficit in goods has been growing over the years. However, after reaching US\$ 196 billion in 2012–2013, it declined slowly to US\$ 112 billion by 2016–2017 – the year of demonetisation. It is observed that except for the lockdown years, when the trade deficit fell due to reduced trade, it has again increased. This indicates that to achieve a trade surplus, the nation needs to export more goods, which means producing more goods and consuming more too.

The analysis highlights a growing trade surplus in services and an increasing trade deficit (i.e. imports higher than exports) in goods. The growing trade surplus in services for India is not enough to cover the trade deficit in goods. This has taken a toll on the rupee. However, when looked at from another perspective, it calls for the strengthening of the domestic manufacturing sector. By doing this, India will achieve a comparative edge in the trade of goods with the aim of 'becoming a manufacturing hub of the world'.

India's Trading Partners

It was observed that during 2017–2018 to 2021–2022, India's merchandise trade partners remained the same. The United States has beaten China to emerge as India's largest trading partner in 2021–2022. This is the position that the United States has occupied during 3 of the last 5 years (Trade, 2022a). If we consider top-10 trading partners, then in FY 2021–2022, Germany is out of this list. India's trade with Iraq and Australia has doubled, whereas there is no European country as a trading partner.

Have a look at the scenario of the Trading Partners of India in FY 2022. As shown in Tables 8.4 and 8.5, all of these allies are important to India given the quantum of trade and mutual benefits arising from this trade. Accordingly, India needs to formulate strategies for its trade allies. Judicious use of foreign trade agreements (FTAs) will be the key to success for India in making it sustainable in international trade.

India's Trade to GDP Ratio

India's TGR was more than 45% in FY 2022, higher than the United States and China. In the pre-liberalisation era, India was less integrated with the world economy. This has made the Indian economy less sensitive to the global financial crisis. However, that has changed in recent years, though the degree or the extent of globalisation (for India) is lower than large European economies such as Germany and France. This is mainly due to the European Union's unified trade regime (TGR, 2023).

The analysis of India's TGR highlights the fact that the denominator (i.e. the GDP) needs to be increased and the numerator (i.e. the imports) needs to be decreased to get a reasonable TGR. This indicates that to increase the GDP, there must be an emphasis on manufacturing (local production) which may result in increased consumption and exports. As a result, this will achieve a trade surplus, indicating that the nation needs to export more goods, which means producing more goods and consuming more too.

This aspect of emphasis on local manufacturing is also always in the talks with the government authorities. Recently, our Hon. Finance Minister (FM) hinted at this aspect to achieve an increase in the GDP. The FM hailed the contribution from the start-ups and start-up ecosystem and asked the manufacturing sector to work together (with them) (mfg, 2022a, p. 11). FM said, '*I would urge the industry to keep a close watch on the innovations coming from the start-ups. The manufacturing sector can benefit from the new energy of the start-ups*'. Further, FM added that the path of Indian industry will be enriched by government policy and the government has taken several measures to attract investments in the manufacturing sector. This includes the production-linked-incentive (PLI) scheme.

Echoing the same opinion, Hindustan Unilever (HUL) CEO and MD, Sanjeev Mehta, presented a joint report on the way forward for India and priorities to the government recently. This report was having proposed plans to establish incubation centres in three states to boost innovations in renewable energy, electric vehicles and water. Mr Mehta said the manufacturing sector will play a key role in maintaining the growth rate of the Indian economy at 7.7% for the next two decades. He urged the government to extend the tax sops for the new manufacturing units (mfg, 2022b, p. 11). According to him, it should be extended for another 5 years because investors always look at the solid foundation on which the policies are based. This is a pivotal moment for the Indian manufacturing sector as many foreign investors are (now) looking at alternatives to China.

It is urgently necessary to develop the industrial sector, particularly in the post-Covid-19 period. After the Russia-Ukraine war, India must have a clearly defined plan of action for the future (Rangarajan, 2022). India's effort to reach a US$5 trillion GDP will unquestionably be driven by the manufacturing sector. According to Dr C. Rangarajan, the former Governor of the Reserve Bank of India, this would be a good short-term aspirational objective given that policy-makers' primary concern will be accelerating economic development. In addition to aiding in job creation, the manufacturing sector will support maintaining consistent growth of 8%–9% throughout the next 10 years.

Implications

Economic Implications

According to a report by Morgan Stanley, the contribution from the manufacturing sector to GDP (in India) could increase from 15.6% currently to 21% by 2031. This can be achievable by encouraging domestic manufacturing, and by achieving a trade surplus. The creation of well-paying jobs for the public is the main economic problem that India faces constantly. This problem calls for more industrial success than has hitherto been the case. Manufacturing is what turns unskilled labourers into semi-skilled, semi-skilled labourers into skilled labourers and skilled labourers into even more skilled labourers. India's industrial sector is crucial to the country's ability to expand economically (Panagariya, 2022a).

According to Batra, services, which are India's strength, should be a significant part of any trade agreement rather than being covered separately because such trade-investment-services ties are engrained in Global Value Chains (GVCs). Because FTAs are designed to facilitate GVC integration with long-term advantages, a trade imbalance need not be problematic. Given the growing integration of services into manufacturing, India must look beyond the limited 'Mode 4 perspective' (Batra, 2022).

It was also suggested that India can attempt to establish cooperation and integration with the 'Factory of Asia', the developed nations in East and Southeast Asia (Batra, 2022). For this, it is required to establish and strengthen India's economic cooperation with the nearby GVC industry groups in East and Southeast Asia. In this context, India may re-evaluate or assess its decision to stay away from the Regional Comprehensive Economic Partnership (RECP). It may be noted that biases about India in the minds of the governments of advanced economies and multinational corporations need to be removed. A strong trade policy with vision and focus can do this. With this strong mechanism put in place, other countries will be in a position to choose India's sizeable market as their preferred alternative for the 'China plus one' plan. Uncertainty in India's discretionary tariff policy may cause investors to reconsider their alternatives and move their money to more stable nations like Vietnam, Thailand, Bangladesh, etc. Moreover, industrialised nations can re-establish domestic production facilities by adding artificial intelligence (AI) and machine learning, industrial robots, 3D technologies, etc.

The integration with GVCs (as indicated by Batra) is on a long-term basis and is aimed at achieving both economic prosperity and supported social inclusion. By doing this, India is predicted to have an imaginative strategy for creating employment (job creation) and economic growth. This is particularly valid in this post-pandemic era. India enjoyed the benefits of the economic boom in the post-1991 period due to its liberalised policies oriented at the reforms. To place the developing India in the 21st century, it is time to revamp India's trade policy.

Social Implications

As stated in section 2 earlier, the social implication of trade is beyond achieving economic growth. This is all about the financial inclusion of low-income workers from sectors such as agriculture and village, cottage industries and household enterprises. In the case of India, no efforts have been made to transform these unskilled workers into skilled ones. Just like what South Korea and China did, India now must help its labour-intensive industries to rise rapidly. It is observed that the most abundant resource is not used and is kept away from making any contribution to (economic) growth and (social) development. Now, it is important that as India grows with say 6%–8% in the economic domain, it must take help from the social domain. It is important to recognise that (social) inclusion is integral to achieving this (economic) progress. Only then India would be able to focus on the policies evenly that would help labour-intensive industries such as apparel, footwear, furniture and other light manufacturing goods grow smoothly. Let us begin by asking (the question) of why multinationals invest in the apparel sector in Vietnam and Bangladesh but not India (Panagariya, 2022b).

India needs to have policies in place to emerge as a strong economy in this post-pandemic era. The government authorities must ensure that the policy initiatives maintain the essential balance between aspirations of speedy (economic) growth, and inclusive social development and job creation. In other words, we can say that India can make strides towards poverty alleviation through suitable future-driven policies, programmes and platforms. This will certainly ensure India's long-term position as a strong and inclusive economy (in the world) with an enhanced rate of employment generation and employment providers (Iyer, 2023, p. 15).

The authors believe that international trade is one of the measures to increase regional cooperation for achieving economic growth as well as social development goals. As stated by the World Bank Group (WBG), it helps its client countries improve their access to developed country markets and enhance their participation in the world economy. The global trading system needs to be strengthened in this situation, according to WBG, to assist developing nations with addressing trade-related growth constraints. The global trade regime's foundations, which are crucial for ensuring trade predictability but have been shaken, need to be reformed because of this. The World Bank Group (WBG) says that the combination of sustainability standards and an open trade policy will be a problem. To ensure that the new guidelines apply to them, developing nations will need to participate. According to WBG, the advancement of sustainable economic growth and the promotion of international trade are not mutually exclusive; rather, they may even work in tandem (WBG, 2022). Global skill shortages are affecting, which can limit the economic benefits of intelligent technology (Baral et al., 2022).

The authors would like to conclude this manuscript/chapter with this quote from the WBG – *'Trade is an engine of growth that creates jobs, reduces poverty, and increases economic opportunity'*. (WBG, 2022)

References

ADB. (2003, July). *Trade and poverty: What are the connections?* Asian Development Bank. https://www.adb.org/publications/trade-and-poverty-what-are-connections#

Baral, S. K., Rath, R. C., Goel, R., & Singh, T. (2022). Role of digital technology and artificial intelligence for monitoring talent strategies to bridge the skill gap. In *International mobile and embedded technology conference (MECON)* (pp. 582–587). https://doi.org/10.1109/MECON53876.2022.9751837

Batra, A. (2022, August 25). *India's trade policy in the 21st century.* Gateway House. https://www.gatewayhouse.in/indias-trade-policy-in-the-21st-century/#

CNBC. (2022, November 9). The rupee gets a boost as govt allows foreign trade payments in INR for export promotion schemes. https://www.cnbctv18.com/economy/rupee-gets-a-boost-as-govt-allows-foreign-trade-payments-in-inr-for-export-promotion-schemes-15128281.htm

Crude. (2022, August 30). Increasing oil, gold imports. *Times of India,* Pune edition, 12.

DFAT. (2018). A report prepared by the Department of Foreign Affairs and Trade; Government of Australia titled "An India Economic Strategy to 2035 – Navigating from Potential to Delivery". https://www.dfat.gov.au/publications/trade-and-investment/india-economic-strategy/ies/overview.html

Drishti. (2022). India & free trade agreements by Drishti IAS. https://www.drishtiias.com/daily-updates/daily-news-analysis/india-free-trade-agreements#

Dutta, B. (2022, December 30). Economy 2023: 6% is pretty good. *Times of India,* Pune edition, 15.

Gates, B. (2022, October 7). At the G20, India can show the way. *Times of India,* Pune edition, 12.

IBEF. (2022, December). About Indian economy, growth rate and others. https://www.ibef.org/economy/indian-economy-overview

ILO. (n.d.). *The social dimension of trade and globalization.* International Labour Organization. https://www.ilo.org/public/english/wcsdg/globali/globali.htm

Iyer, P. (2023, January 9). Gig jobs, green jobs.... *Times of India,* Pune edition, 15.

Khanduri, A. (2023, February 21). Transformation of the Indian trade policy. https://www.linkedin.com/pulse/transformation-indian-trade-policy-akshat-khanduri

Lillis, J. (2022, October 28). *Kazakhstan: Oil-rich west to become green hydrogen hub.* EurasiaNet.

Manufacturing. (2022, September 2). We are back to the future. Article by Soumya Kanti Ghosh. *Times of India*, Pune edition, 10.

McCaig, B. (2011). Exporting out of poverty: Provincial poverty in Vietnam and the US market access. *Journal of International Economics, 85*(1), 102–113.

McCaig, B., & Pavcnik, N. (2014). *Export markets and labor reallocation in a low-income country.* NBER Working Paper No. 20455.

mfg. (2022a, December 17). FM asks India Inc. to focus on manufacturing and learn from the start-ups. *Times of India*, Pune edition, 11.

mfg. (2022b, December 17). Extend tax sops to new manufacturing units: HUL CEO. *Times of India*, Pune edition, 11.

Panagariya. (2022a, December 25). Five big questions for the year ahead: As China, the factory of the world, loses dominance, can India benefit (from the same)? Article by Arvind Panagariya. *Times of India*, Pune edition, 13.

Panagariya. (2022b, November 29). What does inclusion being key to growth mean? Article by Arvind Panagariya. *Times of India*, Pune edition, 13.

Rangarajan, C. (2022, December 24). India will take 20 years, 8%–9% growth to become a developed nation: Rangarajan. *Business Standard*, 14.

Romano, V. (2022, November 8). *EU signs 'strategic partnership' with Kazakhstan on green hydrogen, raw materials.* EURACTIV.com.

TBMS. (2022, July 30). A trade deficit is rising. *Times of India*, Pune edition, 11.

TD. (2022a, June 3). Record trade deficit due to import surge in May. Times News Network. *Times of India*, Pune edition, 13.

TD. (2022b, November 16). Exports shrink as the trade deficit expands to US$27Bn in October 2022. Times News Network. *Times of India*, Pune edition, 14.

TD. (2022c, November 18). Exports and imports data (monthly and quarterly) as available from the Ministry of Commerce, Government of India for the period January 2022 to October 2022. Times News Network. *Times of India*, Pune edition, 10.

TGR. (2023, February 2). India has a higher trade-to-GDP ratio (than China and the US). *Times of India*, Pune edition, 9.

Thakur, A. (2022, August 6). Why the US economy's jitters should worry India? *Times of India*, Pune edition, 10.

TPCI. (2023). India's trade overview and trade policy. https://www.tpci.in/research_report/indias-foreign-trade-policy/

Trade. (2022a, May 30). India's Trade Partners. As provided by the Ministry of Commerce, Govt. of India. *Times of India*, Pune edition, 13.

Trade. (2022b, November 17). Russia is the 5th largest trade partner, jumps from 25th. *Times of India*, Pune edition, 10.

WBG. (2022, April 4). *Trade overview.* The World Bank Group. https://www.worldbank.org/en/topic/trade/overview#

World Bank Group and World Trade Organization. (2018). *Trade and poverty reduction: New Evidence of impacts in developing countries.* World Trade Organization.

Chapter 9

Economic Perspectives on Poverty: Analysing Its Measurement Across Different Economics and Contexts

Vijay Prakash Gupta

Institute of Business Management, G.L.A University, India

Abstract

This chapter investigates the multifaceted nature of poverty, which strips individuals of basic necessities like food, clothing, healthcare, education and sanitation, presenting itself differently across regions and time periods. Each nation sets its poverty standards, impacting its economy through increased healthcare expenses, limited educational access and insufficient services. Poverty, coupled with isolation, lack of education and illness, presents a formidable societal challenge. Despite advancements in poverty measurement and analysis, the World Bank Group continues to refine indicators for its complex dimensions. This chapter conducts a comprehensive exploration of poverty in India and globally, examining its significance, root causes, assessment methods and various initiatives for its alleviation across sectors and economies. Employing rigorous analytical techniques, including secondary data, published reports and international case studies, the author offers a holistic perspective on poverty in developing nations, delving into diverse statistical approaches and strategies used by countries. The resulting findings provide readers with a deep understanding of poverty-related concepts, highlighting real-world causes and consequences, particularly within the context of India. This knowledge proves invaluable to individuals, decision-makers, government entities, researchers and industries that rely on poverty indices for informed planning and the pursuit of sustainable development.

Keywords: Poverty; poverty line; income inequality; Human Development Index (HDI); international poverty comparisons

Creating Pathways for Prosperity, 135–150

Copyright © 2025 Vijay Prakash Gupta

Published under exclusive licence by Emerald Publishing Limited

doi:10.1108/978-1-83549-121-820241010

Introduction

Poverty is a multifaceted issue that includes a lack of food, shelter, healthcare, education and clean water. It impacts people worldwide from various backgrounds. The World Bank and United Nations Development Programme (UNDP) measure poverty differently. It is a complex concept that measures a person, household or community's deprivation. It is a situation, where people are not having enough money to meet their necessities of life. A person who is in the poverty bracket is unable to access clean water, healthy food, education or medical care, etc. It has been found that many people are unable to access their basic needs due to their social, gender, race and regional background. Sometimes economic shocks, medical issues and unemployment also caused poverty. It has been observed that poor people generally indulged in antisocial activities and crime, which is a very serious concern for any nation to kerb it.

The World Bank defines severe poverty as the proportion of people living on less than $1.90 per day. In 2020, 9.2%, or 703 million people, lived in severe poverty, according to the World Bank (2020).

The UNDP's multidimensional poverty index (MPI) considers health, education and living situations. In 2020, 17.2% of the world's population – 1.3 billion – lived in multidimensional poverty, according to the UNDP (2020). The Sustainable Development Goals (SDGs), set by the UN to end all kinds of poverty by 2030, have made progress lately, but more needs to be done.

Current Trends of Poverty

Poverty is complex and quantifiable. The poverty line – the income threshold below which a person or family is considered poor – is a common statistic. Poverty also includes a lack of food, water, healthcare, education and job. The 2019 global poverty rate was 9.2%, down from 36% in 1990. However, the COVID-19 pandemic is reversing decades of poverty alleviation.

Comparing global poverty trends:

Sub-Saharan Africa: Over 40% of sub-Saharan Africans live in terrible poverty. The COVID-19 pandemic will push 32 million people into extreme poverty by 2020.

South Asia: South Asia has reduced poverty from 44.2% in 1990 to 15.7% in 2019. However, the COVID-19 pandemic had driven 52 million people into severe poverty by 2020.

East Asia and the Pacific: East Asia and the Pacific's poverty rate has reduced from 60% in 1990 to 2.1% in 2019, making it one of the most effective areas in poverty reduction. The COVID-19 epidemic, on the other hand, has had a catastrophic impact on the area, with an estimated 38 million people forced into extreme poverty by 2020.

Latin America and the Caribbean: Latin American and Caribbean poverty dropped from 42.8% in 1990 to 21.7% in 2019. However, the COVID-19 pandemic had driven 28 million people into severe poverty by 2020.

Middle East and North Africa: The Middle East and North Africa poverty rate fell from 8.6% in 1990 to 3.7% in 2019. However, conflicts and political uncertainty have caused significant poverty in the area.

- In 2020, the COVID-19 pandemic drove 120 million people into abject poverty. The pandemic has disproportionately afflicted women, children and the poor.
- Poverty remains a severe concern in many regions of the world, and the COVID-19 epidemic threatens to overturn decades of gains in poverty reduction. Continued efforts to eliminate poverty and promote inclusive and sustainable development are critical.
- Poverty is a persistent problem in many areas of the world, with terrible consequences for people, families and entire communities. Here are some current trends in poverty worldwide:
- Global poverty is decreasing. According to the World Bank, global poverty fell from 36% in 1990 to 8.6% in 2018. However, certain regions and nations remain impoverished.
- COVID-19 enhanced poverty. Global poverty rates are affected by COVID-19. According to the World Bank, the pandemic may push 150 million people into extreme poverty by 2021.
- Poverty disproportionately impacts women. In 9 out of 10 single-parent households, women are poorer than men.
- Rural poverty persists. Rural areas are often poorer due to limited resources and economic opportunities. The World Bank estimates that 80% of the impoverished live in rural areas.
- Child poverty is severe. UNICEF reports that one in six children lives in severe poverty.

Sustainable Development Goals and Poverty

The 2030 Agenda for Sustainable Development's 17 SDGs were agreed by the UN in 2015. SDG 1: 'End poverty in all its manifestations worldwide'.

To attain this aim, the SDGs set a series of targets that focus on eliminating poverty, decreasing inequality and encouraging inclusive economic growth. Some of the primary goals include.

- Food, water and healthcare for everybody.
- Providing quality jobs and economic possibilities for everybody.
- Offering social safety and support for the most disadvantaged groups.
- Expanding education and training to develop sustainable livelihoods.
- Improving the resilience of individuals and communities to economic, environmental and social shocks.

The SDGs recognise that poverty involves access to basic services, social isolation and vulnerability to environmental and economic shocks. Thus, the SDGs emphasise tackling several aspects of poverty at once.

Sustainable development must combine economic growth, social inclusion and environmental protection to end poverty. This means addressing poverty and injustice and promoting equitable and sustainable development. Governments, civic society, businesses and people must work together to achieve the SDGs.

SDG and Poverty Goals

Poverty eradication remains a major challenge. Even though extreme poverty was reduced by more than half between 1990 and 2015, too many people still struggle for basic human needs.

736 million people lived on less than $1.90 a day in 2015, many without food, water or sanitation. Despite inequality, rapid growth in China and India has lifted millions out of poverty. Since women have lower wages, education and property ownership, they are more likely to be in poverty.

South Asia and Sub-Saharan Africa, where 80% of the poor live, have also made little improvement. Climate change, war and food insecurity make poverty reduction even more urgent. SDGs seek to end all types of poverty by 2030.

Poverty Rates of the Top 20 Nations of the World

Based on the World Bank's 2020 estimates of the people living below the poverty line (set at $1.90 per day), the top 20 countries' poverty rates are shown in Table 9.1.

Table 9.1. World Bank's 2020: Estimates of the Top 20 Countries' Poverty Rates for People Living Below the Poverty Line.

Rank	Country	Poverty Rate	Rank	Country	Poverty Rate
1	Madagascar	75.4%	11	Malawi	47.9%
2	Central African Republic	70.7%	12	Togo	46.5%
3	Burundi	65.6%	13	Ethiopia	44.9%
4	Mozambique	63.7%	14	Guinea	43.7%
5	South Sudan	58.7%	15	Eritrea	41.9%
6	Sierra Leone	58.1%	16	Yemen	40.0%
7	Afghanistan	56.3%	17	Burkina Faso	40.0%
8	Niger	55.4%	18	Rwanda	38.4%
9	Liberia	50.9%	19	Haiti	38.2%
10	Guinea-Bissau	49.2%	20	Democratic Republic of Congo	37.8%

Source: World Bank. 'Poverty headcount ratio at $1.90 a day (2011 PPP) (% of the population)'. Data accessed on 16 February 2023, from https://data.worldbank.org/indicator/SI.POV.DDAY

Different Approaches to Poverty

Poverty is a complex issue that must be addressed in a multifaceted manner. There are numerous approaches to poverty, and different organisations and governments frequently prioritise different strategies based on their priorities and resources. Here are some popular approaches to poverty.

- *An approach based on charity:* This approach entails providing aid to those in need, such as food, shelter and other necessities. This approach is frequently used in emergencies or to provide immediate relief to poor individuals and communities.
- *Empowerment-based approach:* This approach focuses on developing individuals' and communities' capacity to lift themselves out of poverty. This can include providing education and training, as well as access to financial resources and other opportunities for skill development and the development of sustainable livelihoods.
- *An approach based on human rights:* This strategy addresses structural poverty factors such as discrimination, injustice and lack of resources and services. This strategy prioritises safeguarding and advancing impoverished people's human rights.
- *Sustainable development approach:* Promotes economic growth, social inclusion and environmental sustainability to reduce poverty over time. This method addresses poverty, climate change, economic inequality and social exclusion via integrated and sustainable development solutions.
- *Participatory approach:* This approach involves involving poor people as active participants in the development process. Involving them in decision-making, community organising and advocacy efforts, as well as empowering them to take ownership of their development, can all contribute to this.

Types of Monetary Poverty

Absolute Poverty

Absolute poverty occurs when an individual or family lacks the minimum income, basic needs and resources needed to live comfortably in their community. This means individuals lack food, shelter and healthcare and cannot meet their basic human requirements.

Relative Poverty

Relative poverty, on the other hand, is living below the cultural or communal average. The individual or family may have food, shelter, and healthcare, but they may struggle to meet other social needs like education, transportation and entertainment.

It is important to note that the border between absolute and relative poverty is not always clear-cut since expectations for a decent quality of life vary greatly between communities and time. However, discrimination, lack of social support and restricted social and economic mobility may lead to poverty.

Static Poverty

Static poverty studies assess current poverty in a population. These studies often utilise cross-sectional data to assess the prevalence of poverty at a certain period in time, and they may look at factors like income, education, job status and other demographic factors to detect patterns in poverty.

Dynamic Poverty

Dynamic studies of poverty, on the other hand, seek to comprehend how poverty evolves through time. These studies employ longitudinal data to follow individuals and families over time to determine the variables that cause people to go into and out of poverty, as well as the duration and frequency of poverty spells. Dynamic studies may also investigate how poverty interacts with other life events such as job loss, sickness or the creation of a family.

Transversal Poverty

Transversal poverty, also known as cross-sectional poverty, is defined as poverty quantified at a specific point in time, frequently using a snapshot technique. It gives a comprehensive picture of poverty levels and features for a certain community or group at a specific point in time. This sort of poverty study allows for comparisons across different demographic categories and the identification of individuals who are most vulnerable to poverty.

Long-Term or Chronic Poverty

Long-term or chronic poverty, on the other hand, describes a condition in which an individual or household has been impoverished for a lengthy period, frequently spanning years or even decades. This sort of poverty study examines poverty from a dynamic standpoint, analysing changes in poverty over time and investigating the variables that lead to long-term poor. This method may reveal poverty trends and identify root reasons including low-paying jobs, lack of education and prejudice.

Social marginalisation, low social and economic mobility and bad health may occur. Evaluating the factors that culminate into long time poverty is strategic in framing policy and undertakings that would get people and families out of poverty and towards economic stability. Thus, programs that address the root causes of poverty may reduce poverty more effectively and sustainably.

Poverty dynamic studies may illuminate the causes and impacts of poverty and the efficacy of poverty-reduction strategies. They can help determine what causes chronic poverty and how specific populations or places become impoverished.

Dynamic research may also help policymakers create more effective policies that address the root causes of poverty and support individuals and families in their long-term fight against poverty.

Objective Poverty

Objective poverty is measured by income, assets and access to food, shelter and healthcare. Objective poverty measures use a threshold to define poverty.

The US government uses the poverty threshold to determine eligibility for numerous social assistance programs. The poverty line is adjusted annually for inflation based on the cost of a basic meal and other necessities.

The MPI measures poverty using non-monetary factors including education, health care and basic infrastructure. The UNDP utilises the MPI to assess poverty at the individual and household levels, taking into account a wider variety of criteria.

The advantage of objective poverty measurements is that they are reasonably straightforward to assess and compare across various populations and across time. They are, however, restricted in their capacity to reflect the complex and diverse nature of poverty, including social and cultural elements that may contribute to poverty. Moreover, objective poverty indicators may not completely represent the realities of poor individuals and households, which can be impacted by a variety of subjective and contextual variables.

Subjective Poverty

Subjective poverty is a type of poverty measurement based on an individual's or household's perception of their financial situation and ability to meet basic needs. This method of poverty measurement can account for the social and emotional dimensions of poverty that objective metrics may not completely capture.

Subjective poverty is assessed through surveys in which people or families estimate their economic well-being, capacity to obtain basic requirements like food, housing, healthcare and economic security. These questionnaires may also inquire about feelings of social exclusion, shame or stress related to poverty.

Subjective poverty measures are especially useful for identifying hidden or stigmatised poverty that objective measures may miss. For example, an individual or household may be technically over the poverty line based on objective metrics, yet nevertheless, struggle to make ends meet and satisfy their fundamental necessities. Subjective poverty measures can also assist in identifying the factors that contribute to poverty from the perspective of those who are impoverished.

One major shortcoming of subjective poverty indicators is that they can be impacted by cultural, social and psychological variables, and thus may not always correlate with objective poverty metrics. Subjective poverty measures, on the other hand, can provide a more nuanced understanding of poverty by taking into account the experiences and perceptions of those living in poverty and can be used to inform policies and interventions that are more aligned with the needs and preferences of those living in poverty.

Multidimensional Poverty

Multidimensional poverty assesses income, health, education and infrastructure. The multidimensional approach recognises that poverty is characterised by a lack of money, possessions and access to basic goods and services.

The MPI measures poverty in health, education and living situations. Multiple indicators measure poverty in each category. Health data covers child mortality and nutrition, while education data includes years of schooling and school attendance. Living standards include electricity and water availability. Multi-dimensionally impoverished people or households are inadequate in at least one-third of the MPI indicators. Poverty intensity is also considered by the MPI.

The multidimensional technique may provide a fuller picture of poverty and help locate disadvantaged areas. This may help build poverty-specific policies and interventions and measure success over time.

Comparison of Poverty Measures Used in Different Nations

Table 9.2 delves into the diverse methodologies employed globally to gauge and address poverty's multifaceted dimensions. Through comprehensive analysis, it unveils the intricacies and disparities in poverty measurement techniques, shedding light on varying national priorities and socio-economic contexts. This exploration serves as a crucial tool for policymakers, researchers and advocates striving for more effective and equitable poverty alleviation strategies worldwide.

Non-monetary Aspects of Poverty

Although income is a significant aspect of poverty, it is not the sole element that defines whether a person is poor. Other non-income characteristics of poverty include.

- *Poor people have poor health and limited access to healthcare.* Chronic illnesses, malnutrition and communicable infections may rise. Due to disease, individuals may be unable to work or obtain an education, so contributing to the cycle of poverty.
- *Poverty may persist if education is unavailable.* Children who are brought up in poor living conditions have a lower likelihood of attending school and a dropout risk earlier than their classmates. This can reduce their future employment opportunities and perpetuate intergenerational poverty.
- *Overcrowding, poor sanitation and insufficient housing may harm health and well-being.* It can also impede access to fundamental resources and services, such as clean water and healthcare.

Table 9.2. Comparison of Poverty Measures Used in Different Nations.

Type of Poverty	Definition	Examples of Countries
Absolute poverty	Based on a baseline income or consumption level	India, Bangladesh, Nigeria
Relative poverty	Compared to society's average or median income or consumption.	The United Kingdom, Australia, Canada
Multidimensional poverty	Based on access to education, healthcare and basic infrastructure, not just money.	Mexico, Colombia, Pakistan
Vulnerability to poverty	Refers to the risk of falling into poverty due to events such as job loss, illness or natural disasters	Brazil, Ethiopia, Vietnam
Food poverty	Refers to the inability to access or afford sufficient quantities of food to meet basic nutritional needs	The United States, Uganda, Kenya
Energy poverty	Refers to the absence of power and hygienic cooking facilities.	Sub-Saharan Africa, South Asia, Southeast Asia
Gender poverty	Refers to the disproportionate impact of poverty on women and girls, including lower wages, limited access to education and healthcare and higher rates of violence and exploitation	Sub-Saharan Africa, South Asia, Middle East
Urban poverty	Refers to poverty that is concentrated in urban areas, often associated with informal settlements, limited access to basic services and high levels of unemployment	Brazil, India, South Africa

Source: Self generated by the author.

- *Social exclusion and discrimination:* Women, people with disabilities and ethnic or religious minorities may be discriminated against and excluded from resources and services. This can prolong poverty and exacerbate existing inequality.

Lack of access to basic amenities like water, sanitation and electricity may keep people in poverty. Ultimately, poverty is a complicated problem that demands a comprehensive response. In addition to economic disparity, these non-income components must be addressed in efforts to eliminate poverty.

Assessment Methods for Estimating Poverty

The mechanism used to estimate poverty differs based on the strategy used. Below are some commonly used ways for calculating poverty.

- *Income or consumption-based approaches:* These methodologies quantify poverty by family income or consumption. The most common income-based poverty measure is the poverty line.
- *Multidimensional methods:* Multidimensional techniques measure poverty based on a variety of variables across several dimensions, such as health, education, housing and employment. Typically, these data are weighted and combined to create an index that represents the overall level of poverty.
- *Asset-based methods:* Asset-based poverty measures a household's land, livestock, money and education. This approach recognises that poverty is a lack of assets that may generate money and improve well-being, not a lack of income or consumption.
- *Participatory methods:* Participatory techniques entail collaborating with communities to define and quantify poverty in ways that reflect their own goals and experiences. This might incorporate both qualitative approaches like focus groups and participatory mapping and quantitative methods like household surveys.
- *Proxy means tests:* Proxy means tests measure poverty using household factors that are highly connected with income or consumption, such as household size, education and housing conditions. It is feasible to quantify poverty using these proxies rather than directly measuring income or consumption, which can be costly and difficult to measure.

Ultimately, the methodology for assessing poverty will be determined by the strategy selected and the data provided. A mix of measures may be utilised in many circumstances to create a more full and accurate picture of poverty.

International Indices to Measure Poverty

- *HDI (Human Development Index):* The HDI is a composite statistic that measures a nation's development in three key areas: health (life expectancy at birth), education (school years) and standard of living (gross national income per capita). The UNDP ranks nations by their development using the HDI.
- *Multidimensional Poverty Index (MPI):* The MPI measures wellness, schooling, lodging and work poverty. The UNDP created the MPI to identify vulnerable groups and track poverty alleviation.
- *The Global Multidimensional Poverty Index (Global MPI):* It is a composite statistic that assesses poverty in 105 developing nations. It is comparable to the

MPI, but it contains extra indicators including child mortality, nutrition, access to power and improved sanitation.

- *Poverty and Shared Prosperity Report (PSR):* The PSR is a World Bank yearly study that offers data on poverty levels and trends throughout the world. The study covers income-based and multidimensional poverty indices, as well as data on inequality and shared prosperity.
- *SDGs:* The 17 UN SDGs aim to reduce poverty and promote sustainable development. The SDGs aim to 'end poverty in all its manifestations worldwide', with measures to track progress.

These indicators are just a small sample of the many different measurements that may be used to conduct an analysis of poverty on a worldwide scale. Each index has a distinct set of advantages and disadvantages, and the one that is selected for use will be dependent on the particular circumstances and objectives of the study.

Comparison Chart

Indian and Neighbouring Poors

Table 9.3 highlights the poverty rate of global countries.

It is important to note that poverty estimates might differ depending on the methodology and data sources utilised. Nevertheless, poverty rates may be influenced by a variety of factors such as economic growth, social programs and political stability.

Table 9.3. Comparison Chart Showing the Number of People Living Below the Poverty Line in India and Its Bordering Countries.

Country	Poverty Rate	Source
India	364 million (27.4%)	World Bank, 2017
Pakistan	24.3%	Pakistan Bureau of Statistics, 2018
Nepal	25.2%	World Bank, 2020
Bangladesh	20.5%	Bangladesh Bureau of Statistics, 2019
Bhutan	8.2%	World Bank, 2017
Sri Lanka	4.1%	World Bank, 2016
Myanmar (Burma)	24.8%	World Bank, 2017

Source: Self generated by the author.

Comparison Chart to Measure Poverty

Table 9.4 shows the Comparison Chart of International Indices to Measure Poverty offers a comprehensive overview of various metrics employed globally to assess poverty levels. By juxtaposing indices such as the MPI and HDI, it facilitates cross-country comparisons and identifies areas for targeted intervention.

Indian Income Inequality and Poverty Compared to Other Countries

Below are some instances of income disparity and poverty rates in several nations.

- *The United States:* The top 1% earns more than 20% of total income in the United States, one of the most unequal industrialised nations. Poverty was 10.5% in 2020,

Table 9.4. Comparison Chart of International Indices to Measure Poverty.

Index	Organisation	Dimensions Measured	Geographic Coverage	Data Source
HDI	UNDP	Birth rate, education, GDP per capita.	189 countries	National Statistics Office (NSO), international organisations
MPI	UNDP	Health, education, the standard of living.	105 developing countries	Household surveys, censuses
Global MPI	UNDP	Health, education, the standard of living, child mortality, nutrition, access to electricity and improved sanitation.	105 developing countries	Household surveys, censuses
PSR	World Bank	Income-based and multidimensional measures of poverty, inequality, shared prosperity.	164 countries	Household surveys, censuses
SDGs	United Nations	17 goals related to poverty reduction, including indicators related to income, education, health and access to basic services.	193 countries	NSO, international organisations

Source: Self generated by the author.

with greater percentages for various groups such as Black Americans and Latinos. (Sources: Global Inequality Database, 'United States', accessed 16 February 2023; US Census Bureau, 'Poverty', accessed 16 February 2023).

- *Brazil's* richest 1% earns almost 28% of overall income. The poverty rate was 21.0% in 2021, with considerably higher percentages in rural areas and specific regions. Global Inequality Database, 'Brazil', accessed 16 February 2023; World Bank, 'Poverty and Equity Statistics', accessed 16 February 2023.
- *Japan:* Japan's top 1% earns 6% of total income, compared to other developed countries. Poverty was 16.4% in 2021, with greater percentages for particular categories such as single-parent homes and the elderly. (Global Inequality Database, 'Japan', accessed 16 February 2023; Ministry of Health, Labour, and Welfare, 'White Paper on the Aged', accessed 16 February 2023).
- *South Africa* has the world's largest income inequality, with the top 1% generating more than 20% of total income. Poverty was 32.3% in 2021, with considerably higher percentages for particular categories, such as female-headed families and those residing in rural regions. (Sources: Global Inequality Database, 'South Africa', accessed 16 February 2023; Statistics South Africa, 'South African Poverty Trends', accessed 16 February 2023).
- *China* has seen major poverty reductions in recent decades, although economic inequality remains quite high. In 2021, the poverty rate was 2.3%, while the Gini coefficient, a measure of income inequality, was 0.47, above severe inequality. (World Bank, 'Poverty and Equity Statistics', retrieved 16 February 2023; Global Inequality Database, 'China', retrieved 16 February 2023)
- *India:* According to the Global Inequality Database, the wealthiest 1% of earnings in India account for around 22% of total income. In 2018, the Gini coefficient, which measures income inequality, was 0.51, which is over the threshold for excessive inequality. (Global Inequality Database, 'India', accessed 16 February 2023).
- Poverty In 2021, the World Bank reported 9.2% poverty in India. This statistic, however, conceals substantial heterogeneity among geographies and demographic groupings. India has had rapid economic growth in recent decades, but inequality has not improved. Several studies show that India's economic growth has increased income inequality. According to the International Labour Organization (ILO), the richest 10% of Indian incomes increased their share of total income from 33% to 55% between 2005 and 2015. ILO, 'Global Employment and Social Outlook: Trends 2018', retrieved 16 February 2023.

Poverty and Its Effects on Economic Development

Poverty hinders progress. Because they are less productive and less able to invest in education and training, the poor contribute less to economic progress. Poor individuals spend less, and therefore the economy may experience reduced demand for products and services.

Data and references support this claim:

Eliminating poverty enhances GDP, according to the World Bank. The World Bank predicted in 2016 that reducing severe poverty by 1% may boost GDP growth by 0.2% in low-income nations.

Ending poverty may promote economic growth, according to IMF research. According to a 2016 IMF study, reducing income disparity, which is connected to poverty, may boost economic development (Berg et al., 2012).

The National Bureau of Economic Research (NBER) concluded that poverty reduces economic growth. For every percentage point rise in poverty, economic development is reduced by 1.7% points, according to the 45-year study of 89 nations.

However, NBER concluded that lowering poverty may promote economic growth by increasing human capital (Banerjee & Duflo, 2007). According to studies, a 10% poverty reduction may enhance GDP growth by 0.3% (Acemoglu & Johnson, 2007). These results imply that poverty may inhibit economic development while addressing poverty may improve growth.

Various Programs to Eradicate Poverty

Various Programs to Eradicate Poverty in India

India has several programs to reduce poverty and improve living conditions. Key programs include.

- *MGNREGA:* Every rural family with adult members willing to work unskilled manual labour is given 100 days of paid employment in a fiscal year by law. MGNREGA provides at least 100 days of guaranteed income-based employment in rural regions to improve living standards.
- *Pradhan Mantri Awas Yojana (PMAY):* By 2022, this initiative intends to give affordable homes to the urban poor. The initiative offers eligible participants with financial help for the building of residences.
- *The National Rural Livelihood Mission (NRLM):* It is a poverty-reduction initiative that promotes self-employment and entrepreneurship among rural disadvantaged households. The initiative offers impoverished households with financial and technical assistance in establishing their micro-enterprises.
- *Swachh Bharat Abhiyan (SBA):* The SBA cleans India's cities, towns and rural roads, infrastructure and streets. The campaign's goal is to enhance public health, sanitation and hygiene, as well as to prevent open defecation.
- *National Health Protection Programme (Ayushman Bharat):* The Ayushman Bharat initiative intends to offer poor and disadvantaged households in India financial insurance against catastrophic health spending. More than 100 million poor and disadvantaged households are covered by the plan.
- *Digital India Programme:* Digital India aims to make India a digital society and knowledge economy. The programme comprises activities aimed at improving digital infrastructure, promoting digital literacy and expanding access to digital services, particularly in rural regions.

These are only a few of India's poverty-reduction and quality-of-life programs. These measures have reduced poverty, but they have yet to provide basic amenities to all Indians.

International Poverty-Eradication Programs

Several projects are being launched in many places throughout the world to reduce poverty. Here are a couple of such examples.

* *Conditional Cash Transfer Programs:* Low-income households get financial transfers for meeting criteria like sending kids to school or having regular health exams, e.g. Mexico's Oportunidades and Brazil's Bolsa Familia.
* *Universal Basic Income (UBI)* is a government-funded programme that gives everyone a monthly, unconditional cash payment. The concept is to offer a basic income to all residents, regardless of job status, to ensure that everyone has a basic quality of life. Many nations, notably Finland, Kenya and India, have attempted UBI plans.
* *Microfinance programs* offer modest loans and financial services to low-income households and small companies. The purpose is to assist low-income individuals and enterprises in obtaining loans and establishing financial stability. One of the most well-known examples of a successful microfinance programme is Grameen Bank in Bangladesh.
* *Fair Trade:* Fair trade initiatives connect farmers and workers in developing nations with fair trade purchasers to encourage improved working conditions and higher salaries. Fairtrade certification guarantees that employees are paid a fair wage and that labour rules are followed. Fairtrade items, such as coffee, tea, chocolate and textiles, are available in many nations.
* *Education programs* attempt to enhance access to education, particularly for girls and women, who are frequently marginalised in many regions of the world. The United Nations Girls' Education Initiative, which supports girls' education in underdeveloped countries, and the Malala Fund, which provides educational opportunities for girls in Pakistan, Nigeria and other nations, are two examples.

These are only a few global anti-poverty projects. Each scheme has pros and cons, and what works in one country may not in another. These projects are crucial steps towards a fairer society.

World Bank Group Poverty Eradication Goals

The World Bank Group seeks extreme poverty and shared prosperity goals.

* *Eliminate Extreme Poverty:* The World Bank aims to reduce the global population living on less than $1.90 per day to 3% by 2030. This is ambitious given that over 700 million people live in abject poverty worldwide.
* *Promote Shared Prosperity:* The World Bank aims to boost income growth for the poorest 40% of each country's population to promote shared prosperity. The objective is for the lowest sectors of the population to see faster income growth than the general population.
* To achieve these objectives, the World Bank has devised a three-pillar strategy:

(1) *Accelerating Inclusive and Sustainable Economic Growth:* The World Bank seeks to promote inclusive, sustainable and job-creating economic growth. Infrastructure, education, health and social protection, as well as private sector growth and business climate improvements, are included.

(2) *Investing in Human Capital:* The World Bank invests in human capital through expanding education, healthcare and social safety. Early childhood development, decent education and healthcare access are needed.

(3) *Global Resilience:* The World Bank seeks to assist nations in strengthening their resilience to global shocks and dangers such as pandemics, natural disasters and climate change. This involves enhancing food security, disaster risk management and supporting climate-smart development.

The World Bank Group strives to create a healthy, prosperous society for everyone. For a fairer world, governments, civil society and the private sector must work together to achieve this ambitious goal.

Conclusion

Global poverty is complex. It is often defined by a household's income or consumption, while different methodologies and criteria are used to define poverty in different economies.

In high-income nations, poverty is frequently defined using an absolute poverty line based on a set standard of living, but relative poverty is more usually employed in low-income countries. There are significant discrepancies in how poverty is calculated in urban vs rural locations, as well as for different demographic groupings.

Poverty is a global issue regardless of how various economies define it. Poverty may lead to ill health, educational failure and economic limitations. Multidimensional poverty reduction is needed. This plan should promote economic development, education, healthcare and social safety nets for disadvantaged communities.

References

Acemoglu, D., & Johnson, S. (2007). Disease and development: The effect of life expectancy on economic growth. *Journal of Political Economy, 115*(6), 925–985.

Banerjee, A. V., & Duflo, E. (2007). The economic lives of the poor. *The Journal of Economic Perspectives, 21*(1), 141–168.

Berg, A., Ostry, J. D., & Zettelmeyer, J. (2012). What makes growth sustained? *Journal of Development Economics, 98*(2), 149–166.

United Nations. (2020, January 1). *2020 Global Multidimensional Poverty Index (MPI)*. Human Development Reports. https://hdr.undp.org/content/2020-global-multidimensional-poverty-index-mpi

World Bank. (2020). *Poverty and shared prosperity 2020: Reversals of fortune*. The World Bank.

Chapter 10

An Analytical Study on the Role of Private Sector in Bringing Economic Development and Equality in India

Megha Ojha[a], Rakhi Raturi[b] and Saslina Binti Kamaruddin[c]

[a]JustAuto Solutions Pvt. Ltd., India
[b]NMIMS (Deemed-to-be) University, India
[c]Universiti Pendidikan Sultan Idris (UPSI), Malaysia

Abstract

India's privatisation era is always praised for its capacity to create opportunities and more effective business models to support growth. By excluding the weaker, less skilled and more vulnerable groups in society, private enterprises may also be more likely to exacerbate economic imbalances and inequality, according to the current study. Recent data show that inequality in India has significantly increased in a variety of ways. Additionally, it has been asserted that the private sector makes the wealth gaps worse. In a similar vein, most people would only have limited access to a premium knowledge base or service. This is a worry since the government began disinvesting by selling public sector firms to the private sector, which resulted in a progressive decline in State ownership and control over resources. Privatisation results in the State's loss of control over decision-making and price setting. This may increase the likelihood that expensive, high-quality items and services will be. This study makes an effort to offer solid proof of how the private sector contributes to the country's unequal wealth distribution and low levels of knowledge exchange. This study will also explore if the Indian government can reduce income inequality and poverty rates by enacting sound policies that apply to both the public and private sectors. The results would encourage changes in policy aimed at reducing economic inequality in India and advancing welfare.

Keywords: Privatisation; government policies; inequality; knowledge sharing; wealth distribution; welfare schemes; prosperity and SDG 2030

Creating Pathways for Prosperity, 151–178
Copyright © 2025 Megha Ojha, Rakhi Raturi and Saslina Binti Kamaruddin
Published under exclusive licence by Emerald Publishing Limited
doi:10.1108/978-1-83549-121-820241011

Introduction

At times, India is referred to as an emerging economic superpower. The diverse Indian diaspora, the intellectual capital and management expertise, all contribute to the optimism. Another profile of India, on the contrary hand, is bleak. This country has one of the highest rates of people living in poverty, not being able to read or write and not having jobs. Women and children are plagued by high newborn mortality, morbidity and widespread anaemia (Kurian, 2007). Business and management scholars have recently focused on this trait of inequality. Apart from other factors, industries may also be attributed to a dual role of instilling progress while also causing disparities of various kinds in the country. Given the ever-growing effects of privatisation on individuals, organisations and societies, the rising inequality within firms and society poses a basic ethical quandary of our times (Bapuji, 2020; Kumar, 2022).

The social inequality is not a recent debate. There are various forums where social issues are talked about and remedial measures are discussed. For instance, the notion of the triple bottom line, as described in the Brundtland Report in 1987 (Alhaddi, 2015), emphasised on the significance of economic well-being, social empowerment and environmental conservation (Keeble, 1988). An ethical vision was created by the United Nations Global Commission on Environment and Development to promote the well-being of both present and future generations. The UN Summits in 2002 and 2015, as well as conferences conducted between 1992 and 2012 also discussed the way towards a sustainable world. The Sustainable Development Goals (SDGs) framework was designed with almost 500 indicators to guide the nations and industries to work towards achieving a more self-sustained economy (Jintao Lu, 2020). The SDGs are supposed to be implemented in both developing and developed nations. In this initiative the role of government and industries are crucial and defining. Fortune 500 firms, international organisations and other large corporations may significantly contribute to the fulfilment of the SDGs due to their size, resources, reach, potential to develop knowledge and managerial skills. The SDGs focused on climate changes, financial crisis, energy issues, empowerment, equality and many relevant themes (Anushree Poddar, 2019). These SDGs can easily be incorporated with corporate social responsibility spectrum. But are the companies willing to be part of any social welfare schemes under the purview of SDGs or Corporate Social Responsibility (CSR)? Is the private sector noteworthy in contributing to the local area they may operate or the larger market they cater to?

The private sector's contributions to society are usually judged under the purview of CSR. CSR is a moral approach to improving a company's social and corporate responsibility to its customers, employees and community. For a long time, CSR was regarded as a purely voluntary undertaking rather than something that had to be carried out in accordance with the law (Shuili Du, 2010). Early CSR strategies focused on humanitarian work and random acts of kindness. Publicly traded firms are now required under Section 135 of the Companies Act of 2013 to fund and participate in philanthropic endeavours. They were expected to pay 2% of their net profit to CSR programs such as poverty eradication, employment, education, health care, portable water, sanitation and so on (Narula, 2019). CSR is a moral approach for enhancing a business' social and corporate obligations to its clients, team members and community. Preliminary research of the CSR and sustainability reports revealed that donations were insignificant in recent years, despite the fact that the companies openly declared few CSR activities in their annual reports. Academia laments the fact about how firms may participate in community development initiatives without prior research of the cultural and regional context of the places in which they operate (Anushree Poddar, 2019).

This study highlights how the private sector is contributing towards the CSR initiatives and their level of adherence towards the SDGs. The researchers attempt to provide compelling evidence of how the private sector is instrumental in creating unequal wealth distribution and limited knowledge sharing for the nation rather than working towards a just economy. The findings will assist policymakers in improving the policies aimed at reducing economic disparity in India. There are five sections in this chapter. The first section covers the state of inequality in India, as well as the role of the private sector in attaining the SDGs. The issues of poverty, accessibility and income are highlighted in the next part. Using data and the most recent research that demonstrate how the landscape has altered as a result of the privatisation of important sectors, the facts on private-sector contributions are discussed along with the importance of CSR, community development and funding allocation. The findings are presented in the last Section, with a focus on the crucial success factors and challenges that India must overcome to meet the SDGs and ensure equal opportunities for all residents.

Literature Review

Inequality and Poverty

Poverty is the condition in which a person or household lacks the financial means to maintain even the most basic level of existence. The definition of poverty, however, may change through time and between different nations. The standard method of calculating poverty is to set a minimum amount of money (or income) that must be spent in order to fulfil a set of necessities for a human being. A measurement of multidimensional poverty used in more than 100 developing nations is called the Multidimensional Poverty Index (MPI). It was first made public in 2010 by the United Nations Development Programme (UNDP) and the Oxford Poverty and Human Development Project (OPHI). It assesses deprivation across three dimensions and 10 indicators, such as schooling years, child mortality and nutrition, and access to essential facilities like drinking water, power, fuel, etc., rather than using money as the only indicator of poverty. The role of rural infrastructure in eradicating poverty cannot be understated. Improvements in labour standards support the shift from low-productivity informal work in agriculture to more productive casual work in the non-farm economy. It is necessary for increased income and supports in increasing student enrolment and literacy rates. More funding for rural infrastructure is therefore predicted, especially in developing nations. The socio-economic infrastructure gaps at the Gram

Panchayat level in India were described in Mission 'Antyodaya' 2020. The Ministry of Rural Development's programmes are focused on reducing both household poverty and food insecurity through initiatives such as the Mahatma Gandhi National Rural Employment Guarantee Act (MNREGA), the National Rural Livelihoods Mission (NRLM), the Pradhan Mantri Awas Yojana (PMAY), and the Deen Dayal Upadhyaya Grameen Kaushalya Yojana (DDUGKY). They also target regional poverty through the Pradhan Mantri Gram Sadak Yojana (PMGSY), the Shyama Prasad Mukherji Rurban Mission (SPRM), and the Saansad Adarsh Gram Yojana (SAGY). Apart from Government agencies and trusts, private sectors can facilitate resources to the deprived. This is especially seen in times of natural disasters or epidemics. The private sector should be involved in developing awareness programmes for disaster management, according to the National Disaster Management Framework (NDMF) created by the Ministry of Home Affairs. In a similar spirit, UNDP and the Indian government recommend working together with private businesses (Chadda, 2023). The widely held belief that extreme poverty is a normal state and that it only began to reduce with the growth capitalism based on income statistics and do not sufficiently reflect access to necessities. According to real wage data, extreme poverty historically was rare and mostly appeared during moments of profound social and economic upheaval, especially during colonialism. For example, the land resource which could be used for agriculture and food production is sometimes enclosed for commercial purposes (Sullivan, 2023).

Work Pay Inequality and Spatial Inequality Created by Private Sector

Privatisation strengthens the position of the private sector while weakening that of the public sector. With disinvestment or the selling of government and public sector stock, government enterprises can be converted into private companies (Sangvikar, 2019). Although there seems to be lots of differences in pay method in private sector and government jobs, it is usually assumed that private companies are providing good wages (Glinskaya). However, the differences of salaries are evident in corporate system as well. Work that involves basic literacy and numeracy skills, as well as the ability to complete a few simple and short-term activities under direct supervision, is not expected to be well compensated. With increasing firm size, wage gaps between high- and either medium- or low-skill positions widen, while those between medium- and low-skill positions remain stable or even somewhat narrower. Due to their increased levels of automation, larger organisations pay lower entry-level management wages in exchange for more favourable career prospects, which results in lower wages for 'routine' work duties. This is viewed as part of a global trend towards wider wage gaps (Mueller, 2017).

A situation known as spatial inequality occurs when different geographic or spatial units perform differently on a certain trait of interest, most frequently (average) income. Why should the economic conditions of various geographical areas within a nation differ? Privatisation makes the private sector stronger while making the public sector weaker. Government corporations can become private businesses through disinvestment or the selling of government and public sector stock (which are in steep decline following structural reforms) are significantly less inclined towards such districts. The authors arrive at the opinion that structural reforms increase income inequality in terms of industrialisation and geographic location. Industry concentrations, the availability of dependable infrastructure and better market accessibility are suggested by insights from New Economic Geography (NEG) and regional scientific models. The firm's proximity to market centres, together with its size and density, affects their ability to access those markets. There is no reason why a firm's spatial closeness (i.e. its own district) should limit the scope of its market, as long as appropriate transportation networks connect its products to a larger market area (Lall, 2005). Similar mobility constraints are currently encountered by capitalism society's working poor, the majority of whom originate from demographically disadvantaged communities. Severe spatial mobility restrictions, denial of access to state-based help and civil-society initiatives, normalisation of inequitable and unjust compensation schemes and the ongoing tweaking of laws are all real impediments to advancement (e.g. lower taxes for the wealthy, shareholder dividends and reductions in social services at the lower end of the economic spectrum) (Kumar, 2022). Southern and western States had faster economic and social development as a result of economic reforms than northern and eastern States. As a result, the difference in income, poverty and other measures of progress between the two regions has risen. While big and medium-sized cities have one of the best economies in the world, rural areas have stagnant economies (Kurian, 2007).

The Environmental Imbalance Created by Industries

Environmental justice has rarely been studied in India when it comes to industrial development. More often than not, environmental injustices are viewed in the context of social movement struggles or tragic occurrences like the Bhopal Gas Disaster of 1984. Unfortunately, India's performance in the industrial sphere is largely responsible for its classification as an 'emerging economy', and industrialisation is very bad for the environment. Gujarat, for instance, is one of the top states in western India for both industrial production and the production of hazardous waste. Statistics from several research also highlighted inequalities in Gujarat's society regarding the distribution of hazardous industrial facilities (Chakraborty & Basu, 2019). There are considerable regional and even national differences in environmental regulation (ER) and enforcement. Regional rivalry has raised policymakers' concerns about how environmental policies affect pollution intensive industries (PII) site decisions. China, for example has had remarkable economic growth over the last three decades, but it has also experienced uneven development across its coastline and interior regions. This trend would soon hamper the environment. Environmental restrictions for all industries across globe can prevent the establishment of new pollution intensive hubs (Shen, 2017).

Income Disparity and Wealth Distribution in the Economy

The seminal work by Simon Kuznets to the American Economic Association in 1954 serves as the starting point for most discussions on the differences between the wealthy and the poor in developing countries. Kuznets examines the elements of industrialisation that tend to resist the trend towards an increasing concentration of savings in the hands of the wealthy to investigate the potential causes of this trend in some depth. By analysing data from India, Sri Lanka and Puerto Rico, Kuznets begins the discussion about the applicability of these findings to developing countries. Findings indicate that economic inequality is higher in developing nations than it is in developed nations and that this inequality may be increasing in recent times (Kuznets, 2019).

Some claim that while countries may have grown wealthy, government organisations may not have the same fate with resources (Chancel, 2022). This inequality of income is a significant challenge of modern economies. The gap between the wealthy and poor has been growing in the recent decade. The inequality is further widened by the inaccessibility of education, healthcare and lending facilities. Policies should focus more on deprived if we need to bridge the gap of income divide. Information of assets held by rich segment and corporates reflects the income disparity in the economy. There is also inequality of opportunities in terms of basic needs like food, sanitation, water and greater things like job availability for the skilled class (Dabla-Norris, 2015). Behera emphasised more on agriculture development over urbanisation as the key to wealth and success in India. The expansion of agricultural value added, which reduces economic disparities in India, is a desired trend that is supported by the continued reliance of rural communities on the sector for employment and revenue. In order to maintain development in the primary sector despite a decline in its proportional contribution to gross domestic product (GDP), this emphasises the focus to be on the agriculture and thereby promoting crop research and improving the agricultural practices through better investments. This may empower the rural community (Behera). Poverty and disparity is a major research domain that the World Bank is exploring and has dedicated entirely to studying this with respect to global inequality. The universal desire of international organisation to comprehend and draw attention to economic gaps demonstrates that inequality cannot be avoided in debates about development strategy (Ortiz, 2011).

The pandemic has also reflected the inequality of knowledge scenario. Less mobile social groups stand to gain the most from online schooling. E-learning has the potential to be another effective instrument for gender mainstreaming (Tiwari, 2022). The key to eliminating inequality and eradicating poverty is knowledge sharing. Communities in areas of extreme poverty are, however, frequently divided by different viewpoints and understandings that prevent knowledge exchange. Further complicating the exchange of knowledge are societal fault lines that might erect internal barriers that prevent communication (Qureshi, 2018). Knowledge sharing refers to the exchange of abilities, concepts, viewpoints and comprehension among individuals. The 'digital divide' theory may be applicable in this case due to the differences in internet access and technological resources. According to studies, the high cost of data and an unpredictable power supply are the main problems that impoverished people have when accessing the internet. Inequality could occur for those who reside in distant places without access to electricity or technology (Gamji, 2022).

SDGs and CSR Compliance in India

On 25 September 2015, 193 UN Member States adopted the SDGs to end poverty, safeguard the environment and ensure prosperity. These include mitigating global warming and eradicating poverty. The 17 goals must be met by 2030. Governments are expected to develop national frameworks for implementing the 17 SDGs, as well as to take ownership of the SDGs. Countries are responsible for monitoring and evaluating the outcomes of the Goals' implementation, thus timely, accurate and high-quality data must be collected (Sustainable Development Goals, n.d.). India is committed to the SDGs' accomplishment and has significantly aided their growth. NITI Aayog coordinates India's implementation of the SDGs. NITI Aayog, which also encourages competitive and cooperative federalism between States and Union Territories (UTs), oversees the adoption and monitoring of the SDGs throughout the nation. Instead of only regularly gathering SDG statistics, NITI Aayog's present responsibility is to accomplish its objectives. Ministry of Statistics and Programme Implementation (MoSPI), working with other Ministries, has already started to develop indicators that reflect the SDG objectives (NITI Aayog, n.d.).

To achieve the SDG by 2030, India continues to adopt and put into practise many policies and measures concerning resource efficiency, air pollution, climate change and sustainable development. The 'Swachh Bharat Mission "Beti Bacho Beti Padhao"', 'Smart Cities', 'Pradhan Mantri Jan Dhan Yojana' and'Deen Dayal Upadhyay Gram Jyoti Yojana' are just a few of the initiatives the Indian government has launched to help achieve the SDGs (Press Information Bureau, Government of India, Ministry of Finance, 2019). CSR initiatives serve the objectives of the Companies Act of 2013, but they are not the only ones. As long as those initiatives meet the requirements established in the Companies Act of 2013, CSR in India also refers to actions related with decisions made by the corporate board based on recommendations from the CSR Committee. A description of the company's CSR Committee's spending practises that must be detailed in the yearly action plan (CSR-report, 2019). The Board should receive recommendations from the CSR Committee regarding how much money should be set aside for each CSR initiative and how it should be spent (Govt amends rules governing corporate social responsibility, 2022). The idea that firms should contribute to a country's social development and the idea of enhancing corporate social responsibility have driven many legislative actions in various nations over the past 30 years. Gradually, CSR discussions shifted from charity to shared values and strategic planning. When corporations competed on global markets, ethical business practices gradually lost relevance.

Contributions by the Corporate Sector

Through the sharing of wealth and expertise, Private Sector is considered essential in fostering prosperity through wealth creation and upgradation of life. Businesses have the ability to develop cutting-edge technologies and goods that improve the lives of people and communities by investing in R&D. Businesses can also help people to develop the skills and knowledge necessary for success in the workplace. The employees may receive further benefit of higher education scholarships and training. Additionally, if private business is fair and inclusive then there would be good labour standards, appropriate salaries and medical benefits. Businesses can support economic growth and the public well-being of their communities by investing in research and development, providing education and training opportunities and implementing inclusive and sustainable business practices (Uchida, 2003).

India holds the distinction of being the pioneer in mandating enforceable legal obligations for CSR compliance. The Indian Ministry of Corporate Affairs (MCA) released the Corporate Governance Voluntary Guidelines in 2009 with the aim of promoting the adoption of robust corporate governance principles by businesses on a voluntary basis. In 2011, the MCA formulated the National Voluntary Guidelines on Social, Environmental, and Economic Responsibility of Business. India's implementation of the 2013 amendment to the Companies Act marked a significant milestone as the first nation to enforce rigorous adherence to CSR standards. Section 135 of the Companies Act of 2013, Schedule VII, and the Companies (CSR) Policy Regulations, 2014 provide a framework for businesses to collaborate in addressing the obstacles to national progress. The Indian economy is one of the largest globally and is projected to experience rapid growth. According to the World Bank's GDP growth (annual %) - India, 2021 data, India's nominal GDP stands at $2.73 trillion, which translates to approximately $8,400 per capita in the United States. This figure positions India as the global leader in terms of the fastest growing trillion-dollar economy in 2018 (GDP growth (annual %) - India, 2021).

Companies in India now have a lot more discretion and freedom in how they structure and implement their CSR investments. If they have a net worth of INR 5 billion (US$70 million) or more, INR 10 billion (US$140 million) in annual revenue or INR 50 million (US$699,125) in net profit, they must donate 2% of their three-year average net earnings to CSR (CSR Legislation, n.d.). Section 166 of the Companies Act of 2013 imposes new fiduciary duties on directors, requiring them to pursue the company's goals in the best interests of all parties concerned, including the company, its shareholders, employees, the community and the environment. Businesses can fulfil their CSR Act obligations by contributing a portion of their profits to causes such as hunger, gender equality, poverty and education. Since mandatory CSR compliance was adopted, corporate spending on CSR has increased in India (See Table 10.1). According to a report published in 2019 by the High-Level Committee on Corporate Social Responsibility, India confronts a number of problems in implementing CSR (CSR-report, 2019). The need for more resources, including money, human capital, knowledge and expertise, is one of the major barriers to implementing CSR (CSR-report, 2019).

India's economy is among the fastest growing in the world, but its society is also among the most uneven. The World Inequality Report 2022 analyses several policy options for wealth redistribution and long-term investment in order to address the concerns of the 21st century. It might motivate us to take action before it becomes difficult to resist the progressive concentration of economic

Table 10.1. Evolution of CSR Paradigm in India.

2007	2009	2010	2011	2012	2014
The year of inclusive growth plan as per the 11th 5-year planning	The voluntary guidelines as per the CSR 2009	Standing committee formation/ Companies Bill, 2009	The national voluntary guidelines formulated for environmental and economic responsibilities of firms, 2011	Reporting on business responsibilities	Mandatory CSR under the purview of Section 135 of use the 'Insert citation' button to add citations to this document company's act, 2013. Effective date 1st April 2014

Source: National CSR Portal (n.d.).

(and other) power in the hands of a shrinking minority. The fundamental source of this inequality is the notable difference in growth rates between the top and lowest quartiles of the wealth distribution. We can better understand these inequities by concentrating on the difference between the net wealth of governments and the private sector (Alvaredo, 2018).

Business Environment in India

It was necessary to examine the empirical data provided by the CSR reports to determine the successes and new challenges encountered in achieving the SDGs through CSR initiatives. The data with regard to companies spend on social activities and their reporting mechanism of spending and not spending on various projects is analysed. The share of local area spending, State-wise distribution and accomplishment of few SDGs are also reported. Overall, the purpose was to ascertain whether the companies are spending ample funds on these projects and whether there are defaults in the implementation plans. The willingness and capacity to help the nation's economy by the private sector is ascertained by the facts and information received.

A total of 17,007 businesses spent INR 248.6546 billion on CSR initiatives in Fiscal Year (FY) 2020–2021, according to filings with the MCA (Latest CSR Rules Limit Disclosure of Key Details in Annual Report, 2022) as shown in Table 10.2.

Companies Responsible for CSR in India Based on Their Reporting Status

Companies that must adhere to CSR requirements are included in the total number of liable companies, as shown in Table 10.3. According to the High-Level Committee on Corporate Social Responsibility Report, 2018, there were 16,548 liable companies in India in the FY 2014–2015, 18,290 in 2016 and 19,532 in 2017. These numbers increased to 21,337 in 2017–2018 (CSR-report, 2019).

Table 10.3 displays the trend pertaining to the enterprises that are obligated to report and finance CSR. In the FY 2014–2015, the proportion of businesses that were mandated to engage in CSR and complied with the requirement was 63%. The aforementioned percentage experienced an increase, reaching its highest point at 71% during the 2016–2017 period, followed by a gradual decline to 67% in the same period. The percentage experienced a decline to 54% during the period of 2017–2018. Table 10.3 presents the level of adherence in relation to the aggregate corporate social responsibility expenditure expressed as a proportion of the total required sum for all firms in each financial year. Except for the FY 2015–2016, during which it was considerably elevated, the supplementary data presented in Table 10.3 indicates that the general adherence to the prescribed amount of CSR expenditure, in relation to the total count of companies that are accountable for CSR, has been modest. The rate of compliance experienced a notable upsurge during the financial year 2015–2016, with an increase from 63% to 71%. However, there was a subsequent decline in the two following FYs, with a decrease from 67% to 54%. (CSR-report, 2019).

Table 10.2. CSR Spend by the Companies (In Rs. Cr.).

FY 2014–2015	FY 2015–2016	FY 2016–2017	FY 2017–2018	FY 2018–2019	FY 2019–2020	FY 2020–2021
6043.29	10,477.74	9,819.39	11,454.94	13,617.14	15,542.93	17,853.58

Source: compiled by the authors from (Dynamic CSR Report, 2022)

Table 10.3. Percentage of Liable Companies Reporting on CSR in India.

Financial Year	Total Number of Companies Liable for CSR	Companies Liable for CSR and Reporting	CSR Expenditure by Companies Reporting on CSR (in Rs. Cr.)	CSR Prescribed Amount (in Rs. Crore)	Companies Liable for CSR and Reporting	companies Liable for CSR but Not Reporting	Compliance in Terms of CSR Expenditure (%)
2014–2015	16,548	10,418	10,065.93	17,140.42	63%	37%	59%
2015–2016	18,290	12,955	14,503.65	17,044.45	71%	29%	85%
2016–2017	19,532	13,182	14,312.03	19,789.90	67%	33%	72%
2017–2018	21,337	11,584	13,326.69	23,247.90	54%	46%	57%

Source: Compiled by the authors from (CSR-report, 2019).

State-Wise and Year-Wise CSR Spending in India

Maharashtra leads with the highest spending. In the States where private players are smaller in capacity or unaware of projects, collaborations with trusts & NGOs can be instrumental. These trusts are usually closer to communities and can provide valuable insights and communication to implement CSR-led activities. Moving ahead, Indian corporations should comprehensively declare their CSR alignment with the SDGs in their annual and sustainability reports (CSR-report, 2019) as shown in Table 10.4. Further details are given in Tables A1 and A2 in the appendix.

Table 10.5 shows that the organisations cited multiple reasons:

- challenges in locating a suitable project,
- difficulty in selecting an appropriate implementation agency and
- multi-year projects as reasons for not meeting the mandated CSR amount (CSR-report, 2019).

The number of businesses developing CSR policies rose from FY 2014–2015 to FY 2015–2016 and then fell in the FY 2016–2017. However, the statistics have slightly improved in FY 2017–2018 (CSR-report, 2019) as shown in Table 10.6.

The first proviso to sub-section (5) of Section 135 of the Companies Act of 2013 states that the company must give consideration to the local community where they operate when using the funds set aside for CSR as shown in Table 10.7.

The Indian corporations use their CSR funds on activities, and Table 10.9 shows that the most money is spent on projects connected to education, differently abled people and livelihood. The preceding expenditure category was health, eradicating hunger, poverty and malnutrition, providing safe drinking water, sanitation and so on. Businesses under spent the allocated amounts compared to the budgeted CSR spending. Ganga Project and Other Sectors (Technology Incubator, Benefits to Armed Forces and Admin Overheads) were the most ignored projects.

The CSR Rules, 2014 and the statutory provision are intended to ensure that any actions taken following the CSR policy are related to Schedule VII of the Companies Act, 2013, as stated in General Circular No. 21/2014, dated 18 June 2014, issued by the MCA. To cover the essence of the subjects listed there, the entries in the Schedule VII must be interpreted broadly. The general items listed in Schedule VII of the Companies Act, 2013 are meant to cover a wide range of activities as shown in Table 10.10.

CSR Amendments Under the Companies (Amendment) Act, 2019

The Companies Act of 2013 implemented the mandatory CSR provisions outlined in Section 135, which became effective on 1 April 2014. Prior to the enactment of the Companies (Amendment) Act in 2019, companies were permitted to retain surplus cash reserves and utilise them if their CSR funds were

Table 10.4. State-Wise and Year-Wise CSR Spending in India (FY 2014–2015 to FY 2020–2021).

State	CSR Spent for FY 2014–2015 (INR Cr.)	CSR Spent for FY 2015–2016 (INR Cr.)	CSR Spent for FY 2016–2017 (INR Cr.)	CSR Spent for FY 2017–2018 (INR Cr.)	CSR Spent for FY 2018–2019 (INR Cr.)	CSR Spent for FY 2019–2020 (INR Cr.)	CSR Spent for FY 2020–2021 (INR Cr.)	Total
Andaman and Nicobar	0.29	0.55	0.63	0.73	0.81	1.30	2.86	7.17
Andhra Pradesh	414.28	1,276.73	743.68	575.08	666.03	710.13	715.81	5,101.74
Arunachal Pradesh	11.05	1.48	24.05	11.92	24.55	18.03	10.59	101.67
Assam	134.78	158.97	256.91	211.34	209.99	285.00	167.78	1,424.77
Bihar	36.69	123.81	100.62	106.16	137.56	110.48	79.29	694.61
Chandigarh	1.77	5.34	21.96	20.50	11.47	15.57	13.20	89.81
Chhattisgarh	161.30	239.73	84.66	176.69	149.35	269.68	307.81	1,389.22
Dadra and Nagar Haveli	4.41	12.03	7.36	6.98	13.49	18.34	21.97	84.58
Daman and Diu	20.05	2.39	2.63	20.23	6.25	9.53	5.25	66.33
Delhi	237.44	455.17	460.25	579.36	750.76	829.50	713.58	4,026.06
Goa	27.11	28.16	36.25	53.76	46.77	43.91	41.77	277.73
Gujarat	313.41	547.94	865.29	967.97	1,082.17	984.15	1,443.62	6,204.55
Haryana	187.41	373.44	386.17	363.44	378.11	536.57	542.46	2,767.60
Himachal Pradesh	10.95	52.20	22.83	69.23	78.80	78.61	105.01	417.63
Jammu and Kashmir	38.48	107.80	42.66	50.77	36.44	25.27	35.46	336.88
Jharkhand	79.44	116.92	95.49	109.23	109.81	155.20	210.27	876.36
Karnataka	403.47	771.60	875.40	1,145.42	1,252.19	1,448.08	1,265.06	7,161.22

Kerala	68.23	145.03	133.82	219.73	354.79	298.55	286.52	1,506.67
Lakshadweep	-	0.30	-	2.27	0.39	-	0.01	2.97
Madhya Pradesh	141.85	171.58	161.11	163.92	243.55	215.33	354.49	1,451.83
Maharashtra	1,445.92	2,026.89	2,414.79	2,797.53	3,147.66	3,348.82	3,426.30	18,607.91
Manipur	2.44	6.25	12.35	4.82	7.81	14.21	10.30	58.18
Meghalaya	3.53	5.59	9.75	11.18	16.53	17.66	12.46	76.70
Mizoram	1.03	1.07	0.08	1.28	0.10	0.25	0.97	4.78
Nagaland	1.11	0.96	0.53	1.81	2.13	5.10	3.56	15.20
Odisha	252.18	618.69	325.88	504.21	697.88	716.79	567.63	3,683.26
Pan India (other centralised funds)	624.61	910.73	787.22	799.18	1,155.86	1,789.15	3,417.89	9,484.64
Puducherry	2.02	6.37	7.43	6.08	9.14	11.32	11.97	54.33
Punjab	55.61	69.14	75.04	112.37	166.85	188.52	137.27	804.80
Rajasthan	299.76	483.99	353.22	443.34	595.47	734.10	657.86	3,567.74
Sikkim	1.19	1.45	6.71	7.00	5.87	10.99	15.16	48.37
Tamil Nadu	539.64	588.21	547.94	669.65	877.08	1,072.01	1,145.67	5,440.20
Telangana	101.96	263.60	256.15	380.57	428.05	445.81	624.22	2,500.36
Tripura	1.33	1.39	1.25	1.88	23.06	9.40	9.29	47.60
Uttar Pradesh	148.90	416.99	321.22	435.22	521.33	577.93	870.13	3,291.72
Uttarakhand	74.79	73.12	102.37	85.78	172.31	124.69	155.43	788.49
West Bengal	194.86	412.13	275.69	338.31	382.23	422.95	464.66	2,490.83
Grand Total	6,043.29	10,477.74	9,819.39	11,454.94	13,762.64	15,542.93	17,853.58	84,954.51

Source: Data analysed and compiled by the authors from (National CSR Portal, n.d.).

Table 10.5. Major Reasons Reported for Not/Under-Spending CSR Prescribed Amount.

FY 2014–2015	FY 2015–2016	FY 2016–2017	FY 2017–2018
Suitable project not Found	Delay due to not identifying project	Delay due to not identifying project	Delay in implementation of plan
First year of CSR	Appropriate implementing agencies unable to locate	Delay in implementation of plan	Adoption of Long Gestation CSR Programs/Projects
Multi-year projects	Delay in implementation of plan	Due to multi-year projects	Inability of the company to develop a robust CSR policy
The vast majority of the projects involved infrastructure development in rural areas, which required a lengthy implementation period.	Suitable projects not found	Lack of prior expertise	Lack of prior expertise
Appropriate implementing agencies unable to locate	Delay due to not identifying project		
Delay in implementation of plan			
Appropriate implementing agencies unable to locate			

Source: Compiled by the authors from (CSR-report, 2019).

Table 10.6. Number of Companies Framing CSR Policy out of the Total Companies Liable for CSR (FY 2014–2015 to FY 2017–2018).

FY	Companies Liable for CSR	Companies Framing CSR Policy Out of the Total companies Eligible for CSR	Companies Not Framing CSR Policy Out of the Total companies Eligible for CSR	Companies Not Reported regarding Framing of CSR Policy out of the Total companies Eligible for CSR
2014–2015	16,548	5,086	955	10,507
2015–2016	18,290	7,023	928	10,339
2016–2017	19,532	5,666	426	13,440
2017–2018	21,337	6,326	693	14,318

Source: Compiled by the authors from (CSR-report, 2019).

Table 10.7. Share of Local Area Spending Under CSR (in Rs. Crore) (FY 2014–2015 to FY 2017–2018). Net Donor and Net Recipient States (Top 10 States in India).

FY	CSR Expenditure by Companies Reporting on CSR (in Rs. Cr.)	Share of Local Area Spending under CSR	Number of Projects
2014–2015	10,065.93	2,654.65	28,984
2015–2016	14,503.65	4,601.6	41,318
2016–2017	14,312.03	7,894.77	49,083
2017–2018	13,326.69	7,436.52	44,805

Source: Compiled by the authors from (CSR-report, 2019).

not fully expended within a designated FY. Presently, it is mandatory for organisations and companies to transfer any unutilised CSR funds to one of the funds enlisted in Schedule VII of the Companies Act, 2013 before the culmination of the financial year. As per the recent 2019 amendment, if CSR funds remain unused for three years following their transfer, the amount must be deposited into one of the designated funds. Significantly, in case of non-adherence by corporations, the recent legislation necessitates both pecuniary penalty and imprisonment. In accordance with the penalty provisions, the officer of the company who defaults may be subject to a fine of up to INR 500,000 ($7,023), imprisonment for a period of three years or both. The penalty range varies from INR 50,000 ($700) to INR 2.5 million ($35,000) (htt).

Table 10.8. State-wise CSR Spending (in Rs. Cr.) (FY 2014–2015 to FY 2017–2018).

State-wise CSR Spending (in Rs. Cr.)		Net Donor States (Top 10 Net Donor states)		Net Recipient States (Top 10 Net Recipient States)	
State Name (Top 10 CSR spending states)	CSR Spending (in Rs. Cr.)	Donor States	Amount Donate (in Rs Cr.)	Recipient State	Amount received (in Rs Cr.)
Maharashtra	8,468.28	Maharashtra	10,214.28	Andhra Pradesh	1,635.95
Karnataka	3,014.57	Delhi	8,177.29	Uttar Pradesh	806.55
Andhra Pradesh	2,727.79	Punjab	1,944.39	Rajasthan	798.08
Gujarat	2,499.79	West Bengal	1,398.56	Odisha	667.40
Tamil Nadu	2,330.56	Karnataka	1,361.24	Chhattisgarh	273.29
Delhi	1,773.90	Gujarat	992.93	Uttarakhand	233.82
Odisha	1,660.24	Tamil Nadu	343.35	Haryana	167.49
Rajasthan	1,385.00	Telangana	304.49	Madhya Pradesh	143.09
Haryana	1,196.84	Himachal Pradesh	25.24	Manipur	24.52
Uttar Pradesh	1,184.55	Dadra and Nagar Haveli	16.45	Sikkim	16.80

Source: Compiled by the authors from (CSR-report, 2019).
Note: A State is a net donor if the amount of CSR funds it produces but donates to other States exceeds the amount of CSR funds those other States produce. A State is a net recipient if the amount of CSR funds it produces but receives from other States is lower as shown in Table 10.8.

New CSR Rules Limit Disclosure of Key Details in Company Annual Report

The MCA published the Companies (CSR Policy) Amendment Rules, 2022 on 20 September 2022. It takes effect on the date it is published in the Official Gazette. The regulations allow Indian corporations to limit the sharing of valuable information pertaining to their CSR spending and activities throughout the course of a FY while producing their annual reports. Exempt CSR-related information must be filed on the Ministry of Corporate Affairs website in the CSR-2 form (Govt. amends rules governing corporate social responsibility, 2022) as shown in Table 10.11.

Findings and Discussion

Major findings of the data retrieved are: Business spend on CSR is increasing year by year. From 2014 to 2018, the financial year 2016–2017 has shown the maximum of

Table 10.9. Development Sector-wise and Financial Year-wise CSR Spending in India (INR Cr.).

Development Sector	CSR Spent for FY 2014–2015 (INR Cr.)	CSR Spent for FY 2015–2016 (INR Cr.)	CSR Spent for FY 2016–2017 (INR Cr.)	CSR Spent for FY 2017–2018 (INR Cr.)	CSR Spent for FY 2018–2019 (INR Cr.)	CSR Spent for FY 2019–2020 (INR Cr.)	CSR Spent for FY 2020–2021 (INR Cr.)	Total
Any other fund	277.10	334.35	419.99	292.73	731.06	931.97	1,564.89	4,552.09
Clean Ganga fund	5.47	32.82	24.37	33.96	8.11	6.63	13.39	124.75
Education, differently abled and livelihood	2,233.58	3,611.02	3,876.54	4,957.52	5,463.33	6,108.44	5,730.40	31,980.83
Encouraging sports	30.24	67.56	93.68	164.57	182.16	164.59	122.59	825.39
Environment, animal welfare and conservation of resources	351.76	745.36	730.02	1,011.50	1,079.38	1,177.16	1,071.08	6,166.26
Gender equality, women empowerment, old age homes and reducing inequalities	119.70	243.35	337.12	390.70	429.66	476.58	373.37	2,370.48
Health, eradicating hunger, poverty and malnutrition, safe drinking water and sanitation	1,948.34	3,458.39	2,696.93	2,980.01	3,697.48	4,669.85	5,709.44	25,160.44
Heritage art and Culture	77.35	94.44	254.11	281.61	156.99	162.94	181.22	1,208.66
Other sectors (technology incubator and benefits to armed forces and admin overheads)	5.81	24.16	38.48	28.70	55.64	60.18	61.95	274.92
Others	159.62	621.51	214.36	2.04	4.84	28.62	72.78	1,103.77
Prime ministers national relief fund	228.18	218.04	158.80	200.42	321.19	797.13	1,678.76	3,602.52
Rural development	487.57	687.76	744.90	800.91	1,486.60	869.41	1,025.75	6,102.90
Slum area development	4.71	13.46	46.03	38.20	50.70	36.01	87.11	276.22
Swachh Bharat Kosh	113.86	325.52	184.06	272.07	95.50	53.42	160.85	1,205.28
Grand Total	**6,043.29**	**10,477.74**	**9,819.39**	**11,454.94**	**13,762.64**	**15,542.93**	**17,853.58**	**84,954.51**

Source: Data analysed and compiled by the authors from (National CSR Portal, n.d.).

Table 10.10. SDG and CSR Compliance in India (Mapping of SDGs With Schedule VII of the Companies Act, 2013) (FY 2014–2015 to FY 2017–2018).

Schedule VII Areas	SDG Mapping With Schedule VII of the Companies Act 2013	Cumulative CSR Spend (in Rs.cr)	% of Total CSR Spend
Environment, animal welfare and conservation of resources (including Clean Ganga fund)	15, 14, 13, 11,7,6,	4,554.03	8.72
Education, differently abled and Livelihood	8,4,2,1	19,291.47	36.95
Health, reduction of hunger, poverty, and malnutrition sanitation and safe drinking water (Swachh Bharat Kosh)	6,3,2,1,10	14,846.50	28.44
Encouraging sports	8	600.89	1.15
Heritage, art and Culture	11,9	824.90	1.58
Gender equality, women empowerment, Nursing Homes and inequality reduction	10,5,1	1,484.04	2.84
Rural development	9,4,3,2,1,	5,442.84	10.43
Slum area development	9,7,6,3,2,1	197.53	0.38
Prime Minister's national relief fund and any other fund	15,6,4,3,2,1	2,037.55	3.90
Other sectors (Technology incubator and benefits to armed forces and admin overheads)	8,4,3,12,13,9	152.00	0.29
Not mentioned	Not mentioned	2,779.28	5.32

Source: Compiled by the authors from (CSR-report, 2019).

71% but dropped next year not showing a consistent improvement. Major reasons cited by companies for not implementing social tasks were Suitable Implementing Agencies Not Found, Delay in Implementation of Plan, Suitable Projects Not Found, lack of expertise, etc. Most of the reasons do not look sufficient for not undertaking a single CSR project for a year. Major spends is on education, differently abled and livelihood. However, there is negligible CSR spending on sports. Reliance Industries Limited and Tata Consultancy Services Limited are major contributors.

In order to prevent and manage inequalities (of all kinds) in developing countries, the private sector can and should play a role. It can do this within its own sphere of influence and by helping governments with funding distribution and other CSR activities. The researchers of this study drew on their collective wealth of practical experience in this area as well as expertise acquired from in-depth readings of relevant literature, discussions and presentations on economic growth and equal chances for all stakeholders. The top priority categories that receive the greatest funding, according to the High-Level Committee Report for 2019, are education, differently abled, livelihood, health, poverty, hunger and health and sanitation.

Table 10.11. CSR Contribution by Companies in FY 2016–2017 to 2020–2021 (Top 10 Companies).

FY 2016–2017		FY 2017–2018		FY 2018–2019		FY 2019–2020		FY 2020–2021	
Company Name	Amount (INR Cr.)	Company Name	Amount (INR Cr.)	Company Name	Amount (INR Cr.)	Company Name	Amount (INR Cr.)	Company Name	Amount (INR Cr.)
Reliance Industries Limited	649.26	Reliance Industries Limited	745.04	Reliance Industries Limited	849.32	Reliance Industries Limited	908.71	Reliance Industries Limited	922
Oil and Natural Gas Corporation Limited	504.91	Oil and Natural Gas Corporation Limited	482.07	Oil and Natural Gas Corporation Limited	586.85	Tata Consultancy Services Limited	602	Tata Consultancy Services Limited	674
Tata Consultancy Services Limited	380	Tata Consultancy Services Limited	400	Indian Oil Corporation Limited	468.15	Oil And Natural Gas Corporation Limited	582.07	Tata Sons Private Limited	545.83
HDFC Bank Limited	305.42	HDFC Bank Limited	374.55	HDFC Bank Limited	443.78	Tata Sons Private Limited	548.83	HDFC Bank Limited	534.03
Infosys Limited	289.44	Indian Oil Corpn. Limited	331.04	Tata Consultancy services Limited	434	HDFC Bank Limited	535.31	Oil and Natural Gas Corporation Limited	531.45
NTPC Limited	277.81	Infosys Limited	312.6	Infosys Limited	342.04	Indian Oil Corporation Limited	518.49	Indian Oil Corporation Limited	445.09
ITC Limited	275.96	ITC Limited	290.98	Mahanadi Coalfields Limited	334.29	Infosys Limited	359.94	NTPC Limited	418.87

(Continued)

Table 10.11. *(Continued)*

FY 2016–2017		FY 2017–2018		FY 2018–2019		FY 2019–2020		FY 2020–2021	
Company Name	**Amount (INR Cr.)**	**Company Name**	**Amount (INR Cr.)**	**Company Name**	**Amount (INR Cr.)**	**Company Name**	**Amount (INR Cr.)**	**Company Name**	**Amount (INR Cr.)**
Oil India Limited	216.74	Mahanadi Coalfields Limited	267.53	ITC Limited	307	Power Grid Corporation of India Limited	346.21	Infosys Limited	361.82
Indian Oil Corpn. Limited	213.99	NTPC Limited	241.54	Tata Steel Limited	305.47	Bharat Petroleum Corporation Limited	345.55	ITC Limited	335.43
Wipro Limited	186.31	Tata Steel Limited	231.62	NTPC Limited	285.46	ITC Limited	326.49	Wipro Limited	246.99

Source: Data compiled by the authors from (National CSR Portal, n.d.).

Rural development is another sector that receives a lot of cash. A sizeable percentage of the budget is allotted to Rajasthan, Uttar Pradesh and Andhra Pradesh from FY 2014 to FY 2018. However, there is a clause for spending in the neighbourhood and in the communities close to the businesses. This may be the case for a number of reasons as the business wants to have a beneficial social influence elsewhere. Additionally, local spending as a proportion of overall spending was 26% in FY 2014–2015, 31% in FY 2015–2016 and 54% in FY 2016–2017.

The wealth created by predatory capitalism and inheritance has been absorbed by the wealthiest. They are acquiring riches at a much faster rate, whereas the poor are still having difficulty getting by and having access to good healthcare and education. The fundamental issues in India that need to be addressed by efficient policies are the rural–urban split, poverty, malnutrition, difficulty in education and health, etc. There have been numerous requests for businesses to assume responsibility for their acts beyond philanthropy from the position of their social duty to address these difficulties and challenges are caused by unequal economic growth (Sangvikar, 2019).

Conclusion

It seems plausible that the contributions by private sector would be more promising as outlined by the CSR policy. Although, there is a proper mechanism of project allocation and fund allocation in the policy, it's not working at the optimal level. Although, in times of disaster and pandemics, private companies have supported the government wholeheartedly, in normal times it needs more contributions. The researchers attempt to demonstrate that private-sector initiatives are typically inefficient at addressing societal issues. This article takes a more cautious stance on privatisation as the only way forward. Despite the rhetoric of private-sector efficiency, honest government projects would prioritise welfare while private ventures focus on profits. Political factors, on the other hand, may also exhibit corrupt behaviour. This is a critical situation that requires a stringent regulatory structure specifying not only obligations but also harsh penalties for social initiatives that are stalled or delayed. We are not concerned with large-scale industrial projects or private sector expansion to comprehend our chances for growth. Our goal is to give all citizens a long-term, incremental empowerment through access to better healthcare, education and finances sufficient to maintain a basic standard of living.

References

Alhaddi, H. (2015). Triple bottom line and sustainability: A literature review. *Business and Management Studies*, 6–10. https://doi.org/10.11114/bms.v1i2.752

Alvaredo, F. (2018). *World inequality report 2018*. Harvard University Press.

Anushree Poddar, S. A. (2019, March 14). A study of corporate social responsibility practices of the top Bombay Stock Exchange 500 companies in India and their alignment with the Sustainable Development Goals. https://doi.org/10.1002/csr.1741

Bapuji, H. (2020). Understanding economic inequality through the lens of caste. *Journal of Business Ethics, 162*(3), 533–551.

Chadda, V. M. (2023). Corporate response to disaster resilience: Examining problems and potential for Indian CSR regime. In *5th World Congress on Disaster Management* (Vol. III). Taylor & Francis.

Chakraborty, J., & Basu, P. (2019). Linking industrial hazards and social inequalities: Environmental injustice in Gujarat, India. *International Journal of Environmental Research and Public Health, 16*, 42. https://doi.org/10.3390/ijerph16010042

Chancel, L. E. (2022). *World inequality report 2022*. Harvard University Press.

CSR Legislation. (n.d.). https://www.csr.gov.in/content/csr/global/master/home/aboutcsr/csr-legislation.html

CSR-report. (2019). *Report of the high level committee on corporate social responsibility, 2018*. Government of India, Ministry of Corporate Affairs. https://www.mca.gov.in/Ministry/pdf/CSRHLC_13092019.pdf

Dabla-Norris, M. E. (2015). *Causes and consequences of income inequality: A global perspective*. International Monetary Fund.

Dynamic CSR Report. (2022). *Ministry of corporate affairs*. Government of India. https://www.csr.gov.in/content/csr/global/master/home/ExploreCsrData/dynamic-csr-report-search.html

Gamji, M. B. (2022). The challenges of digital divide and the use of web 2.0 platforms as knowledge sharing tools among Nigerian academics. *Information Development, 38.1*, 149–159.

GDP growth (annual %) - India. (2021). The World Bank.

Govt amends rules governing corporate social responsibility. (2022, September 23). *The Economic Times of India*. https://economictimes.indiatimes.com/news/economy/policy/govt-amends-rules-governing-corporate-social-responsibility/articleshow/94381725.cms

Invitation for public comments for High Level Committee on Corporate Social Responsibility 2018. (n.d.a). https://www.mca.gov.in/Ministry/pdf/InvitationOfPublicComments HLC_18012019.pdf

Jintao Lu, L. R. (2020). *Exploring the relationship between corporate social responsibility and firm competitiveness* (pp. 1621–1646).

Keeble, B. R. (1988). *The Brundtland report: 'Our common future*.

Kumar, A. B. (2022). "Educate, agitate, organize": Inequality and ethics in the writings of Dr. Bhimrao Ramji Ambedkar. *Journal of Business Ethics, 178*, 1–14. https://doi.org/10.1007/s10551-021-04770-y

Kurian, N. (2007, October). Widening economic & social disparities: Implications for India. *Indian Journal of Medical Research, 126*(4), 374–380.

Kuznets, S. (2019). *Economic growth and income inequality. The gap between rich and poor* (pp. 25–37). Routledge.

Lall, S. C. (2005). Industrial location and spatial inequality: Theory and evidence from India. *Review of Development Economics, 9*, 47–68. https://doi.org/10.1111/j.1467-9361.2005.00263.x

Latest CSR Rules. (2022, October 15). *Limit disclosure of key details in annual report*. https://indiacsr.in/latest-csr-rules-limit-disclosure-of-key-details-in-annual-report/

Mueller, H. O. (2017). Wage inequality and firm growth. *The American Economic Review, 107*, 379–383. https://doi.org/10.1257/aer.p20171014.

Narula, A. P. (2019). A study of Corporate Social Responsibility (CSR) and Sustainable Development Goal (SDG) practices of the states in India. In *Mandated corporate social responsibility* (pp. 85–94). Springer. https://doi.org/10.1007/978-3-030-24444-6_5

National CSR Portal. (n.d.). *Ministry of corporate affairs*. https://www.csr.gov.in/content/csr/global/master/home/aboutcsr/history.html

NITI Aayog. (n.d.). https://www.niti.gov.in/niti-aayogs-role#:~:text=NITI%20Aayog%20has%20the%20twin,realise%20the%20goals%20and%20targets

Ortiz, I. a. (2011, April 6). *Global Inequality: Beyond the Bottom Billion – A Rapid Review of Income Distribution in 141 Countries*. https://doi.org/10.2139/ssrn.1805046

Press Information Bureau, Government of India, Ministry of Finance. (2019, July 4). *India follows a holistic approach towards its 2030 Sustainable Development Goals (SDGs)*. https://pib.gov.in/Pressreleaseshare.aspx?PRID=1577014

Qureshi, I. C. (2018). The transformative power of knowledge sharing in settings of poverty and social inequality. *Organization Studies*, 1575–1599.

Sangvikar, B. P. (2019). Comprehending the pre and post economic turbulence calamity of India: The realization message from the nineties. *Journal of Critical Reviews*, *6*(6), 345–349.

Shen, J. Y. (2017). The impact of environmental regulations on the location of pollution-intensive industries in China. *Journal of Cleaner Production*, *148*(2017), 785–794.

Shuili Du, C. B. (2010, January 15). Maximizing business returns to corporate social responsibility (CSR): The role of CSR communication. *International Journal of Management Reviews*, 8–19. https://doi.org/10.1111/j.1468-2370.2009.00276

Sullivan, D. a. (2023). Capitalism and extreme poverty: A global analysis of real wages, human height, and mortality since the long 16th century. *World Development*, *161*(2023), 106026.

Sustainable Development Goals. (n.d.). https://www.un.org/sustainabledevelopment/development-agenda-retired/un.org

Tiwari, S. P. (2022). Information and communication technology initiatives for knowledge sharing in agriculture. *arXiv preprint arXiv:2202.08649*.

Uchida, C. P. (2003). Privatisation and economic growth in developing countries. *Journal of Development Studies*, 121–154.

https://www.mca.gov.in/Ministry/pdf/AMENDMENTACT_01082019.pdf

Appendix

Table A1. State-Wise and Development Sector-Wise CSR spending (INR Cr.) from FY 2014–2015 to FY 2020–2021.

State	Education, Differently Abled, Livelihood	Encouraging Sports	Environment, Animal Welfare, Conservation of Resources	Gender Equality, Women Empowerment, Old Age Homes, Reducing Inequalities	Health, Eradicating Hunger, Poverty and Malnutrition, Safe Drinking Water, Sanitation	Heritage Art And Culture	Other Sectors (Technology Incubator and Benefits to Armed Forces and Admin Overheads)	Others	Rural Development	Slum Area Development	Grand Total
Andaman and Nicobar	0.51		0.47	0.44	3.05	0.25		0.03	2.42		7.17
Andhra Pradesh	1,521.27	11.32	682.29	144.43	1,894	26.93	1.08	231	585.12	4.19	5,101.7
Arunachal Pradesh	45.95	0.4	11.95	13.89	13.96	0.07		8.83	6.62		101.67
Assam	694.62	12.14	89.3	25.75	453.4	13.71	0.8	27.3	95.32	12.4	1,424.8
Bihar	171.42	2.47	291.47	18.8	119.3	3.34	1.58	19.6	66.26	0.43	694.61
Chandigarh	21.15	2.93	2.12	22.74	31.83	0.49	5.7	1.1	1.59	0.16	89.81
Chhattisgarh	505	20.66	124.95	20.64	554.9	15.44	1.69	17.6	128.09	0.26	1,389.2
Dadra and Nagar Haveli	24.8	0.02	21.35	0.8	27.11	0.16		0.67	9.67		84.58
Daman and Diu	37.86	1.57	0.55	1.1	19.55	0.09		0	5.61		66.33
Delhi	1,753.97	56.35	397.61	186.07	1,353	81.86	62.12	28.7	98.56	7.79	4,026.1
Goa	144.25	2.99	11.51	10.46	85.43	2.96	0.86	1.38	17.52	0.37	277.73
Gujarat	2,393.59	17.76	342.41	146.53	2,316	390.3	16.77	21.7	544.32	15.5	6,204.6
Haryana	1,491.59	20.84	180.83	99.36	772.2	11.88	2.38	16.1	170.7	1.75	2,767.6
Himachal Pradesh	151.1	9	38.83	13.32	132.4	16.48	0.71	7.59	44.4	3.85	417.63

Jammu and Kashmir	90.64	1.4	56.37	9.71	160.2	1.8	1.57	4.4	10.67	0.15	556.88
Jharkhand	194.17	32.39	46.09	29.07	441.8	5.34	2.35	12	112.3	0.93	876.36
Karnataka	3,396.17	91.08	1,144.6	197.82	1,678	97.72	26.68	112	393.69	23.5	7,161.2
Kerala	418.83	14.2	133.94	66.52	671.1	12.85	2	39.7	142.8	4.72	1,506.7
Lakshadweep	0	0.12	0.43	0.01	2.26		0			0.15	0	2.97
Madhya Pradesh	522.37	8.33	98.22	43.9	447.7	9.75	3.23	36.6	280.99	0.74	1,451.8
Maharashtra	8,408.61	191.5	1,046	612.64	7,072	105.9	70.66	165	915.82	20.3	18,608
Manipur	32.49	6.91	1.41	1.82	11.61	1.04		0.96	1.94	0	58.18
Meghalaya	29.29	0.14	5.02	9.85	16.99	0.1		4.23	10.35	0.73	76.7
Mizoram	1.29	0	0.02	0.82	1.14			0.59	0.92		4.78
Nagaland	3.36	3.5	1.58	0.06	5.39			0.3	1.01		15.2
Odisha	1,615.28	97.49	166.75	42.69	862.1	58.48	0.57	15.7	802.42	21.8	3,683.3
Puducherry	26.4	1.08	3.87	0.97	17.74	0.12		0.25	3.9		54.33
Punjab	265.01	7.63	127.9	35.14	289	22.3	2.07	3.38	50.27	2.14	804.8
Rajasthan	1,492.31	80.1	287.81	156.67	996.8	106.6	9.44	91.4	337.66	8.97	3,567.7
Sikkim	24.91	1.21	1.08	0.56	14.59	0.27		1.21	4.54		48.37
Tamil Nadu	2,633.53	86.8	375.88	151.04	1,606	101.9	27.13	44.5	405.88	7.45	5,440.2
Telangana	1,113.52	13.24	123.48	77.07	749.7	16.61	9.58	12.2	254.65	130	2,500.4
Tripura	10.43	0.21	1.3	0.91	32.22	0.02	0.04	0.54	1.93	0	47.6
Uttar Pradesh	1,385.2	12.13	236.95	86.8	999.3	18.14	14.87	143	392.19	3.51	3,291.7
Uttarakhand	349.23	1.12	28.07	60.05	256.6	7.43	1.67	11.1	73.25		788.49
West Bengal	1,010.71	16.38	83.79	82.03	1,053	78.47	9.37	23.7	129.37	4.36	2,490.8
Pan India (other centralised funds)											9,484.6
Grand total	31,980.8	825.4	6,166.3	2,370.5	25,160	1,209	274.9	1,104	6,102.9	276	84,955

Source: Data compiled by the authors from (National CSR Portal, n.d.).

Table A2. Pan India CSR spending (INR Cr.) From FY 2014–2015 to FY 2020–2021.

Pan India CSR Spending	(INR Cr.)
Clean Ganga fund	124.75
Swachh Bharat Kosh	1,205
Prime Ministers National Relief Fund	3,603
Any Other Fund	4,552.09
Pan India (Other Centralised Funds)	9,484.6

Source: Data compiled by the authors from (National CSR Portal, n.d.).

Chapter 11

Sustainable Poverty Alleviation Strategies: Sustainable Environment with Respect to Go Green

Rakesh Kumar and Archana Saxena

Uttaranchal University, India

Abstract

The globe faces a difficult job in maintaining a sustainable ecosystem. Sustainable development goal (SDG-2030) is an important agenda for United National Organization. By 2030, the United Nations aims to have eliminated hunger, poverty, social protection, environmental protection, social security and inequality as described in different goals of SDG-2030. This cannot be accomplished without diligent work from each member. This study focuses on the strategy to removal of poverty with go green concept. The study is based on secondary data which was collected from different websites and previous research papers. This is analyst-based research. The go green notion is stressed in this chapter as aim to achieved SDG-1. The go green idea and its supporting industries were stressed in this chapter as a means of achieving SDG-1. This chapter discussed the many forms of poverty and an examination of their causes, as listed in SDG-1. Environment degradation is crucial for the SDGs. This chapter links SDG-1, 2, 6 and 7, which are concerned with hunger, clean water and sustainability of energy sources. This study explores achieving SDG while protecting the environment. This chapter explains how green growth policies, technology, good healthcare equipment, a strong education sector and effective communication technologies can all work together to achieve SDG-1 in a sustainable manner. This study focused on the resources needed to eradicate poverty in various regions. It is a crucial component of sustainable endeavours that help preserve a healthy environment for coming generations. Human development was dependent on a healthy environment. This study emphasised green growth, eco-friendly transportation and clean energy concept while achieving SDG-1. The study analyses different parameters to remove poverty with go green concept.

Creating Pathways for Prosperity, 179–196

Copyright © 2025 Rakesh Kumar and Archana Saxena

Published under exclusive licence by Emerald Publishing Limited

doi:10.1108/978-1-83549-121-820241012

Keywords: Green economy; poverty; technology; environment; energy; education; health care; digital

Introduction

A sustainable society is the main agenda of United Nation Organizations (UNO). There are some parameters of SDGs that encompasses around People, environment, success society and harmony. The SDGs seek to protect the environment and natural resources that all life depends on; promote economic growth and development; reduce inequality and poverty; advance peaceful and inclusive societies; increase countries' capacity against violence, extremism and pursue knowledge that can result in more eco-friendly and ethical business practices. Goals aim to achieve sustainable and peaceful society. By reducing electricity and waste disposal expenses, green construction techniques may reduce building running costs as well as ongoing maintenance costs. Sustainable development means advancing society without permanently harming the resources essential to the life of our species (Tartaruga & Sperotto, 2021). The Sustainable Development Goals Summit is expected to 'mark the beginning of a phase of accelerated progress towards the Sustainable Development Goals'. It is important to mention here that we must pace with time to achieve our goal and be ready to face some undesirable activities like natural disasters.

The corporate sector is also a big player in achieving SDGs. This can be measured through environmental, social and governance (ESG) programme launched by the company. This method of assessing businesses is based on how well they operate in these three categories (Ballesteros-Vivas et al., 2021). Companies are becoming held to higher standards in terms of their environmental, social and governance activities as ESG investment gains popularity around the world. In India, the top 1,000 listed firms by market capitalisation are now required to comply with the new business responsibility and sustainability reporting (BRSR) standards. Companies are required to disclose information regarding their governance procedures, as well as their environmental and social impacts.

The word poverty is a wide term which is defined in different manner by different organisations. Low wages for low class people is also involved in poverty concept. There are many workers who work only for meal which will be deprived from education services. Aspects of poverty are also said to include poor levels of health and education, inadequate access to clean water and sanitation, inadequate physical security, lack of voice and a lack of resources and possibilities for improving one's position in life. Consumer spending surveys, according to the Indian Planning Commission, can be used to assess a nation's level of poverty (Calicioglu & Bogdanski, 2021).

Literature Review

Water, sanitation and disaster management are the main topics of Poverty Reduction Strategy Papers (PRSPs) and Progress Reports, whereas voluntary sustainability standards work to assure the ecologically and socially sustainable production of commodity crops (Ramzan et al., 2023). Findings indicate that relationships significantly affect how the families choose to make a living. This study offers a theoretical framework for understanding the connections between a relational society, targeted poverty reduction and household livelihood options. Many other countries also integrated with sustainable products which are ultimate eco-friendly. CO_2 emission is a major concern for the whole world. On the other side, mineral sources are limited and hazardous for humans as well as nature (Zanellato & Tiron-Tudor, 2021). Go green concept provides clean energy which leads to achieve SDG-7. Government policy must be effective in sustainable environment issue and pace with SDGs. Results from different conferences are to be required integrated effort towards SDGs (Suparjo et al., 2021). To accomplish both pro-poor and sustainability goals, this research investigates the sustainability stances of significant pro-poor tourist players. It implies that, in the absence of a serious effort to address structural injustices, the potential of tourism must be fundamentally re-evaluated. It also investigates the synergies and trade-offs of adaptation and mitigation choices as they relate to the two-way interactions between sustainable development and climate measures in a 1.5°C warmer future. Lastly, it investigates environmental sustainability within modern methods to poverty alleviation and evaluates policies on social and sustainable development. It contends that social justice and human development will likely always take precedence over environmental justice, and that the best we can do is learn from experience by recording the work that social workers are doing to advance sustainable social change (Rakhmangulov et al., 2017). A study was conducted in China to examine regional environmental vulnerability and livelihood resources in China's Longman Municipality. The study aimed to find out vulnerable livelihood in specified region of China. It divided 27 poverty-stricken regions into 10 subcategories that considered environmental vulnerability and all five sources of livelihood, as well as two levels of environmental vulnerability and four classes that combined natural and human capital. The Rio Declaration encourages lawyers and legal professionals to think creatively about the legal preparedness for the green economy. The two-way causal relationships between poverty alleviation and natural tropical forests are examined in this research, with the hypothesis that increasing poverty might either hasten or slow down forest decline. Yet there aren't many 'win-win' synergies between national poverty reduction and natural forests, which might be the reason why tropical forest loss is still happening (Georgeson et al., 2017). Removal of Poverty and hunger is topmost priority of SDGs. Poverty is defined in different ways by UNO which is related to food, shelter, basic healthcare service and education. Information technology is a useful tool for supporting SGDs. Society is derived from clean water and sanitisation. SDGs −6 aim to provide clean water. These goals relate to each other for sustainable society (Singh, 2022).

Objectives

UNO aims to achieve all goals by 2030. It is important here to achieve this goal in a sustainable environment. However, many governments are active with sustainable environment policy but still many countries are not supporting sustainable environment development policy. Sustainable society can only be achieved by achieving these goals. It requires integrated effort from all members. Greenhouse gas emission is major issue which increases overall temperature of earth. Clean and green technology is an important factor which is related to goal 7. However, the foremost requirement is to remove poverty and hunger, i.e. goal 1 and goal 2. This study connected with go green concept removed poverty. However, the go green concept also touched on goal 6, i.e. related to clean water and sanitisation and goal 7, i.e. related to clean energy. This chapter emphasised achieving SDG-1 with sustainable environment policy, i.e. go green concept. Objective of this study are as follows:.

- To study and analyse SDGs with respect to achieving SDG-1 with sustainable environment.
- To study and analyse go green concept contribution to removal of poverty.
- To study and analyse different parameters to achieving SDG-1.
- To study and analyse poverty alleviation strategies with sustainable equipment.

Sustainability Development Goal (SDG)

Present level of climate change, inequality and poverty research and suggest directions for advancement that might help achieve three of the 17 SDGs (end poverty, reduce inequality and climate action). The findings demonstrate that little study has been done on the topic, and there are large disparities between the many places examined. Sustainability-related issues have the biggest number of publications, and more vulnerable communities are more at risk from climate change's consequences than others. Moreover, understudied topics like energy poverty and food security may benefit from the circular economy. The major goals of this strategy are to get rid of bad externalities, particularly the socio-economic inequities that are present in the current linear economy model. It is important to mention here that the goals are related to human development with sustainable environment (Dong et al., 2021). Present development being compromising environmental protection issues which is not suitable for future generation. We have limited mineral sources which can be ended in the next 100 years. Conservation of these mineral resources is important for future generation. The 17 SDGs aim to achieve removal of poverty, removal of hunger social security, social protection, equality and conservation of mineral resources for future generations (Montesano et al., 2023).

Achievement of these goals is an integrated effort from all members of UNO. Greenhouse gasses emission is emitted by developed countries and impact of gas emission is faced by whole world. Conference and agreement on climate change are under documents and not showing impact on climate. Social securities like right to equality, right to accessibility, affordable service, etc., are some important issues in society. Deprived society being facing of food shelter, education services, affordable health services. Fear of Terrorism, violence, extremist and fraud lead to poverty in the society. Good healthcare system, education system, technology, transportation and information technology will be important factors to achieve SDGs. Go green concept developed sustainable society.

Poverty Concept according to SDG

The multifaceted phenomenon of poverty is characterised by the denial of essential human requirements as well as a lack of access to sources of income and useful resources. The majority of people who participated in the survey believed it to be a danger to all of the goals of the 2030 Agenda, and it is considered a significant obstacle to its implementation. With an emphasis on food, safe drinking water and sanitation as well as finding solutions to climate change and conflict, SDG-1 seeks to eradicate poverty in all its manifestations. As the SDGs are a voluntary agreement rather than a legally enforceable treaty, governments have the option to set goals with a broader scope and more ambitious aspirations. The SDGs' stated goal is to provide a 'supremely ambitious and revolutionary vision' that will enable us to 'envision a world free from poverty, hunger, sickness and lack, where all life can thrive'. The SDGs may be criticised in a variety of ways; however, this chapter will assess the SDGs against the benchmark established by its own authors, with an emphasis on SDG-1 ('end poverty in all its manifestations everywhere'). The author contends that SDG-1 deserves respect for clearly outpacing the Millennium Developmental Goals (MDGs') primary target of eradicating poverty.

Analysis Target of SDG-1 With Respect to Sustainable Environment

SDG-1 includes the eradication of extreme poverty, the reduction of all poverty by half, the implementation of social safety systems, the guarantee of equal rights and the development of disaster resilience as seven objectives and 14 indicators to track progress. SDG Tracker by Our World in Data is the primary data source for SDG-1 indicators, which also includes maps. The targets cover a wide range of subjects, such as eradication, halving poverty, implementation, ensuring equitable access to real estate, basic services, technology and financial resources, constructing resilience against natural and man-made disasters, and mobilising resources to end poverty (Giuliani et al., 2021). Although targets specify the goals, indicators act as the measurements by which the world measures its success. According to this analysis, three key factors – a group of norm entrepreneurs; the Open Working Group's institutional framework and operating procedures; and fresh perspectives on the value of the environment and an integrated approach to sustainable development – all had a significant impact on the environmental content of the SDGs (OWG). These variables significantly influenced the goals and targets, but they had far less of an impact on the indicators, which were chosen through a distinct process with a different institutional framework and important players who had different backgrounds. Although many objectives are ambitious and environmental goals are included into all the other goals, this chapter argues that the influence of the SDGs on stakeholder activities and decision-making may be difficult. All targets are shown in Fig. 11.1.

- *Eradicate Extreme Poverty:* This is Target 1.1 and aim of this target is to remove extreme poverty within the timeframe. There are number of indicators set for this target. Extreme poverty is defined on the basis of Food and shelter. This target can be achieved with help of other goal like goal no 2, i.e. hunger. Further sustainable agriculture also plays an important role in this target. Biochemicals are major concern in go green concept. Production capacity has to increase without harm to the nature through the use of chemical.
- *Reduce Poverty by Half of Total:* This is Target 1.2 which aims to reduce poverty by at least half the percentage of men, women and children of all ages living in poverty. This target lags due to the pandemic. But still this target is pacing with time. It is important to analyse difference between extreme poverty and poverty. This concept defines as people living below poverty line. This comprises two indicators, i.e. based on the percentage of populace and national standard. This concept is based on food, shelter, education and health care facility.

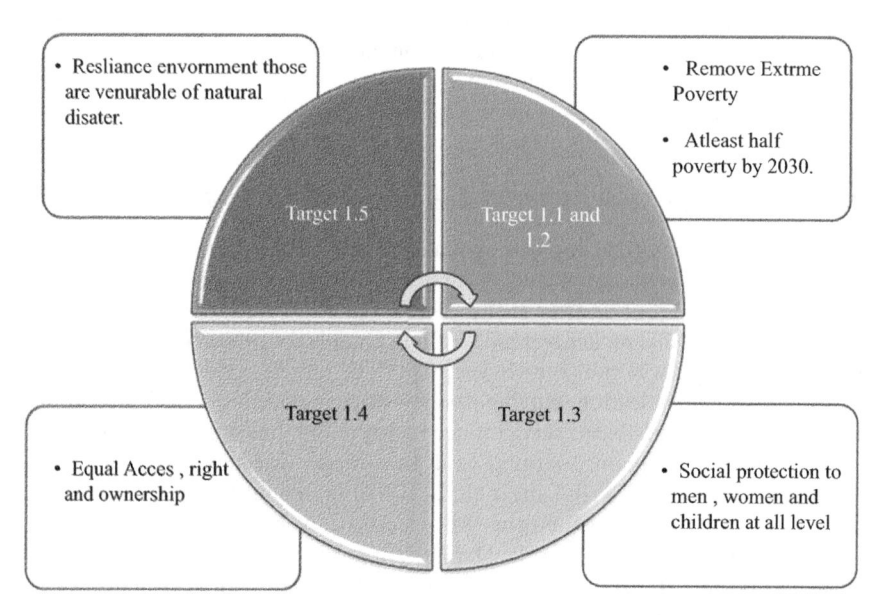

Fig. 11.1.   Target of Goal 1. *Source:* Prepared by the Authors.

- *Implement Nationally Appropriate Social Protection Systems:* This target is related to social security systems that are suitable for each country. Social security is an important facet in society. There are number of parameters involved like security of food, shelter, health, education and accessibility of resources. Better security in terms of education, health, information technology and transport services are concerned with this target. Technology based equipment support in healthcare sector and education sector are important factors to achieve this target.
- *Equal Rights to Ownership, Basic Services, Technology and Economic Resources:* This objective calls for equal access to economic resources, ownership of and control over land and other kinds of property, inheritance and natural resources for all men and women. The lowest and most vulnerable people are disproportionately affected by this. Two measures of this are the percentage of people who have access to necessities and the percentage of adults who have secure land tenure. Accessibility and equality for men, women and children are also signs of human growth.
- *Build Resilience to Environmental, Economic and Social Disasters:* This target improves the resilience of the deprived and those in precarious situations while reducing their exposure to and susceptibility to natural catastrophes, economic shocks and social upheavals. Four indicators point in this direction: the number of fatalities, missing persons and disaster-related personal economic loss as a percentage of global gross domestic product (GDP); the adoption and implementation of national disaster risk reduction plans; the proportion of local governments that adopt and implement local disaster risk reduction strategies; and research programmes for climate-related disasters.
- *Mobilisation of Resources to End Poverty.* This aims to gather funding from various sources. Fund is an important facet for every project. There are number of issues for SDG like poverty, hunger, living standard, etc. Growth of a country also depends upon sustainable society which required more fund. This concept mobilised fund from developed countries to developing nations for reduction of poverty. UNO also launched many programmes in least development country for upliftment of poor people. During pandemic, many countries send medical facility to other country.
- *Establishment of Poverty Eradication Policy Frameworks at All Levels.* Creating effective policy frameworks at the national, regional and international levels based on pro-poor and gender-sensitive development policies is the goal of this target, which intends to promote increasing investment in efforts to eradicate poverty. It is necessary to make policy for spending on pro-poverty policy. Right spending of fund will help to remove of poverty. It is also important that policy framework shall be effectively utilised for eligible people.

Go Green Concept With SDGs

The phrase 'going green' describes the search for knowledge and practices that can lead to more environmentally and ecologically aware decisions and lifestyles, helping to protect the ecosystem and its natural resources for both current and future generations. Creating a sustainable world is a crucial component of going green (Muhammad & Habib, 2023). Going green is the practice of living sustainably and in harmony with the environment. It might also mean preserving the ecological equilibrium of the world, together with all of its natural systems and resources. In general, those who practice sustainability make efforts to reduce the damage they cause to the ecosystem, such as the carbon footprints they leave behind. Several specific, measurable, achievable, realistic and time bound (SMART) components are absent from the SDGs. Goals are frequently wide, all-encompassing, ambitious, qualitative and possibly transformational, yet they might not be achievable soon. The stated global goal of limiting climate change to 2 degrees, as well as the aspirational 1.5-degree objective for climate adaptation is absent. The SDGs specifically include air pollution; however, its significance is diminished in comparison to other environmental media, such as land and water, or climate. Although there is just one mention of gender concerns in goal 6.2 on sanitation, environmental difficulties and pollution are very intimately tied to gender issues. Although goal 16.10 does not expressly address environmental information, access to information is a critical environmental concern.

UN aim to achieve SDG by 2030 through sustainable environment. However, along with goal no 1, i.e. related to poverty, other goals also support environment and clean energy. For example, goal no 6 is clean water and sanitation and goal no 7 is related to clean energy. In this process each goal is connected with each other. On the other hand we can define that one goal depends on the other goal. The concept of go green is related to achievement of SDG without harm of nature. Achieving of SDG-1, flowing goals is also considered in go green concept. Fig. 11.2 Shows achieving of SDG-1 through go green concept.

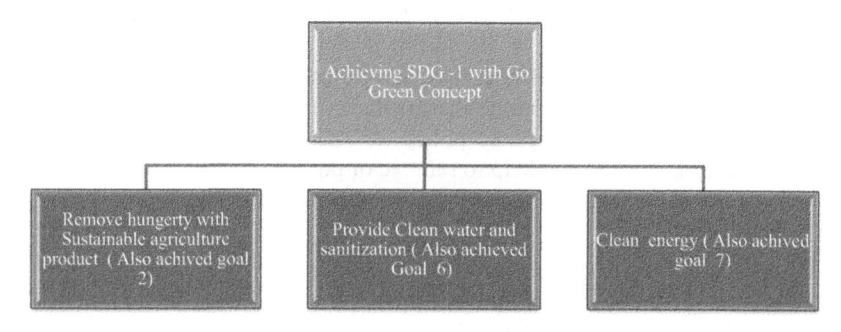

Fig. 11.2.   Achieving of SDG-1 With Go Green. *Source:* Prepared by the Authors.

Digital Contribution to Removal of Poverty Through Go Green

Right access to information technology leads to access of welfare scheme. The government launched several schemes for poor people and society which cannot access by eligible people. Digitisation is an important tool for accessibility of information. But there are some sustainable nature issues in digital equipment which harm nature. Sustainable technology can remove these issues. Eco-friendly and affordable equipment will help to achieve SDGs with relation to removal of poverty.

Food, health and shelter are three main issues for poor people. Government in pro-Poverty policy provides free ration, free health and free shelter for eligible poor people. But they are still unable to access this facility. Information technology (IT) is the only platform to connect these schemes with poor people. In this way IT equipment shall be cheaper, eco-friendly and easy to use for every individual. Go green concept also integrated with technology which provides sustainable equipment. Extreme poverty is different from poverty, which can be removed easily with these schemes launched by the government.

- *App-Based Agriculture Services.* Access to information is a big issue for poor people. Social welfare scheme is launched by the government for poor people. It is important to access these schemes by poor people. Technology can integrate these schemes with poor people. Digital platforms are valuable in terms of health, food, climate change and sustainable environment (Lee, 2020). Technology is helpful in Agriculture production like information about seasonal change, rain, drought and new avenue for business. Artificial Intelligence (AI)-based application provides information about rate of food grain, availability of stores, new bazar and prediction of market. Geographic information system (GIS)-based technology provides information about land health and water information (Savchenko & Borodina, 2020).
- *AI-Based Water Quality Measurement.* Clean and cost-effective water is big challenge for poor people. AI can measure water quality and provided clean water to poor people. As shown in Fig. 11.3, digitalisation can provide clean and cost-effective water which reduced poverty through go sustainable strategies.
- *Cost-Effective Renewal Energy Sources.* As shown in Fig. 11.3, clean energy is a big issue in climate change. There are many AI-based applications which provide information about gas emission and level of hazardous. Further green technology is also based on AI-based equipment. For instance, there are many home appliances installed like solar energy, monitoring cameras, electric control device, etc., helpful in clean and green energy. Technology is the base of renewal energy production. Presently electric vehicles are being used effectively in the society. Technology is a big player in this clean energy technology. There are many other technologies used in renewal energy sources like solar power control devices which replace traditional energy sources. Industry 4.0 provides 24/7 accessibility service without any interruption. Technology enables us to provide robot-based service without human effort which is accurate in speed

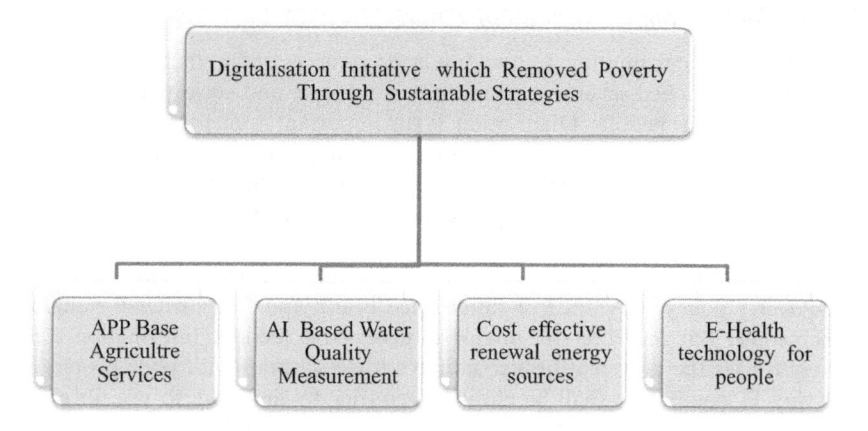

Fig. 11.3.   Digitalisation Initiative Which Removed Poverty Through Sustainable Strategies.

prediction. People can easily get tickets at the railway platform without standing in queue.

• *E-Health Technology for People.* As shown in Fig. 11.3, technology can provide information related to health issues. In Present time, poor people are deprived from cure of normal disease. As a result the society becomes poor due to health issues. Digitalisation can provide e-health service which is very cost effective and reduces poverty in the society.

The earth's temperature is increasing after a time. Technology is helpful to predict earth temperature in an accurate manner and recorded data. In this way, a deliberate planning can be made to observe earth temperature with the help of technology. Department of research and technology predicts overall chart to control earth temperature.

As mentioned above, technology provides valuable information to people, new avenue in agriculture production, base for renewable energy sources, monitoring of earth temperature and robotic-based services to people. These are all related to sustainable society. It is also important that accessibility of these technologies must be of reach to poor people. In this way technology is a strong factor to remove poverty.

Good, Affordable and Eco-friendly Healthcare Facility

According to World Economic Forum, AI technologies, for example can help reduce inefficiencies (care delivery errors, overtreatment and improper care delivery), resulting in significantly more efficient and cost-effective health environments (Sakai et al., 2022). Robotic-based systems reduced human effort and provided accurate result. Good health care systems provide best consultation which prevent from number of diseases. Biomedical products are also majorly connected to medical industry. It is important here to use go green concept in medical sector. Essential of good healthcare sector is shown in Fig. 11.4. There are four methods where technology can increase the effectiveness, eco-friendly and affordability of healthcare:

- *Influencing treatment decision:* AI-enabled systems can track outcomes and diseases within a moment. Technology also can predict recovery time. This can help in speedy and accurate treatment of patients.
- *A more accurate prognosis:* technology based on AI and robotic systems which reduced human effort and provide result based on outcome of machine. In this process, the result is more accurate than manual perception and suggests way of treatment.
- *Optimising clinical studies and developing new medications:* Technology not only benefits in health care equipment but is also useful for production of drug. COVID-19 is a recent example where vaccine has been developed within short span of time and with accurate prediction.

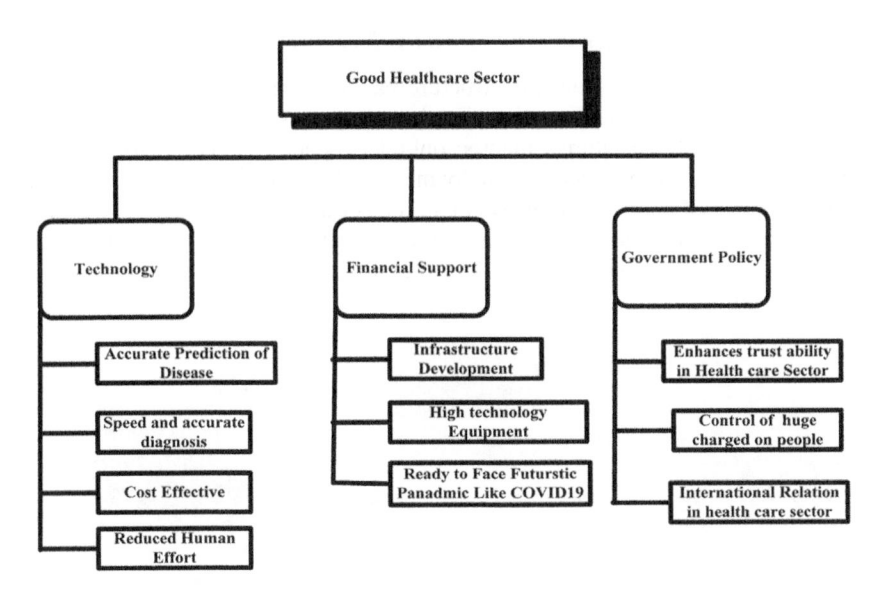

Fig. 11.4.   Health Care Sector Achieving SDG-1. *Source:* Prepared by the Authors.

- *Patient empowerment:* Technology gives better opportunities to discuss with consultants and doctors without moving from home.

Green Growth Policy

A possible route of economic growth that is ecologically sustainable is referred to as 'green growth.' It is fuelled by the shift to sustainable energy systems and is strongly tied to the ideas of the green economy and low carbon or sustainable development. Green growth policy proponents contend that effectively implemented green policies may open job prospects in industries like renewable energy, organic agriculture and sustainable forestry (de Carvalho Figueiredo & Rotaru, 2021). The phrase 'green growth' has been used to characterise national or worldwide efforts as part of the economic recovery from the COVID-19 recession by several nations and international organisations. Green growth is criticised for failing to adequately account for the underlying economic system changes required to address the climate problem and biodiversity loss. Public and private investment in infrastructure and resources that lower carbon emissions and pollution, increase energy efficiency, conserve biodiversity and provide ecosystem services is what fuels growth in employment and income in a green economy. Fig. 11.5 shows parameters related to SDG-1 with go green concept.

Affordable, Clean Energy and Eco-friendly Transportation

Investment in transportation infrastructure has long been thought to indirectly help reduce poverty, but recent empirical research has supported the idea that transportation infrastructure's macroeconomic impact is essential for assuring continued growth in production, employment and income. Affordable transport facility connected people from urban area, industrial area to rural area and poor people. This will reduce poverty among society and economic system of country will be stronger (Hasan & Syahruddin, 2022). Electronic vehicle concept is going

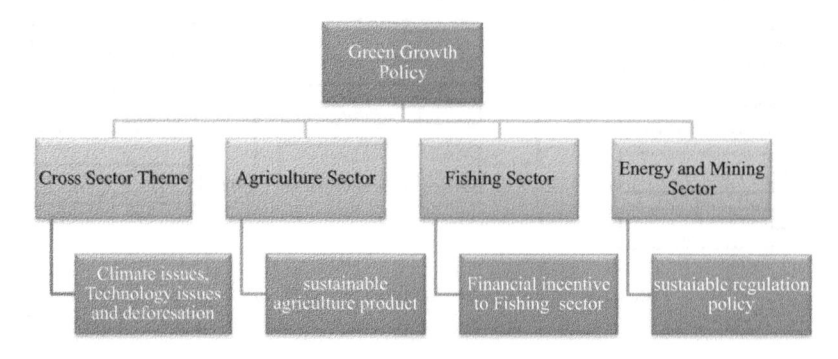

Fig. 11.5.   Green Growth Policy. *Source:* Prepared by the Authors.

green concept which support clean energy. Through cutting input costs and improving access to loans, extension services and output markets, transportation infrastructure may directly help to the elimination of poverty. Moreover, advancements in rural transportation reduced the cost of moving people and products for the poor, produced cash for farms, encouraged non-farm activities and broadened the variety of alternatives for wage work. The fundamental advantage of investing in transportation infrastructure is the reduction in operating expenses, which must be distributed to the underprivileged in the form of reduced tickets or freight rates.

A key challenge is the lack of effective maintenance in developing nations, which denies the community of chances for income and employment, hinders the ability of the poor to maintain improvements and results in significant efficiency losses and spending problems. The connectivity between two nations is possible through affordable transport facility. Interaction of society exchanges their ideas which remove weakness with each other. Poor society will be lifted when it integrated with other developed society. Further clean energy concept is also connected with transportation. Electric vehicle concept is going on in society but these vehicle are costly than existing vehicle. Affordable electric vehicle can provide clean energy to society.

As mentioned above, transportation is connection between developed to developing society. It is important to provide affordable transport facility to poor people so that they can access opportunity of employment in other city as well as other country. Also, we must keep in mind about clean energy sources in transportation sector. All these issues will be led to SDG-1 and SDG-7. This is effective tool of physical communication when poor people got employment as per their skill. Further, electric vehicle concept makes sustainable nature. The International Maritime Organization (IMO) is limiting ship-sourced greenhouse gas emissions and the SDGs aim to promote sustainability.

Affordable and Eco-friendly Information and Communication Technology

Information and communication technology (ICT) may relieve poverty by increasing poor people's access to government, financial and health services, but it requires rigorous project planning and policy development. The availability of information and services that cater to the needs of the poor, as well as local ownership, are facilitated through grassroots intermediaries and community engagement. Without access to ICT, the impoverished in rural India rely on informal networks of reliable family, friends and local authorities for information. ICT might increase access to information; however utilising new technology is challenging for those with low levels of knowledge. ICT can reduce poverty by improving poor people's access to education, health, government and financial services. Grassroots intermediaries and community involvement are key factors to foster local ownership and the availability of content and services that meet the needs of the poor. According to UN meeting held on 9th march 2023, Women and girls' participation in digital technology and innovation is essential for economies, poverty removal and sustainability. India's Minister for Women and Children Development, Smriti Irani, stated, that approximately 123 million girls are enroled in programmes that support science and technology education in schools, while other initiatives aim to teach rural women and those from marginalised groups of society how to use mobile phones and other essential tools (Acosta et al.2020). The participation of men and women in STEM fields is almost equal in her nation, in contrast to much of the rest of the world. She mentioned the 'STEM Stars' online campaign, which celebrates women who have made names for themselves in science and technology while outlining several government initiatives in that field.

Green and Clean Energy for Living Standard

Real Life Options (RLO) is an opportunity for staff, service users and families to make a real contribution to the environment through their ideas, skills and passion. This will give them a sense of pride and help reduce waste and CO_2 emissions. Go digital, switch lights off, re-use before recycling, get sharing and switch computers off to reduce energy consumption. This will save money and unnecessary manufacture. Recycle, save water, cut unnecessary travel, use RLO Skype or teleconference facilities, green the commute, bring your own lunch and use dual-flush toilets or water saving devices for toilet cisterns. Green technology incentive is important for development of green energy. Green building concept is environment friendly which generates everything from building. It is important here to introduce effective and trustable policy for clean energy. Many countries like Canada given tax-based incentive for green building project (Shehata et al., 2022).

RLO is an opportunity for those people who are actual users and families providing actual inputs to the environment through their ideas, skills and passion. This will give them a sense of pride and assist in bringing down wastage and Carbon di oxide flux. Go digital, switch lights off, re-use before recycling, get sharing and switch computers off to reduce energy consumption. This will save money and unnecessary manufacture. Recycle, save water, cut unnecessary travel, use RLO Skype or teleconference facilities, green the commute, bring your own lunch and use of toilets which have double flush buttons, or we can say a device which can save water in toilets (Zhou et al., 2020). To raise public awareness of green buildings, the government should fund energy-saving technology research and development as well as raise the standard of property management. Market regulation may drive green buildings in a better direction by developing expert green building consulting firms, ensuring market information is transparent and implementing market competitive procedures. High efficiency light fixtures, windows, insulation, timers, motion detectors and natural light operation sensors reduce energy use and light pollution. Solar energy is harvested at the top of a green building to supplement conventional energy, natural light is harvested on intermediate floors to reduce electricity use and solar energy is harvested at the bottom of a green building to supplement conventional energy. Concepts for green buildings may assist the environment, the economy, human health, public safety and the community while consuming less energy and operating costs.

Discussion

Poverty is defined in different manners by different organisations. UNO divided poverty into two-part: extreme poverty and poverty. Extreme poverty is related to food and shelter. A basic requirement of an individual is food, clean water and shelter. SDG-1 is about removal of poverty within a given timeframe. Many targets and indicators are prepared to achieve this goal. This study finds out that how SDG is achieved through go green concept. This goal is also connected with other goals like removal of hunger, clean water, clean energy and sanitisation in different parameters. These are integrated with the green energy concept. Goods healthcare sector can effectively treat patients. But it shall be affordable and eco-friendly. Many poor people are not getting good health care services due to the high cost. This is one important factor which helps to achieve SDG-1.

Technology is rooted everywhere. Access to information is again lacking with poor people. There is much information which are out of reach with poor people. Technology can solve this issue. It is important here to provide affordable and sustainable products to poor people. Many poor people are unable to afford this technological equipment due to high cost. Information technology reduces poverty and provides information about welfare schemes.

Better education always leads society and removes poverty. Eco-friendly affordable educational service equipment is an important issue to removal of poverty. There are many costly courses that are unable to reach by poor people. This can be solved with the help of technology where a huge amount of infor-mation is available related to affordable courses. Sustainable educational as well as sustantiable equipment will help to clean and green energy concept.

Clean energy is an important component of a sustainable society. This is cost-effective sources which is an essential strategy for poverty alleviation. Solar energy is an example of cost effective and easily accessible energy which improves the living conditions of poor households.

Findings

SDG-1 is an important goal for human development. Poverty is defined in different manner in this chapter as extreme poverty and poverty. The aim is to remove extreme poverty completely and poverty at least 50% by 2030. This study finds out how this can be achieved with a sustainable environment. Go green concept shall be adopted along with this goal. Study finds out following areas to achieve this goal with go green concept.

- Conservation of mineral resources for future generations leads to a sustainable environment. This is also connected with SDG-7 that is the use of clean energy ideas. This can be achieved thorough green technology with go green concept.

Electrification of vehicles, solar energy and renewal energy sources are important component to of sustainable environment.

- Efficient and sustainable healthcare equipment reduces overall cost which will positively impact on consumer. Good healthcare system along with sustainable equipment which conserve environment support go green as well-affordable diagnosis for people. Low class people can avail themselves of any type of medical facility.
- The education and information technology sector shall also adopt eco-friendly equipment which can be accessed in an affordable manner by every person. Access of information helps to achieve SDG-1. Cost-effective education information can be provided to all class of people.
- Smart home technology shall be adopted in an affordable manner which will improve living standard along with sustainable environment. Clean and efficient energy can be used.
- Green growth policy shall be adopted in Agri-based product and other sectors which connect with biotechnology. This will help to conserve technology and support SDG.

Conclusion and Implications

The natural environment has recently become a significant global issue. Due to growing industrial and human effects on the environment, environmental problems intensify and spread more widely. Businesses need to treat the environment and their corporate goals equally in this regard. Green stimulus is described as short-term fiscal stimulus that also has an environmental or 'Go Green' concept and its implication in sustainable environment. Sustainable energy, sustainable healthcare sector, sustainable transportation, sustainable agriculture products, etc., are important component to achieve SDG-1 through go green concept. Information technology is an effective platform to provide valuable information like welfare schemes for poor people, agri-based product information and climate change issues.

Many recently passed national stimulus plans shave sizeable 'green' elements. Companies are prioritising and addressing environmental, social and governance issues because of ESG investing and the BRSR requirements in India. The corporate sector is also contributing to green technology through CSR activities which help to achieve SDGs. Companies are attempting to raise their ESG performance and satisfy stakeholder expectations through variety of methods. Through proper access to food, financial assistance and necessities for households and families living below the poverty line, Poverty Alleviation Programmes seek to lower the rate of poverty in the nation. Many schemes are launched at national as well international levels for poor people, which can be easily accessed through IT. This study emphasised SDG-1 through go green concept. Clean energy technology is a major issue in the present day. Traditional energy sources are limited way and harmful for nature. In this way, the green energy concept is an important player in society. This study covered the use of go green concept in health care sector, education sector and transportation sector. Poverty alleviation along with sustainable environment can be achieved through go green concept.

References

Acosta, L. A., Maharjan, P., Peyriere, H. M., & Mamiit, R. J. (2020). Natural capital protection indicators: Measuring performance in achieving the Sustainable Development Goals for green growth transition. *Environmental and Sustainability Indicators, 8*, 100069.

Ballesteros-Vivas, D., Socas-Rodríguez, B., Mendiola, J. A., Ibanez, E., & Cifuentes, A. (2021). Green food analysis: Current trends and perspectives. *Current Opinion in Green and Sustainable Chemistry, 31*, 100522.

Calicioglu, Ö., & Bogdanski, A. (2021). Linking the bioeconomy to the 2030 sustainable development agenda: Can SDG indicators be used to monitor progress towards a sustainable bioeconomy? *New Biotech, 61*, 40–49.

de Carvalho Figueiredo, F., & Rotaru, C. S. (2021). From Green Growth to the Blue Growth in the 2030 Agenda Goals. *Bulletin of the Transilvania University of Braşov. Series VII: Social Sciences Law*, 23–30.

Dong, L., Liu, Z., & Bian, Y. (2021). Match circular economy and urban sustainability: Re-investigating circular economy under sustainable development goals (SDGs). *Circular Economy and Sustainability, 1*, 243–256.

Georgeson, L., Maslin, M., & Poessinouw, M. (2017). The global green economy: A review of concepts, definitions, measurement methodologies and their interactions. *Geo: Geography and Environment, 4*(1), e00036.

Giuliani, G., Petri, E., Interwies, E., Vysna, V., Guigoz, Y., Ray, N., & Dickie, I. (2021). Modelling accessibility to urban green areas using Open Earth Observations Data: A novel approach to support the urban SDG in four European cities. *Remote Sensing, 13*(3), 422.

Hasan, N. F., & Syahruddin, S. (2022). Enhancing Green Waqf for carbonization technology: Opportunities for Sustainable Development Goals (SDGs) in Indonesia. *El Barka: Journal of Islamic Economics and Business, 5*(2), 235–251.

Lee, J. W. (2020). Green finance and Sustainable Development Goals: The case of China. *Journal of Asian Finance Economics and Business, 7*(7), 577–586.

Montesano, F. S., Biermann, F., Kalfagianni, A., & Vijge, M. J. (2023). Can the sustainable development goals green international organisations? Sustainability integration in the International Labour Organisation. *Journal of Environmental Policy and Planning, 25*(1), 1–15.

Muhammad, L., & Habib, R. (2023). Green marketing is not a choice but a pre-requisite for Z generation: A case of green campus initiative in Capital University of Science & Technology, Pakistan. In *Sustainability and social marketing issues in Asia* (pp. 57–65). Emerald Publishing Limited.

Rakhmangulov, A., Sladkowski, A., Osintsev, N., & Muravev, D. (2017). Green logistics: Element of the sustainable development concept. Part 1. *NAŠE MORE: znanstveni časopis za more i pomorstvo, 64*(3), 120–126.

Ramzan, M., Abbasi, K. R., Salman, A., Dagar, V., Alvarado, R., & Kagzi, M. (2023). Towards the dream of go green: An empirical importance of green innovation and financial depth for environmental neutrality in world's top 10 greenest economies. *Technological Forecasting and Social Change, 189*, 122370.

Sakai, K., Hassan, M. A., Vairappan, C. S., & Shirai, Y. (2022). Promotion of a green economy with the palm oil industry for biodiversity conservation: A touchstone toward a sustainable bioindustry. *Journal of Bioscience and Bioengineering.* https://doi.org/10.1016/j.jbiosc.2022.01.001

Savchenko, A. B., & Borodina, T. L. (2020). Green and digital economy for sustainable development of urban areas. *Regional Research of Russia, 10*, 583–592.

Shehata, N., Mohamed, O. A., Sayed, E. T., Abdelkareem, M. A., & Olabi, A. G. (2022). Geopolymer concrete as green building materials: Recent applications, sustainable development and circular economy potentials. *Science of the Total Environment*, 155577.

Singh, V. K. (2022). Regulatory and legal framework for promoting green digital finance. In *Green digital finance and sustainable development goals* (pp. 3–27). Springer Nature.

Suparjo, S., Darma, S., Kurniadin, N., Kasuma, J., Priyagus, P., Darma, D. C., & Haryadi, H. (2021). Indonesia's new SDGs agenda for green growth: Emphasis in the energy sector. *International Journal of Energy Economics and Policy, 11*(3), 395–402. https://www.zbw.eu/econis-archiv/bitstream/11159/7723/1/1771707690_0.pdf

Tartaruga, I. G. P., & Sperotto, F. Q. (2021). Rethinking clusters in the sense of innovation, inclusion, and green growth. In *Rethinking clusters: Place-based value creation in sustainability transitions* (pp. 101–110). Springer International Publishing.

Zanellato, G., & Tiron-Tudor, A. (2021). Toward a Sustainable University: Babes-Bolyai University Goes Green. *Administrative Sciences, 11*(4), 133.

Zhou, M., Govindan, K., & Xie, X. (2020). How fairness perceptions, embeddedness, and knowledge sharing drive green innovation in sustainable supply chains: An equity theory and network perspective to achieve sustainable development goals. *Journal of Cleaner Production, 260*, 120950.

Chapter 12

Restructuring Sustainable Strategies for Alleviation of Poverty Through a Dynamic Approach

Abhiraj Malia, Aurodeep Kamal, Bhubaneswari Bisoyi, Biswajit Das and Ipseeta Satpathy

KIIT University, India

Abstract

This chapter explores into the understanding of poverty and mitigating the challenges by revisiting for a sustainable alleviation of the scales of economy. Eventually insufficient income and spending is the bastion of natural deprivation for household problems. Effective measures are critically examined to redefine the obstacles that are key to upliftment and eradication of poverty. It essentially aims to bridging the gap, analysing the SDG goals through a trend analysis for a time period. These strategies will introspect into overcoming the emerging areas of concern with a futuristic development. Evidently global challenges in the social, economic, political and cultural ecosystem require newness of intervention and initiatives to achieve the triple bottom line, revisiting the dimensions of poverty. Essentially it will anatomise into the causes and consequences of poverty through certain measuring yardsticks in the context of different economies globally. These social, economic, political, legal and technological interventions through their novel strategies can empower and create inclusion for the sharing of equitable wealth distribution, ensuring justice and supporting human rights, providing social security to the poorest of the poor. This study shall innovatively scan through the new entrepreneurship models to understand the skillsets across the globe in order to foster good governance in a win-win environment. Nevertheless, the aspects of poverty alleviation and sustainable order for mitigating the challenges of poverty shall be addressed in the spectrum of climate change and volatility, uncertainty, complexity and

Creating Pathways for Prosperity, 197–213
Published under exclusive licence by Emerald Publishing Limited
doi:10.1108/978-1-83549-121-820241015

ambiguity (VUCA) environment. Basically, in review of the aforesaid dimensions, this study shall vividly examine on the Sustainable Developmental Goals (SDGs) pertaining to poverty alleviation worldwide to adjust for the seamless and uninterrupted continuation trend analysis of the periodic plans of action. It shall adjudge into the befitting global trend admissible under the uncertain future.

Keywords: Sustainable Development Goals (SDGs); poverty alleviation; e-Governance; environment; socio-economics

Introduction

Approaches to development policy and programming have changed during the past 40 years. Our comprehension of the problems that underlie development strategies and programming has been aided by experience. As a result, the intricate dynamics that affect developing economies are more clearly understood. Notably, the relationship between gender and the environment has been highlighted, as has the interaction between economic, sociocultural and political influences. The foundation of development policy has been called into question by the increasing emphasis on sustainability. The Brundtland Commission, also known as the World Commission on Environment and Development, is credited with popularising sustainable development. In its 1987 report, the Brundtland Commission urged for growth that fulfils the requirements of current society without compromising the requirements of future generations. It emphasised the necessity of addressing environmental and developmental issues concurrently in policy and programmes. The idea of sustainability has now been broadened to encompass more than only environmental concerns. Currently, development professionals handle issues relating population, sustainability and poverty alleviation. This strategy clarifies the connection because poverty reduction is a prerequisite for both achieving and maintaining ecologically sustainable development. Therefore, in order for economic assistance to benefit the poor, the relationship between sustainability and poverty reduction must be thoroughly recognised.

The Sustainable Developmental Goals (SDGs) consists of 17 development objectives formulated by UN with the intention of achieving certain socio-economic and ecological goals by the year 2030. The SDGs are broader objectives built on the preceding Millennium Development Goals (MDGs), framed in 2000. They deal with issues including economic development, fair employment, environmentally sound cities and communities, industrialisation, wetlands, ecological systems power, the effects of climate change, environmentally friendly production and consumption, harmony equity and justice. The set of quantifiable goals is meant to direct and monitor regional, national and international efforts to accomplish sustainable development. Human society's common goal is to achieve global sustainability. The 2030 Agenda for Sustainable Development (SDGs) has two main objectives: 'No Poverty' and 'Zero Hunger', along with prerequisites for attaining the objectives associated with 'Decent Work and Economic Growth Industry' as well as 'Innovation and Infrastructure'. China has been working very hard to accomplish the No Poverty goal.

Since the vast bulk consisting of structure of the energy outtake is dependent on fossil fuels, faster cost-effective growth aiming to lower severe level of poverty is creating progressive energy consumption and consequently, the environment quality in developing countries (Papakonstantinidis, 2017). Although the connection between poverty and wealth inequality and environmental degradation has not yet been established in developing nations, particularly those in Asia, they have opted to ignore it. Due to the majority of developing countries' great vulnerability and limited ability to mitigate the effects of the environment, the degradation of the environment could have a noteworthy impact (Apergis et al., 2018).

When developing appropriate, efficient policies and defining poverty as transient or chronic while evaluating the growth towards such targets, knowledge of poverty dynamics is essential. Due to complexity as well as diversity of poverty's motivators, there is a need for unique solutions and policies that focus on Transient Poverty (TP) (Groover, 2011). As a result, in order to build the best policies that may successfully address various forms of poverty, policymakers should understand intrinsic complication of families and classify motivating indicators. By focusing on TP, we might potentially lessen global poverty, mitigate long-term effects and create benefits that will help us achieve SDG 1 and the other SDGs. According to this viewpoint, researching TP with context to sustainable development will expand the possibility of anti-poverty policy and take into account the complexities of living in scarceness. Thorat et al. (2017) noted that compared to chronic poverty, fleeting poverty appears to receive less attention in the research. By giving a broad impression of the issue through sustainability telescope, this study fills up this knowledge gap. Addition of a bibliometric analysis to assess incorporation of TP with the discourse on sustainable development, it builds on earlier research.

Review of Literature

Poverty is defined as being without food and shelter. It is being ill and unable to get medical attention. Poverty is characterised by a lack of resources, representation and freedom. It has a variety of faces that change over time and space (Lipton & Ravallion, 1995). Poverty and environment offers a comprehensive static mathematical model to represent the poverty-environment trap. They showed how the distribution of income has a substantial impact on the association between poverty and the environment. The five issues namely agricultural growth, rural poverty, environmental devastation, participatory rural development and market reforms with regard to agriculture were interconnected and concluded that the environment and growth and poverty interacted with one other in intricate ways. The connections between poverty, the environment and development are highly intricate and lend themselves to broad generalisations. A common belief, particularly in the West, is that poverty, which prevents people from using natural resources sustainably, is the primary cause of environmental damage (Duraiappah, 1998). In turn, it is thought that degradation causes poverty to worsen.

The goal of sustainable development, which continues as an intricate occurrence, associating many actors (administrations, development agencies, universities and NGOs, to name a few), is to enable nations to begin a path of advancement marked by self-sustaining dynamics, ensuring its persistence. So, achieving sustainable development entails continuing to build programmes whose advantages last forever. Globally, emerging nations are frequently seen as being characterised by extreme poverty, which has negative effects on long-term development. The characteristics of poverty in emerging nations are pervasive, affect many dimensions and continue to obstruct initiatives for sustainable development and disturb livelihoods (Cobbinah et al., 2015). The following characteristics of poverty continue to be the most common, despite the fact that there are many others: illiteracy, poor health, gender inequality, disparities between rural and urban areas and bad governance.

Sustenance depletion, which allows people to attain their most grassroot requirements, is widely studied in the milieu of financial evolution. The papers of Blasi et al. (2022) and Strulik (2010) are closely related. Both come up with solutions to the utility maximisation conundrum using the usual AK-type production technology and Stone-Geary preferences. These settings, however, fail to take into account the fact that many low-income developing nations have abundant natural resources (Barbier, 2005), have high development demands and have slower growth than developed nations (Gaitan & Roe, 2012). The Department of Health and Social Security (DHSS) framework has been thoroughly examined in another body of research using some particular presumptions. Benchekroun and Withagen (2011) and others have used the Cobb Douglas constant returns to scale production structure using repeatable resource input and human-made capital. In a utilitarian manner, Antony and Klarl (2019) incorporate minimum subsistence consumption into the DHSS model.

Regarding income inequality, it has a variety of effects on various socio-economic strata in the regions (La Rovere, 2017). Since the majority of disadvantaged members of society are among the most exposed and susceptible populations in the area, they are the ones who are most adversely affected by economic inequality. Because it may cause policy concerned with environmental protection, income disparity may result in reduced protection for the environment's quality and, ultimately, increased hazardous emissions (Grottera et al., 2017). Furthermore, it unintentionally raises mortality and morbidity rates among the poor. Otherwise, improving the environment might be accomplished through decreasing extreme poverty, particularly with context to expanding economies of the province. It has been found that poverty, in addition to sustainability are closely associated, likely as a result of how much poor people depend on the surroundings and resources from nature. Because of their dependence on natural resources, underprivileged people abuse and manipulate their quality in unsustainable ways, which worsens pollution and the environment's quality. In addition, extreme poverty, urbanisation and rapid population increase degrade the capacity for absorption and lower the value of natural as well as environmental resources (Schleicher et al., 2018).

The connection between resources, growth and development is another aspect of our strategy. First, as Nayak (2012) among others, have claimed the connection between resources, growth and development is another aspect of our strategy. First off, as recommended, among other sources, by Nayak (2012) and Van der Ploeg and Venables (2011), some resources-abundant developing countries can be using resource rent footfalls to raise finance and speed development. This is due to a lack of both physical and human resources. They contend that a higher return on domestic capital is implied by capital scarcity. Therefore, it might be better to capitalise in physical and people capital rather than elsewhere. Empirical data from Venables (2016), however, seem to indicate that this is not the case. According to the 2030 Agenda, each of the 17 SDGs is interlinked to the others (van Soest et al., 2019), meaning, the advancement of one target affects the standing of the others. Additionally, development demonstrates intricate shared opinion interactions among several SDGs, which include collaborations (advantages) and trade-offs (disadvantages). By examining the trade-offs and collaborations, Mitra et al. (2013) predicted developments in and exchanges between SDGs until 2030. Using an SDG databank of 166 nations, Nilsson et al. (2016) employed an inverse network method to investigate SDG interactions. At both low and high sustainability levels, he found significant positive and negative relationships across SDGs, although at intermediate levels, they tended to group into more isolated clusters with positive meanings. Researchers investigate how particular objectives link with other goals or affecting factors in conjunction with concentrating the overall SDGs network and the compromises and collaborations between them (Bisoyi & Das, 2015).

Although the drop in vulnerability to poverty and the diminution of poverty are seen as significant advances, concerns about resolution of transient poverty exist. Differences involving acute as well as chronic poverty are crucial, especially when viewed from a policy perspective, as different reactions as well as actions must sufficiently tend to each person's unique requirements (Baulch & Hoddinott, 2000). According to Hulme and Shepherd (2003), chronic poverty describes 'people who have suffered poverty for long periods, or maybe all of their lives'.

However, the availability of quality as well as quantity employment aspects determines how much work decreases poverty. The International Labour Organization (ILO) and SDG 8 advocated towards fair and equal job prospects for all in recognition of the significance of these two components (Gammarano, 2019). The amount of work required by an individual to lead a respectable living is referred to as their quantity of employment (Das, 2015). When a person is properly covered by someone else's in contrast to when an individual is if they are employed, they will very certainly earn a definite wage that reduces struggles and drudgery. However, the issue with vulnerable employment is that it comes with a lot of doubt and does not ensure sufficient employment. As a result, it is called 'vulnerable employment'. In some instances, the amount of labour that employees receive is still susceptible to economic ups and downs. Thus, it is improbable that a vulnerable Employment significantly lowers the rates of poverty in these countries. However, the value of employment denotes the working environment (Panigrahi et al., 2015). People who work in safe environment and earn a living wage are less likely to fall into poverty and they are also protected by sufficient social security. There is a wealth of research indicating that this type of job is linked to deplorable wages and hazardous working conditions, variables that negatively impact employees' ability to meaningfully overcome poverty (Cazes & Verick, 2013).

The lack of natural resources, income inequality and poverty are three topics that have gained a lot of discussion over the years and have been the subject of many debates. Over the past few years, research on the economics of environment and sustainability has steadily highlighted the complex nature as well as relevance of the relationship among inequality of income, poverty and environmental conditions. The UN's SDGs are tough to achieve in countries that are developing, where the majority of humanity lives in unstable circumstances and inequality of income and poverty (Gulzar et al., 2020).

This progression begins with the Industrial Revolution and the Malthusian Stagnation, and it concludes with a steady increase in per capita income (Galor, 2005; Galor & Weil, 2000). In the scale of unified growth theory model, population increase has an impact on natural resource scarcity in a manner similar to ours (and labour productivity). In their 2015 article, Peretto and Valente (2015) explore a Schumpeterian growth model with endogenous fertility with a focus on population dynamics and resource constraints.

Despite practical and sensible efforts to accomplish the SDGs for the abolition of poverty and income inequality, the majority of developing countries continue to see rises in poverty and income inequality. Finding ways that eliminate severe poverty, income inequality and environmental conservation are complicated and difficult problems for both developed and developing nations. One possible solution to such policies that encourage economic growth is because it is generally believed that economic growth helps to reduce poverty (Akinlo & Dada, 2021). It is possible to 'kill two birds with one stone' by reducing extreme poverty, rising income disparity and environmental destruction (De Neve & Sachs, 2020; Dhrifi et al., 2020) Therefore, comprehending theoretically abstruse topics like wealth inequality, poverty and environmental pollution for ensuring a better future.

Bibliometric charting has been recognised as a necessary area for study. The conception of bibliometric maps in association with graphical display of such maps can be seen as two distinct facets of the mentioned methodology. The creation of bibliometric maps receives the most focus in the bibliometric literature (Börner et al., 2003). For instance, VOSviewer is a software designed for map creation of authors or journals based on data from co-citations or create maps of keywords based on data from co-occurrence. The software includes a viewer that enables in-depth analysis of bibliometric maps. A map can be depicted via VOSviewer in a variety of ways, each emphasising a distinct feature of the map. Its zooming, scrolling and searching capabilities make it easier to examine a map in depth (Van Eck & Waltman, 2011). VOSviewer's viewing capabilities are particularly helpful for maps with at least a relatively significant number of elements (Zougmoré et al., 2016). The majority of bibliometric mapping software does not display such maps in an acceptable manner.

Research Methodology

As it is crucial to gather a wide range of data on TP, the current study incorporates a bibliometric analysis (Bello et al., 2021).With the help of Scopus database, a widely recognised database of academia and literature, bibliometric analysis was carried out for specified key phrases. Over 24,000 papers and more than 5,000 journals are included in the database (Scopus 2021). This platform has been used to carry out previous bibliometric evaluations connected to the current study.

Quantitative method in order to evaluating conceptual framework of a specific field of study is bibliometric analysis. The effectiveness of particular themes, authors and other category delineations can be assessed using this technique by compiling citations (Donkor & Chitakira, 2022). Science mapping and performance analysis are the two main applications of the method. According to Zupic and Čater (2015), performance analysis strives to evaluate both individual and organisational research and publishing performance. With the help of a variety of approaches, such as word count analysis, citation and co-citation analysis, it is possible to give information on the scope and influence of research. Additionally, it can count articles according to the unit of analysis, including author, nation and affiliation.

The bibliometric approach was utilised in this study to identify frequently used TP and sustainable development subjects. The software VOSviewer was used for text mining to find phrases that frequently occur together. In April 2021, research questions and data collecting were carried out. In the beginning, only the phrases 'Sustainable' OR 'SDG' AND 'transient poverty' OR 'transitory poverty' OR 'transient poor' or 'transitory poor' was used for scouting documents. Variations of the search queries were also studied. The provided new strings were generally created for catching pertinent papers as feasible in order to continue the bibliometric assessment:

> Query 1: (TITLE-ABS-KEY (sustainable* AND development)) AND (TITLE (poor OR poverty))
> Query 2: TITLE-ABS-KEY ('Transient Poverty') OR 'transient poor' OR 'transitory poverty' OR 'transitory poor')

For first query, the search resulted in 107 results, and second query, 1,838 sources as mentioned in the Table 12.1. Table 12.1 depicts the analysis of the query strings and the count of keywords observed in the SCOPUS database. The co-occurrence analysis was carried out using each of these samples. The findings are shown as a network diagram, with the link breadth representing degree of associations between two terms and the node distance reflecting the regularity of recurrence of a string. Due to their frequent co-occurrence, terms that appear

Table 12.1. Query Strings Criterion and Count of Keywords Observed in SCOPUS Databank.

Search Query	Count of Research Articles	Out of
(TITLE-ABS-KEY (sustainable* AND development)) AND (TITLE (poor OR poverty))	1,838	1,995
TITLE-ABS-KEY ('Transient Poverty') OR 'transient poor' OR 'transitory poverty' OR 'transitory poor')	107	1,957

Source: Own Source, 2023.

adjacent by one another have been assumed to be related and correlate to such clusters. Additionally, this strategy can solve some restrictions brought on by bibliometric analysis used in isolation.

Results and Discussions

There are four subsections to the results and discussion. The first section addresses the overall research backdrop that the researchers have studied poverty and sustainable development. The phenomenon of transient poverty is specifically addressed in the second section. The following subsection connects the preceding two sections and expands on the concept of transient poverty to include SDGs and sustainable development.

Poverty and Sustainable Development

Although poverty cannot be completely eradicated by economic progress, the impoverished often do far worse when it does not occur. The impoverished are the first to be evicted in a contracting or stagnant economy, and they are particularly susceptible since they have no reserves. Sustainable economic growth with special consideration for the underprivileged and a shift in the priority of rural invest-ments are necessary for the decrease of poverty. For at least three decades, the majority of the world's impoverished will live in rural areas (Jena & Ghosh, 2013). Majority of the low-income nations that successfully reduced significant levels of poverty are formed by providing resources to the poor and increasing the pro-ductivity of those resources. As a result, there was an increase in local income from both self-employment and inexpensive, productive work. The poor must be given more power by building assets and increasing savings in order for rural areas to flourish sustainably. A household may be able to engage in economic activity through time and financial saves (by entering a savings or loan organi-sation), time savings (by requiring less time to gather water and wood) and the purchase of useful assets like livestock, a kitchen or a plot (Masron &

Subramaniam, 2019). They will only be able to join and benefit from a labour-intensive economic growth that creates new employment prospects if they have these beginning assets.

Healthcare, nourishment, appropriate drainage, safe drinking water, social marginalisation, poor education, substandard living conditions, crime and a lack of efficient energy supply systems are some of the variables that contribute to poverty as it is experienced by the poor. Fig. 12.1 illustrates various multilevel issues associated with alleviation of transient poverty. The association is established between social, economic and environmental aspects that contribute towards the upliftment.

These intricate cases of poverty necessitate various approaches to reducing it and tailored regulations (Jalan & Ravallion, 1998). An analysis of poverty in relation to socio-economic difficulties, healthcare, education and food security was done in number of papers. Since employment is the principal locus of remuneration for the poor, preserving as well as improving the employment standards is crucial to ensuring access to healthcare and educational opportunities. Studies on how education affects reducing poverty have demonstrated the various advantages including individuals and communities. Healthcare has been discussed in context with the result of poverty and as a way to combat it. Skilled personnel are frequently discussed in the literature as a catalyst for economic

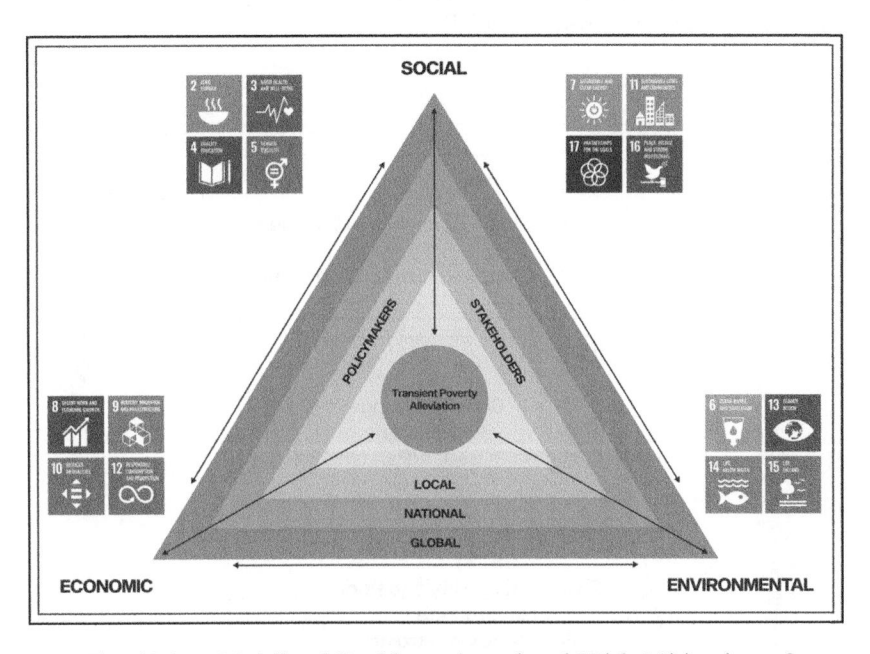

Fig. 12.1.   Multilevel Problems Associated With Mitigation of Transient Poverty. *Source:* Own Source, 2023.

growth and progress, and enhancements in health also help to raise service quality (Cichos & Salvia, 2018).

The main debate is how sustainable development's poverty problem is addressed in the literature. Global warming, regional development, decision-making, environment, habitat, forest, deforestation, CO2, landscape use, water management and irrigation are therefore the primary concepts associated with it. The issue of potential climate change effects on the farming sector, farmed animals system, as well as fishing industry production in Africa, highlighting the significance of programs to reduce political and social effects of climate change. Last but not least, the socio-economic as well as planning are two of its key concepts and they relate to energy usage, environmental policy and optimisation. Absence of political will and quality of governance to adopt laws can provide people in developing nations with contemporary energy services. The multifaceted nature of poverty makes a better energy supply a crucial element in the region's efforts to reduce poverty (Bhide & Monroy, 2011).

Transient Poverty

According to the results of the TP evaluation, prior research has concentrated on evaluating poverty as a whole and has only partly addressed the traits of people who are predisposed to moving from TP to severe poverty or to escape poverty. Fig. 12.2 represents the tri-levels of TP.

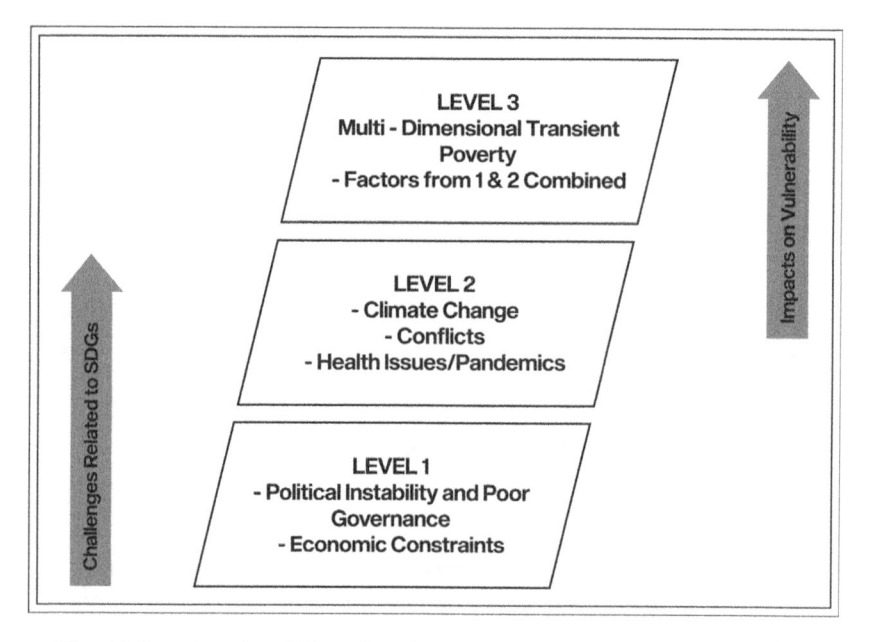

Fig. 12.2.   Levels of Transient Poverty. *Source:* Own Source, 2023.

Education and gender are typically the main factors when the factors that contribute to TP have been considered and addressed since they can be used to forecast the likelihood of a directional change away from TP.

Fig. 12.3 establishes the coinciding bibliographic clusters that are associated with poverty. Numerous studies have linked male employment in weak economic sectors and educational level with continued poverty. The definition of TP has been discussed as an environmental stressor, irrespective of personal traits, and that its distinguishing aspects are more indicative of its persistence. This would be consistent with the idea that the length of TP will have an impact on mental state of health and participation of employment and traits associated with transitory states. Sharma et al. (2014) demonstrated that empowered women have a favourable impact on the fight against poverty since they are important players in the global socio-economic development. Change initiatives should put a focus on pragmatic gender requirements, such as female's earnings and physical assets, because empowering women promotes women's rights (SDG 5) and eliminates inequities (SDG 10). Additionally, it is crucial to address the core causes of TP, such as the marginalisation of women as a result of social systems (Zaman, 1999).

Significance of Transitional Poverty From the Sustainable Development Perspective

Poverty is a dynamic phenomenon, as was said in the preceding section, rather than a static one. These processes are visible in the shifts in socio-economic

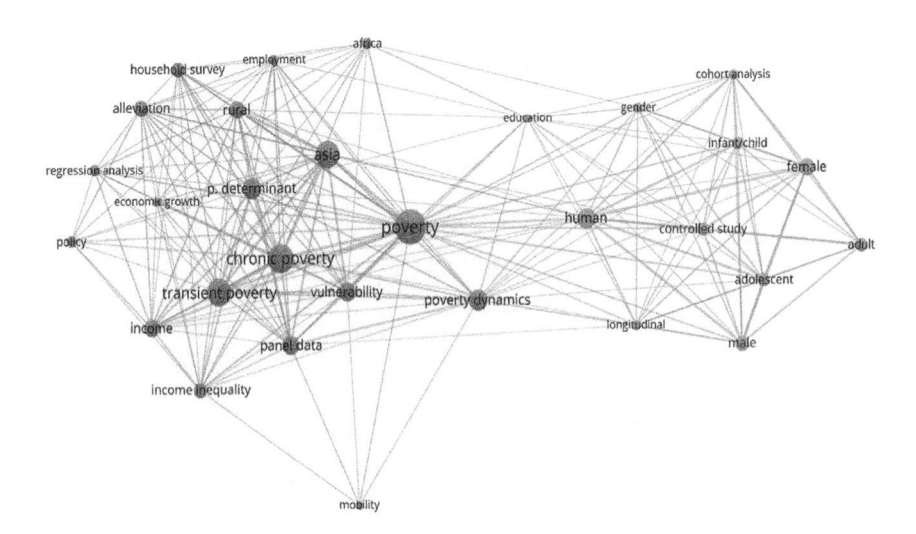

Fig. 12.3.   Transient Poverty Clusters Using VOS Viewer Output.
Source: Own Source, 2023.

position and general well-being that people experience over time. Fig. 12.4 represents the multiple incidences of terms coinciding (Sustainable Development, Poverty).

People may therefore move in and out of poverty depending on the scope and nature of the hazards they face as well as their capacity to handle them. The 17 SDGs are interdependent, thus progress in one area has positive spillover effects in other areas. Since the SDG main objective, which trails, 'end poverty in all its manifestations everywhere', it follows making real progress towards attaining the SDGs necessitates tending to poverty's intersecting problems. As governments prioritise progress for those who are most behind, this also has co-benefits for the global agenda. However, extreme poverty makes individuals desperate and compels them to forgo sustainability concerns in order to survive (Sengupta, 2018).

Additionally, a sizeable portion of the world's population still has challenges in meeting their most fundamental needs, including access to food, clean water to drink and sanitary conditions. As a result, the SDGs for ending hunger as well as providing admission to drinking water and sanitary conditions are jeopardised by negative consequences for the 2030 global agenda as a whole (Bisoyi & Das, 2016). Due to its intersection with and aggravation by the cumulative outcomes

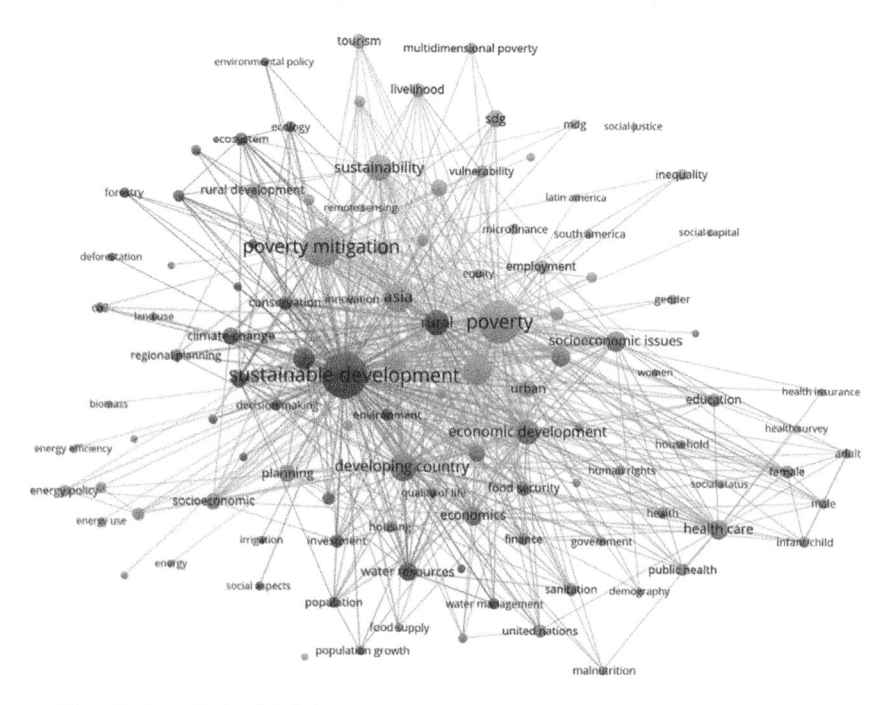

Fig. 12.4.   Coincidal Occurrence of Terms Sustainable Development and Poverty Using VOS Viewer Output. *Source:* Own Source, 2023.

concerning environment changes as well as COVID-19 pandemic, the detrimental consequences of poverty on sustainable development have become an important issue.

Interventions aimed at reducing poverty must use a multifaceted, integrated strategy to be successful. In this context, combining public assistance and private initiatives is one effective way to combat TP, among others. One of the main topics of the SDGs is knowledge generation to inform policy, which highlights the necessity for reliable data and assessment techniques to direct policy formation.

Literature on the interaction between TP and climate change is scarce. Despite this gap, there are obvious connections between the two ideas that merit more investigation. Climate change may potentially contribute to poverty entrenchment or TP in households that wouldn't have otherwise experienced it. This is crucial since the poorest people in the world suffer the most from the COVID-19 epidemic due to their insecure living conditions. As a result, sustainable development and climate change interact dynamically. When climate policies are included in the broader plan of action for global sustainable development, they can be more effective (Hasan et al., 2020). Last but not least, just as climate change reworking is utilised to alleviate poverty, it can also be used as a beset approach to lessen TP.

Conclusion

The resolve of this research was to advance understanding of Transient Poverty in the framework of sustainable development. Conducted bibliometric study demonstrates the literature mostly examines the poverty issue from a wide outlook and frequently fails to distinguish between TP and chronic poverty. Additionally, there is no doubt that throughout time, knowledge associated with links among the poverty phenomena and sustainable development has grown. The relationship to the theory of sustainable development appears to be missed in publications that cover concepts related to 'transient poverty', and there is a lack of an interdisciplinary argument. Application of bibliometric analysis of poor and sustainable development also showed basic needs insecurity affects poverty in addition to income deficits. A few connections between severe poverty, revenue and economic inequality were also revealed by the bibliometric analysis of 'transient poverty'.

The methodologies used in this study have certain inherent limitations. One of them is the failure to give careful thought to the several socio-economic issues that affect it because of the focus on temporary poverty. Another drawback is that the study did not examine how temporary poverty might develop into chronic poor in specific situations. Despite these drawbacks, the study adds to the body of knowledge in that it advances our knowledge of the causes and effects of temporary poverty, particularly the factors that motivate it from an interdisciplinary standpoint. Finally, there is a pressing need for public measures that go beyond a money-based approach to reducing the vulnerability to temporary poverty. This necessitates that policymakers recognise the intrinsic complication of the 2030 Schema and the connections among the 17 SDGs of the UN, and that even though there are many different reasons of transient poverty, a deeper comprehension of its causes is crucial in classifying the tenacities to resolve it.

References

Akinlo, T., & Dada, J. T. (2021). The moderating effect of foreign direct investment on environmental degradation-poverty reduction nexus: Evidence from sub-Saharan African countries. *Environment, Development and Sustainability*, 1–21.

Antony, J., & Klarl, T. (2019). Non-renewable resources, subsistence consumption, and Hartwick's investment rule. *Resource and Energy Economics*, *55*, 124–142.

Apergis, N., Jebli, M. B., & Youssef, S. B. (2018). Does renewable energy consumption and health expenditures decrease carbon dioxide emissions? Evidence for sub-Saharan Africa countries. *Renewable Energy*, *127*, 1011–1016.

Barbier, E. B. (2005). *Natural resources and economic development*. Cambridge University Press.

Baulch, B., & Hoddinott, J. (2000). Economic mobility and poverty dynamics in developing countries. *Journal of Development Studies*, *36*(6), 1–24.

Bello, B. G., Rapetti, E., Delmonte, M., Merlino, M., Palumbo, M., & Pivetta, V. (2021). Gender and social barriers to STEM education and training among children in situations of educational poverty in Italy. In *Proceedings of the 2nd International Conference of the Journal Scuola Democratica "Reinventing Education, Learning with New Technologies, Equality and Inclusion* (Vol. 2, pp. 1053–1067). ASSOCIAZIONE "PER SCUOLA DEMOCRATICA".

Benchekroun, H., & Withagen, C. (2011). The optimal depletion of exhaustible resources: A complete characterization. *Resource and Energy Economics*, *33*(3), 612–636.

Bhide, A., & Monroy, C. R. (2011). Energy poverty: A special focus on energy poverty in India and renewable energy technologies. *Renewable and Sustainable Energy Reviews*, *15*(2), 1057–1066.

Bisoyi, B., & Das, B. (2015). Adapting green technology for optimal deployment of renewable energy resources and to generate power for future sustainability. *Indian Journal of Science and Technology*, *8*, 28.

Bisoyi, B., & Das, B. (2016). Necessitate green environment for sustainable computing. In *Proceedings of the Second International Conference on Computer and Communication Technologies* (pp. 515–524). Springer.

Blasi, S., Ganzaroli, A., & De Noni, I. (2022). Smartening sustainable development in cities: Strengthening the theoretical linkage between smart cities and SDGs. *Sustainable Cities and Society*, *80*, 103793.

Börner, K., Chen, C., & Boyack, K. W. (2003). Visualizing knowledge domains. *Annual Review of Information Science & Technology*, *37*(1), 179–255.

Cazes, S., & Verick, S. (2013). *The labour markets of emerging economies: Has growth translated into more and better jobs?* International Labour Office and Palgrave McMillan. Springer.

Cichos, K., & Salvia, A. L. (2018). Sustainable Development Goal 1. In *SDG1–No poverty* (pp. 51–61). Emerald Publishing Limited.

Cobbinah, P. B., Erdiaw-Kwasie, M. O., & Amoateng, P. (2015). Rethinking sustainable development within the framework of poverty and urbanisation in developing countries. *Environmental Development, 13*, 18–32.

Das, B. (2015). Housing and urban infrastructure management: Sustainable and green development. *International Journal in Management and Social Science, 3*(9), 355–365.

De Neve, J. E., & Sachs, J. D. (2020). The SDGs and human well-being: A global analysis of synergies, trade-offs, and regional differences. *Scientific Reports, 10*(1), 1–12.

Dhrifi, A., Jaziri, R., & Alnahdi, S. (2020). Does foreign direct investment and environmental degradation matter for poverty? Evidence from developing countries. *Structural Change and Economic Dynamics, 52*, 13–21.

Donkor, F. K., & Chitakira, M. (2022). Nexus of Water, Sanitation, and Hygiene (WASH) and Sustainable Development Goals. In *Clean water and sanitation* (pp. 453–461). Springer International Publishing.

Duraiappah, A. K. (1998). Poverty and environmental degradation: A review and analysis of the nexus. *World Development, 26*(12), 2169–2179.

Gaitan, B., & Roe, T. L. (2012). International trade, exhaustible-resource abundance and economic growth. *Review of Economic Dynamics, 15*(1), 72–93.

Galor, O. (2005). From stagnation to growth: Unified growth theory. *Handbook of Economic Growth, 1*, 171–293.

Galor, O., & Weil, D. N. (2000). Population, technology, and growth: From Malthusian stagnation to the demographic transition and beyond. *The American Economic Review, 90*(4), 806–828.

Gammarano, R. (2019). *The working poor. Or how a job is no guarantee of decent living conditions. A study based on ILO's global estimates of employment by economic class.* ILOSTAT Spotlight on Work Statistics.

Groover, K. D. (2011). *Distinguishing between Chronic and Transient Poverty in Mozambique.* Doctoral dissertation.

Grottera, C., Pereira Jr, A. O., & La Rovere, E. L. (2017). Impacts of carbon pricing on income inequality in Brazil. *Climate & Development, 9*(1), 80–93.

Gulzar, S., Ghauri, S., Abbas, Z., Hussain, K., & Jibril, A. B. (2020). Antecedents of employee wellbeing in the banking sector: The moderating role of working environment. *Problems and Perspectives in Management, 18*(4), 36.

Hasan, M. A., Abubakar, I. R., Rahman, S. M., Aina, Y. A., Chowdhury, M. M. I., & Khondaker, A. N. (2020). The synergy between climate change policies and national development goals: Implications for sustainability. *Journal of Cleaner Production, 249*, 119369.

Hulme, D., & Shepherd, A. (2003). Conceptualizing chronic poverty. *World Development, 31*(3), 403–423.

Jalan, J., & Ravallion, M. (1998). Transient poverty in postreform rural China. *Journal of Comparative Economics, 26*(2), 338–357.

Jena, S. K., & Ghosh, K. (2013). MGNREGA-"silver bullet" for sustainable poverty eradication-a case study of Koraput District of Odisha. In *Proceedings on Rural Development in India: issues, Progress and Programme Effectiveness RGU, Archers and Elevators, Bangalore.*

La Rovere, E. L. (2017). Low-carbon development pathways in Brazil and 'Climate Clubs'. *Wiley Interdisciplinary Reviews: Climate Change*, *8*(1), e439.

Lipton, M., & Ravallion, M. (1995). Poverty and policy. *Handbook of Development Economics*, *3*, 2551–2657.

Masron, T. A., & Subramaniam, Y. (2019). Does poverty cause environmental degradation? Evidence from developing countries. *Journal of Poverty*, *23*(1), 44–64.

Mitra, T., Asheim, G. B., Buchholz, W., & Withagen, C. (2013). Characterizing the sustainability problem in an exhaustible resource model. *Journal of Economic Theory*, *148*(5), 2164–2182.

Nayak, S. (2012). Sustainable mineral-intensive growth in Odisha, India. *Journal of the Institution of Engineers (India): Series D*, *93*, 43–51.

Nilsson, M., Griggs, D., & Visbeck, M. (2016). Policy: Map the interactions between Sustainable Development Goals. *Nature*, *534*(7607), 320–322.

Panigrahi, J., Das, B., & Tripathy, S. (2015). Paving the path from Education to employment. *Parikalpana: KIIT Journal of Management*, *11*(1), 113.

Papakonstantinidis, L. A. (2017). The "win-win-win Papakonstantinidis Model": From social welfare's philosophy towards a rural development concept by rural tourism approach: The WERT case study. *International Journal of Innovation and Economic Development*, *3*(5), 7–25.

Peretto, P. F., & Valente, S. (2015). Growth on a finite planet: Resources, technology and population in the long run. *Journal of Economic Growth*, *20*, 305–331.

Schleicher, J., Schaafsma, M., & Vira, B. (2018). Will the Sustainable Development Goals address the links between poverty and the natural environment? *Current Opinion in Environmental Sustainability*, *34*, 43–47.

Sengupta, M. (2018). Transformational change or tenuous wish list?: A critique of SDG 1 ('End poverty in all its forms everywhere'). *Social Alternatives*, *37*(1), 12–17.

Sharma, V., Reddy, B., & Sahu, N. (2014). Sustainable rural livelihoods approach for climate change adaptation in Western Odisha, Eastern India. *Development in Practice*, *24*(4), 591–604.

Strulik, H. (2010). A note on economic growth with subsistence consumption. *Macroeconomic Dynamics*, *14*(5), 763–771.

Thorat, A., Vanneman, R., Desai, S., & Dubey, A. (2017). Escaping and falling into poverty in India today. *World Development*, *93*, 413–426.

Van der Ploeg, F., & Venables, A. J. (2011). Harnessing windfall revenues: Optimal policies for resource-rich developing economies. *The Economic Journal*, *121*(551), 1–30.

Van Eck, N. J., & Waltman, L. (2011). Text mining and visualization using VOSviewer. arXiv preprint arXiv:1109.2058.

van Soest, H. L., van Vuuren, D. P., Hilaire, J., Minx, J. C., Harmsen, M. J., Krey, V., Popp, A., Riahi, K., & Luderer, G. (2019). Analysing interactions among sustainable development goals with integrated assessment models. *Global Transitions*, *1*, 210–225.

Venables, A. J. (2016). Using natural resources for development: Why has it proven so difficult? *The Journal of Economic Perspectives*, *30*(1), 161–184.

Zaman, H. (1999). *Assessing the impact of micro-credit on poverty and vulnerability in Bangladesh.* The World Bank.

Zougmoré, R., Partey, S., Ouédraogo, M., Omitoyin, B., Thomas, T., Ayantunde, A., Ericksen, P., Said, M., & Jalloh, A. (2016). Toward climate-smart agriculture in West Africa: A review of climate change impacts, adaptation strategies and policy developments for the livestock, fishery and crop production sectors. *Agriculture and Food Security, 5*(1), 1–16.

Zupic, I., & Čater, T. (2015). Bibliometric methods in management and organization. *Organizational Research Methods, 18*(3), 429–472.

Printed and bound by CPI Group (UK) Ltd, Croydon, CR0 4YY

10/06/2025

14687083-0002